TWENTIETH CENTURY

TIME
LIFE
BOOKS
®

LIFE WORLD LIBRARY

LIFE NATURE LIBRARY

TIME READING PROGRAM

THE LIFE HISTORY OF THE UNITED STATES

LIFE SCIENCE LIBRARY

INTERNATIONAL BOOK SOCIETY

GREAT AGES OF MAN

TIME-LIFE LIBRARY OF ART

TIME-LIFE LIBRARY OF AMERICA

FOODS OF THE WORLD

GREAT AGES OF MAN

A History of the World's Cultures

TWENTIETH CENTURY

by

JOEL G. COLTON

and

The Editors of TIME-LIFE BOOKS

TIME-LIFE BOOKS, NEW YORK

THE AUTHOR: Joel G. Colton, chairman of the Department of History at Duke University, did his undergraduate work at the College of the City of New York and received his master's and doctoral degrees from Columbia University. Professor Colton has been honored with fellowships from the Guggenheim and Rockefeller Foundations and, since 1947, has been affiliated with Duke University. He is the author of *Compulsory Labor Arbitration in France* and *Léon Blum*, and co-author with R. R. Palmer of *A History of the Modern World*. He is a contributor to *The American Historical Review* and other learned journals.

THE EPILOGUE: William H. McNeill, former chairman of the Department of History at the University of Chicago, is the author of the 1963 National Book Award winner, *The Rise of the West*. Professor McNeill received his doctoral degree from Cornell University and is the author of a number of scholarly books, which include *A World History*, *The Contemporary World* and *Past and Future*.

THE CONSULTING EDITOR: Leonard Krieger, University Professor at the University of Chicago, was formerly Professor of History at Yale. Dr. Krieger is the author of *The German Idea of Freedom* and *The Politics of Discretion*, and co-author of *History*, written in collaboration with John Higham and Felix Gilbert.

THE COVER: A detail from Louise Nevelson's *Sky Cathedral III*—a subjective ordering of discarded pieces of turned, carved and torn wood, arranged in compartments—suggests both the fragmentation and the unity of 20th Century life.

TIME-LIFE BOOKS

EDITOR
Maitland A. Edey
EXECUTIVE EDITOR
Jerry Korn
TEXT DIRECTOR   ART DIRECTOR
Martin Mann   Sheldon Cotler
CHIEF OF RESEARCH
Beatrice T. Dobie
PICTURE EDITOR
Robert G. Mason
Assistant Text Directors:
Harold C. Field, Ogden Tanner
Assistant Art Director: Arnold C. Holeywell
Assistant Chief of Research: Martha Turner

PUBLISHER
Rhett Austell
Associate Publisher: Walter C. Rohrer
General Manager: Joseph C. Hazen Jr.
Planning Director: John P. Sousa III
Circulation Director: Joan D. Manley
Marketing Director: Carter Smith
Business Manager: John D. McSweeney
Publishing Board: Nicholas Benton,
Louis Bronzo, James Wendell Forbes

GREAT AGES OF MAN

SERIES EDITOR: Russell Bourne
Editorial Staff for *Twentieth Century:*
Text Editors: Anne Horan, Robert Tschirky
Picture Editors: Jean Tennant, Edward Brash
Designer: William Rose
Staff Writers: George Constable,
Lucille Schulberg, Edmund White
Chief Researcher: Peggy Bushong
Researchers: Carol Isenberg,
Susan Grafman, Kathleen Brandes,
Alice Baker, Nancy Cabasin,
Val Chu, Millicent Greenberg,
Helen Lapham, Don Nelson,
Sigrid von Huene, Johanna Zacharias,
Arlene Zuckerman
Art Assistant: Anne Landry

EDITORIAL PRODUCTION
Color Director: Robert L. Young
Assistant: James J. Cox
Copy Staff: Marian Gordon Goldman,
Barbara Hults, Florence Keith
Picture Department: Dolores A. Littles,
Joan Lynch
Traffic: Arthur A. Goldberger

The following individuals and departments of Time Inc. gave valuable aid in the preparation of this book: Editorial Production, Robert W. Boyd Jr.; Editorial Reference, Peter Draz; Picture Collection, Doris O'Neil; Photographic Laboratory, George Karas; TIME-LIFE News Service, Richard M. Clurman; Correspondents Maria Vincenza Aloisi (Paris), Ann Natanson (Rome), Margot Hapgood (London), Traudl Lessing (Vienna), Elisabeth Kraemer (Bonn), Erik Amfitheatrof and Takiko Kato (Tokyo), Friso Endt (Amsterdam), Ernest Shirley (Sydney), Louis Kraar (Bangkok), Amir Daud (Djakarta) and Felix Rozenthal (Moscow).

CONTENTS

INTRODUCTION

To become "a citizen of the world" has ever been one of the noblest dreams of man. But only in the 20th Century have the barriers preventing worldwide community been successfully bridged and the old ideal of a global fraternity become a practical possibility. Indeed the beams and girders of a new civilization, rising above the confines of nation and continent, are being set in place at this very moment. They constitute a peculiarly modern international culture, one that corresponds to none of the patterns that history has provided.

The world culture of the 20th Century has at its center neither a Greek design nor a Roman ideal. It recalls neither Alexander the Great's vision of an *oikumene* (the whole inhabited world) that transcends boundaries by stressing the fundamental unity of mankind, nor the empire of Augustus that bound together varied peoples without inhibiting their rich variety. It is, rather, an internationalism based on the brash realities of technology, and one must wonder whether that is the stuff of which great civilizations are built.

The Greek ideal of union existed before Alexander's conquests, dating back at least to the formation of the Boeotian League in the Eighth Century B.C. Inspired by the superb rationalism of the Greek mind, it and later unions were logical, efficient and politically responsible: the Achaian League of the Third and Second Centuries B.C. regulated coinage, standards of weight and measures, and, through its Assembly, commissioned ambassadors and settled the questions of war and peace. But the Greeks sought more than uniformity of administration. The Fourth Century philosopher Zeno propagated the idea of the common qualities and the fusibility of peoples. And the Fifth Century poet Aristophanes (better known for his bawdy comedies) favored the coming to-gether of the Greek city states and likened that process to weaving:

> Then you should card it and comb it and
>   mingle it all in one basket of love and
>   of unity,
> Citizens, visitors, strangers and sojourners—
>   all the entire, undivided community.

The Roman system for pulling the known world together was altogether different. It made no ef-fort to capitalize on the fundamental unity of mankind; on the contrary, it recognized the dif-ferences among peoples and nations, and within a grand imperial framework of elite administrators, upheld local traditions and peculiar ways. The Pax Romana endured for some 500 years, holding together a world that at its height stretched from the Irish Sea to the Persian Gulf in the network of common laws, broad highways (whose extent has been estimated at 50,000 miles), secure harbors and unavoidable taxes. Man in more recent times has formed no government to match it.

Our own technological community has neither Greek wit nor Roman sense. Yet it is our best hope; it is the thrust of our culture. For the first time in the history of the world a glittering, hum-ming transmission network has been established, permitting one culture to communicate quickly and effortlessly with another, often to extraor-dinary effect—allowing the Chinese to conspire with the Cubans, the Scandinavians to consult about anthropology with the Peruvians, even the American Indians to coordinate attacks on dis-crimination with the American Negroes. The na-tions of the world are united in development projects (such as Egypt's Russian-financed Aswan Dam), in scientific quests (such as the International Geophysical Year) and in artistic pursuits (such as the sudden, global popularity of Indian music and rock 'n' roll). They have become freely and culturally interlaced. Yet they coexist fearfully, under the shadow of their destructive weapons.

This final volume in the Great Ages of Man Se-ries analyzes the emergent world culture of today from the two points of view required to understand it. In his admirably succinct history of the 20th Century, Professor Joel Colton of Duke University shows how the reality of men's lives expanded from a regional self-dependence to a worldwide interdependence. In gauging the contemporary re-sults and exploring the future possibilities, Pro-fessor William McNeill, of the University of Chicago, shows how men simultaneously seek the technological culture while rejecting its total domi-nation, how they flock to modernized cities while promoting old-fashioned traditions.

There is one undeniable achievement of our still-forming 20th Century culture: most men have been stirred to make new decisions and to find new ways of living. It is true that all too often the men of our times exercise that choice not by broadening their perspectives but by retreating to parochial considerations, but the challenge none-theless exists. Technology, with its obliteration of space and time, has accelerated enormous cultural changes, bringing timeless ways into question, making ancient laws inapplicable. We live, thus, in an unstable, dangerous age. But as Alfred North Whitehead wrote, "It is the business of the future to be dangerous." The benefit of in-stability, as the creative citizens of Greece, Rome and other changing societies demonstrated, is that this can be the rock-strewn route to greatness.

RUSSELL BOURNE
Series Editor
GREAT AGES OF MAN

a composite of the

TWENTIETH CENTURY

showing the human, scientific and technological
forces that have helped to form a world culture

1
THE WEST IN COMMAND

Newspapers and magazines remind us daily of the shrinkage of the globe and the intermingling of the world's cultures. American families adorn their homes with African sculpture, and clothes designers embellish fashions with African motifs. Medical scientists use ancient Indian herbs to produce tranquilizer drugs; Zen Buddhism wins adherents in the United States. Young Americans on Peace Corps missions fan out through Nigeria, Cameroon, Ethiopia, Malaysia and Korea. Teenagers from Brazzaville to Prague wear the miniskirt and carry ballpoint pens. The sheiks of Middle Eastern oil kingdoms air-condition their palaces and limousines. An American baseball team tours Japan—and is defeated at its own game. The stream of culture flows both ways.

It was not always so. Although cultural exchange is the overwhelming fact of current history, only recently has global unity begun to emerge. A century ago culture flowed one way—from West to East. The civilization that rose in the West long ago reached out in the 19th Century to make a vital impact on all the cultures of the world, often diluting or destroying them.

When we speak of Western civilization, we mean the civilization of which Western Europe was the founder, a civilization based on science, technology and a world economic market; but we mean also a civilization that extols human freedom and equality, and social justice. It is a civilization with a secular faith, a faith in progress and in the idea that men can find happiness on earth. Western civilization introduced the concept of self-government, the promise of economic betterment and the vision of cooperation among all nations. Western civilization introduced the sovereign national state, a political entity that owes allegiance to no other but claims allegiance from its own citizens. And out of the sovereign national state has come the spirit of nationalism, a powerful force that has repeatedly threatened to destroy the very civilization from which it sprang.

Paradoxically, even as it has expanded, European civilization has declined. Two world wars, the rise of powers outside Europe, a terrible economic depression and the end of old colonial empires have removed the nations of Europe from the

A COLLAGE OF CULTURES, posters on a wall in Hong Kong reflect the interplay between East and West. Interspersed among notices of apartments for rent are ads for Philip Morris cigarettes and Kolynos dental cream.

supreme position they held before 1914. But their civilization has nevertheless triumphed; the institutions and the technology that began in Western Europe have sunk roots all over the world.

The origins of the modern world go back half a century or more before 1914, to the Age of Imperialism, when Western culture made its sharpest impact on the rest of the world. That age was a time of unprecedented material progress in technology, industry and science. European civilization, which had been expanding since the explorations of the 15th Century, spread in the 19th to the inner recesses of Africa, to Asia and across every ocean. Europe established global supremacy and brought the entire world under its influence.

For Europeans and Americans this was an age of rising standards of living, longer life spans, more comfort and better health, growth in democratic government and personal liberty, humanitarian advances and a flowering of literature and art. All these gave to the Western world pride of accomplishment, exuberance and a belief in the inevitability of progress. But at the same time, rivalry between the competing nations planted seeds that were to yield a harvest of unparalleled human destruction. And European colonialism began to germinate resentment that would one day end the white man's rule over the world.

The phenomenon of imperialism, which goes back a long time, entered a new phase in 1882, when the British government sent warships to bombard Alexandria. Egypt was nominally part of the Ottoman Empire, which had been disintegrating for more than a century. By 1882 Egypt was "Westernizing." It had helped build the Suez Canal and was acquiring railroads. But to do so the Egyptian government had borrowed heavily from the British and the French, and Egypt therefore grew increasingly dependent on the Europeans—a fact that caused dismay among Egyptians beginning to feel the spirit of nationalism. In June of 1882 an army officer, Colonel Ahmed Arabi, denouncing the Egyptian rulers as European puppets, led a nationalist insurrection. In retaliation the British bombarded Alexandria, landed troops and established a protectorate over Egypt. The British asserted that the arrangement was only temporary, but they remained in Egypt until after the Second World War.

The French, resenting the British intrusion in North Africa, where French influence had been growing since the early part of the century, consolidated their control over Algeria, assumed a protectorate over Tunisia and moved into Morocco. The Italians conquered Libya in a war against Turkey. All of these areas in North Africa were part of the dying Ottoman Empire. The struggle for the spoils of that empire embittered relations between the European powers and contributed to the friction that led to the First World War.

Few parts of the world escaped Western expansion in the Age of Imperialism, but the most dramatic intrusion took place in Black Africa, south of the Sahara, and the full weight of European colonialism was felt there. In the last two decades of the 19th Century the European powers transformed the map of Africa. Flaunting their superior technology and their military power, they staked claims to whatever territories struck their fancy, sometimes in collaboration with their fellow-Europeans, sometimes in opposition to them.

Since the 15th Century, Europeans had been trading on the coasts of Africa—paying tribal chieftains in rum they brought from their Caribbean colonies in exchange for gold, ivory and spices, and in guns, which the tribal chieftains could use for rounding up another of their exports—human slaves. There had been a few well-organized kingdoms in Africa—among them Ghana and Mali, which had flourishing cultures in the period known to the West as the Middle Ages—but these had disappeared under the impact of internecine warfare and Arab conquests from the north. The inner continent was uncharted, dark and mysterious, and until the last third of the 19th Century few white men ventured into its vast stretches. But in time, as enlightened men came to see the infamy of the slave trade, a movement for abolition gained; then Europeans began to think of Christianizing the Africans, and missionaries set forth for the Dark Continent. Explorers, scientists and colorful adventurers also flocked from the West to find out what mysteries lay beyond the coasts. They sent back tales of rich natural resources, and investors and governments followed them into the continent.

As entrepreneurs arrived in Africa, they set up trading posts or mining camps, and each planted the flag of his country. Soon there was a rush for territories, a rush in which no government allowed itself to be outdone. Inevitably, quarrels arose.

Foreseeing international disaster if the situation were not checked, the "Iron Chancellor" of Germany, Count Otto von Bismarck—whose country was late to enter the colonial race—called a conference in Berlin in 1885. There the European powers established the ground rules for the occupation of Africa. By the terms of the Berlin Conference, any nation already established on the coast had rights in the interior. To claim these rights it had only to prove its occupation by sending administrators or troops there, planting its flag and serving notice to the world of its claims.

The result was a frantic scramble for Africa. In a brief period following 1885 almost the entire continent south of the Sahara was partitioned among the British, French, Belgians and Germans. The Portuguese, who had been in Africa since the earliest explorations in the 15th Century, retained and expanded their old trading stations in Angola and Mozambique. By 1914 there were only two independent states in all of Africa: Liberia, which had been established by freed American slaves in 1822 and was practically an American protectorate, and Ethiopia, which alone among African territories had been able to resist conquest. The boundaries of the new map of Africa were laid out according to the claims of the European empires; they usually bore little relation to ethnic or linguistic divisions of the peoples who lived on the land—a fact that was to cause political difficulties in the middle of the 20th Century.

The intrusion of Western culture upset virtually all of Africa. The Africans lived by ancient modes of farming and cattle tending. They had few written languages, but they had eloquent bronze sculpture, wood and ivory carvings, and noble rock paintings. Untouched by modern technology and competitive economic pressures, the Africans were unacquainted with European ideas of government, law and property. They lived under an ethos quite unlike the Europeans' worship of work and wealth. In many societies the women of the tribe did the work of tilling the fields while the men hunted and fought tribal wars.

The Europeans, greedy for the vast natural resources of the continent, exploited the native labor and altered the established ways. Having arrived in Africa after perilous, costly journeys, they intended to make their colonial ventures pay. They did so with inexcusable brutality. The civilized Europeans had rejected chattel slavery at home and outlawed the slave trade, but in Africa they unhesitatingly used forced labor that was tantamount to slavery. For building roads, operating mines and tilling plantations, they conscripted labor gangs, demanding long hours of work on a regular basis, a concept totally alien to tribes used to doing as their spirits moved them. The Europeans established rubber and cocoa plantations on the most fertile lands—lands that the natives had been accustomed to use for grazing, hunting and temporary settlement.

To get the land and the labor they wanted, the Europeans carried off whole tribes, whom they herded into "protected" areas. Sometimes they imposed a hut tax or head tax on able-bodied men, payable in money, which could be earned only by working on the plantations or in the mines. They separated men from their families and sent them off to work and live in compounds under miserable conditions and for pitiful wages that scarcely paid the taxes exacted from them. And the most brutal of the European masters punished slackers by cutting off their hands or shooting them.

In all fairness, it must be said that many Europeans honestly wished to bring the benefits of medicine, sanitation and literacy to the African peoples. But they carried out their self-assumed mission with an air of insufferable condescension. They saw themselves as sharing with the "little black brother" the advantages of the West. Rudyard Kipling, writing of the Philippines in 1899, spoke of the "white man's burden" and the French spoke of the *mission civilisatrice*; both envisioned a crusade of carrying the blessings of the West to the farflung peoples of the world. Europeans never thought to question whether Western "blessings" were indeed blessings—or whether the recipients wanted to be so blessed. Not surprisingly, they left among the colonial peoples a sting of resentment that has persisted, despite some good that the imperialists did—such as ending tribal warfare, building cities and introducing Western medicine, hygiene and education.

The same drive for expansion developed in Asia in the 19th Century. In Asia European merchants and armies imposed Western culture by superior force on peoples who, though inferior to Westerners in technology and power, had highly

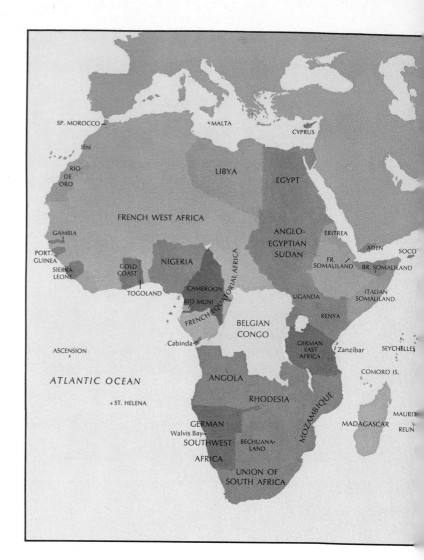

civilized nations with complex urban societies and a wealth of art and literature.

China was the chief victim. The Chinese, for their part, had no interest in the Europeans, whom they considered "barbarians." They traded grudgingly with the West, because they wanted opium, which the English produced in India. They had plenty of tea and silk to give in exchange, and when those ran out there was silver. But commerce was the limit of foreign intercourse, and even that was heavily restricted. A European merchant could trade only with one of the Thirteen Hongs, licensed merchants in Canton who alone transacted foreign business and controlled the

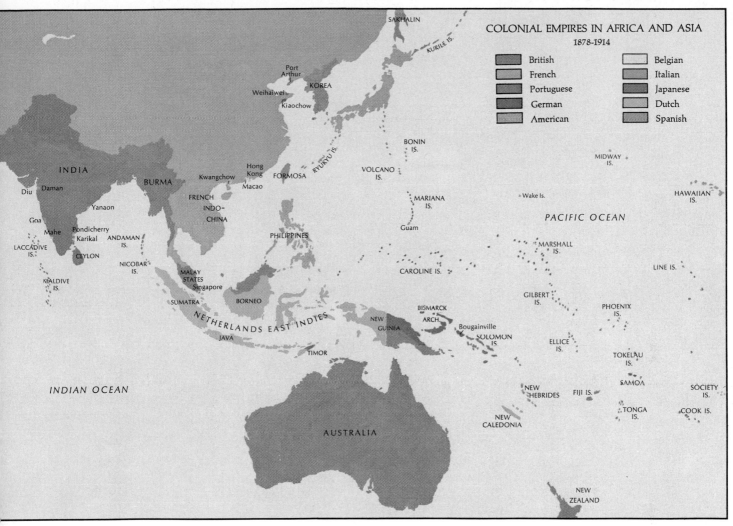

THE COLORS OF IMPERIALISM *spread rapidly across the unindustrialized world after the Berlin Conference of 1878. The interior of Africa, rich territories in Asia and the islands of the Pacific became politically consolidated within 10 major empires. Of these the largest was the British, which more than doubled in size before the end of the 19th Century.*

relations of the foreigners with the local authorities. The Chinese guarded their culture jealously; they forbade the teaching of their language to foreigners, for instance. When Robert Morrison, the first Protestant missionary, settled in Canton and persuaded a native to give him lessons, the teacher had to come disguised as a cobbler returning a pair of shoes—and he carried a flacon of poison to drink in case he was caught.

In the 19th Century the Chinese nation was in dire financial straits. Opium was being imported in such quantities that the drain of silver was bringing the country to bankruptcy. Twice the ailing government made feeble attempts to curb the use of the vicious drug, and both times the English retaliated by shelling several Chinese cities. These incidents became known as the Opium Wars. In the second of these wars the English, together with the French, landed troops, then looted and burned the Emperor's dazzling Summer Palace, a veritable storehouse of gold and silver, jade and pearl.

It took three days for the two armies to carry the treasures away, even though they were aided by hordes of Chinese peasants who, hearing that the palace had fallen, poured over the walls and joined in the plunder. Count Maurice d'Hérisson, an officer of the French Army, recorded in his memoirs the "strange and unforgettable vision [of] the swarming of men of all types and colors . . . on a heap of spoils, hurrahing in all tongues of the world. . . . Some soldiers had buried their heads in the red lacquered chests of the Empress, others were half hidden among heaps of embroidered fabrics and silkware, still others were filling their pockets, shirts and kepis with rubies, sapphires, pearls and pieces of crystal, or again were loading their chests with necklaces made of large pearls. . . . All [the noise] was now and then drowned out by our easily amused soldiers roaring with laughter. . . . Before sunrise, the looting began all over again."

Out of the Opium Wars came the so-called treaty system that the English, later joined by the French, the Germans and the Russians, foisted upon the hapless Chinese. It governed Chinese relations with the West until World War II. Under it the Chinese were required to open more than a dozen port cities to foreign trade. The Europeans gave themselves special privileges, among them the right of extraterritoriality, which placed a European in China above local law; while residing or traveling anywhere in China, he was subject only to the laws of his own government. Import duties in the ports specified by the treaties were limited to a minimal five per cent.

The huge markets opened up by the treaty system inspired English merchants to grandiose but often ill-starred ventures. One jubilant Britisher exclaimed that if every person in China would buy a cotton nightcap a year, the British mills would be kept busy. Another, a manufacturer of musical instruments, shipped a boatload of pianos in the mistaken belief that a million Chinese ladies should do as their European sisters did and learn to play; and a cutlery firm sent thousands of knives and forks, supposing that the Chinese could be lured away from chopsticks. Both these

entrepreneurs were wide of the mark and spent the next several years paying for storage space instead of raking in profits.

In this new forced trade, European advisers collected China's own customs duties, some of which they appropriated as indemnities for the Opium Wars instead of turning them over to the Chinese government for its use. For almost a century the Chinese lived under these degrading treaties, an organized system of subordination so offensive to the Chinese that it has poisoned their feelings toward the West down to the present day.

The treaty system was not the only humiliation China had to endure. In prouder days China had been an empire. Though it did not rule foreign territories in the way of 19th Century European powers, it claimed fealty from its neighbors. Manchuria, Korea, Burma, Cambodia and Laos paid China token tributes periodically, and they submitted the names of new kings for Chinese approval.

China was robbed of these honors in the 19th Century as it was of control of its trade. The British took over Burma. The French helped themselves to Cambodia, Laos and what is today Vietnam, and reorganized the three areas as French Indochina. The Russians also exploited the Chinese; they sailed down the Amur River through Siberian territory belonging to China and founded Vladivostok on the edge of Manchuria.

The West was able to exploit China because the imperial court had fallen into decay. Since the 17th Century China had been ruled by the Manchu Dynasty, so called because its founders had come down into China from Manchuria. By the end of the 19th Century, power was in the hands of the Emperor's aging and capricious aunt, a former concubine of the late Emperor and now Empress Dowager, a role she had made for herself by her skill at palace intrigue. What power she did not have was wielded by feudal warlords who acknowledged no authority but their own. The Emperor, a young man who had inherited the throne as an infant, spent most of his time with dancing girls while the people starved and rebellions racked the country.

Exploitation by the West was bad enough; even harder for the Chinese to swallow was exploitation by their neighbors in Japan, whom the Chinese had for centuries scorned as "Dwarf Pirates." Now the Japanese moved in on China—after they had modernized.

The modernization of Japan is a remarkable story. For two centuries, until 1854, Japan had been isolated from the West, ignoring it completely except for some trade with the Dutch in such items as sugar, medicine, books and paintings.

Like China, Japan had large cities and a sophisticated culture of arts and letters but no industrial technology. The country was nominally headed by an emperor, a semi-divine being who, according to Shinto religious teachings, was the Son of Heaven. But the Emperor was only a figurehead, for the country was ruled by the Tokugawa clan, a family that had held sway over people and emperor alike since 1603. One of its members always held the office of shogun, or military dictator. Under the shogun there were a number of feudal lords who had little political power but a great deal of land, wealth and social distinction.

The Tokugawa were as suspicious of foreigners as the Chinese. In the 17th Century they had outlawed Christianity—brought into the country by Portuguese Jesuit priests—because they saw in the alien religion a means of foreign domination. They also heavily restricted foreign trade—partly because they were suspicious of outside influences, partly because they feared to let their vassals grow rich and powerful on gold and guns, partly because they believed that foreigners had only superfluous luxuries to barter for necessities that Japan could scarcely do without.

But in 1853, at a time when American foreign trade was expanding, four U.S. Navy warships under Commodore Matthew Perry steamed into Edo Bay. Perry demanded that the Japanese open commerce with the West and threatened bombardment if they would not. The Shogun acceded, and a year later trade was under way.

The Western powers forced Japan, as they had China, to sign treaties surrendering control of its trade and tariff policies. Foreigners residing in Japan, as in China, received extraterritorial privileges that exempted them from Japanese laws. In 1862, when a Japanese lord dared to lead an attack on foreign vessels in the straits of Shimonoseki, a naval force consisting of British, French, Dutch and American vessels destroyed the Japanese forts and ships and exacted a heavy indemnity. Japan was no longer master of its destiny.

But the Japanese did not take their misfortunes meekly. Before long, a number of lords took matters into their own hands. Conscious that their predicament was due partly to the weakness of the Shogun, and largely to Japanese lack of modern technology, they resolved to oust the former and to learn the secrets of the West. In 1867 they forced the Shogun's resignation and restored the imperial throne to authority. They were fortunate in having ready for the crown Mutsuhito, the 15-year-old son of the late Emperor; he was malleable enough to allow these men to put their ideas into practice. Mutsuhito's reign, which lasted until 1912, came to be called the Meiji, or "Enlightened," Era.

The Westernization of Japan in the Meiji Era represents the most spectacular example of cultural transformation in recent history. It was the first instance of modernization by a non-Western people.

In the space of hardly two decades, the Japanese

put their small country on a footing with the West. They adopted the Gregorian calendar and minted a new national currency based on the decimal system. They sent students abroad to learn the ways of the West first hand. They erected cannon foundries, cotton mills and other factories designed like those of the West. They laid miles of railroad tracks and instituted mail and telegraph services. They conscripted a state army, which they modeled on that of Prussia, and founded a navy modeled on that of Britain. They sent a mission abroad in the hope of persuading the Western powers to abandon the practice of extraterritoriality; and when the mission failed because Westerners found Japanese jurisprudence backward, they hired a Frenchman to help them draft a modern legal code of justice.

One reason that Japan was able to modernize so rapidly was that the country already had a remarkably high rate of literacy. But further attention to education was a fundamental part of the modernization program. The Japanese promptly founded a military academy, several agricultural colleges and universities, and more than 250 new secondary schools. They established a primary school for every 600 children in the population and made primary education compulsory.

Alongside the industrial and cultural revolution went the expansion of foreign trade; the Japanese bought ships and firearms until they learned to make their own, and they imported plants, seeds and farm implements.

The new rulers of Japan also drafted a constitution and founded a parliament. But these steps did not give the country democracy; the government fused Western and Eastern practices and ideals. Ministers governed in the name of the Emperor, without responsibility to the parliament. The revival of the ancient veneration of the Emperor served the cause of a new nationalism. And

COMMODORE MATTHEW PERRY, *the American emissary who forced Japan to open its doors to the West, was portrayed in 1854 by a Japanese artist who gave him the big Caucasian nose that Asians found so amusing. The caption reads: "Portrait of a high official of the North American Republic."*

the military arm of the government played a large role as it had in the past; by 1883 conscripted soldiers served 12 years and stood always ready to put down resistance to the new ways.

Japan lost no time in showing the Western nations its intention of resisting foreign encroachment and of competing for wealth and power on equal terms with the Europeans. Looking covetously around, Japan went to war with China in 1894, and easily won. The Western world was astonished at Japan's new strength. Russia, because of its interests in Manchuria, reacted quickly, persuading Germany and France to join in forcing Japan to return some of the gains to China.

But the meager returns did little to salve the feelings of China, which was humiliated beyond endurance by the Japanese victory. At last the feeble Chinese government made an effort to modernize, and to that end secured large loans from Europe. But even in this China was victimized.

As security for the loans, the European nations demanded that China pledge its tariffs. Then France demanded mining and railroad-building rights in China and a piece of territory to add to Indochina. England planted officials in the Yangtze River valley and in the port of Shantung. Germany appropriated the port of Kiaochow and mining and railway rights in the province of Shantung. And Russia, on the pretext of "protecting" China from further encroachment, sent a fleet of ships to Port Arthur, then made plans to build a railroad connecting the city with Russia.

These events took place in 1898, the year when the United States had taken, among other colonial territories, the Philippine Islands. Now it, too, had an interest in Pacific affairs. Lest China be divided up like Africa, the United States formulated, with British backing, the so-called Open Door policy, which was intended to keep China "open" to all powers wishing to trade there. The Open Door policy saved China from the fragmentation Africa had suffered, but it did not diminish the privileges the Western powers enjoyed. While the Manchu government stood by helpless, foreign customs officers collected revenues at Chinese ports and foreign gunboats maintained law and order on the Yangtze River.

Law and order were a problem, for the country was rife with revolutionary societies, some of them plotting against the corrupt and vulnerable Manchu government, others against foreign intrusion, which was beginning to rankle more and more. One of the latter groups burst out in May 1900 with one of the bloodiest of several uprisings; this was the celebrated Boxer Rebellion, so called from the name of the society that incited it, the Society of Righteous and Harmonious Fists, loosely translated as Boxers. With their heads wrapped in red scarves bearing the legend *Fu,* or "Happiness," with their chests emblazoned with a red coat

of arms and their wrists and ankles done up in red bands, the Boxers dedicated themselves to overthrowing the "Western devils." In June 1900 they stormed the foreign legations in Peking, plundered foreign shops, tore up railroad tracks—the most visible sign of Western intrusion—and wantonly murdered both foreigners and Chinese Christians.

The Empress Dowager, seeing a chance to strike the hated foreigners a blow, gave the Boxers her blessing and ordered the Chinese armies to aid them. But so divided was the country that some of the warlords refused to help and offered their services to the foreigners instead. The armies of no fewer than eight nations moved in to put down the rebellion—England, France, Germany, Russia, the United States, Japan, Italy and Austria. Once they had done so, they stationed troops in Peking and exacted heavy indemnities from the Chinese government. Weak, divided, heavily in debt, exploited by outsiders, China fell into worse chaos than before.

Japan, in the meantime, forged ahead with its program of modernization, growing in industry, arms and self-confidence. By 1905 the tiny country felt sufficiently sure of itself to wage war on a Western power: Russia.

Both sides had chips on their shoulders. Japan wanted Manchuria as a buffer against Russia; Russia wanted it to assure access to the ocean. Japan wanted raw materials for its burgeoning industry, and it wanted imperial prestige such as the West enjoyed; Russia looked with apprehension on the growing Japanese power. Japan had been smoldering with resentment against Russia for its role in the disappointing conclusion of the war with China 11 years earlier. And Russia, troubled at home over criticism of the czarist regime, welcomed the diversion of a foreign quarrel.

In 1904 the two countries went to war. Japan attacked Port Arthur, Russia's acquisition in

Manchuria, then moved inland to fight and win a stunning battle at Mukden, and next dispatched its brand new navy to sink the Russian fleet, which had sailed almost all the way around the world from the Baltic Sea to engage the Japanese.

The Japanese victory in the Russo-Japanese War was momentous; it drove home to peoples all over the world the practical value of Western technology. For the first time in the modern era a non-Western country had defeated a European power. Japan had won by "Westernizing," by adopting the scientific, industrial and military techniques developed in the West, and by forging a strong sovereign national state like those of the West.

The consequences of the Russo-Japanese War reverberated all over the world. Other peoples were already rankling under foreign exploitation, and they looked on the Japanese with mixed envy and hope. If the Japanese could throw off foreign domination, forge a national state and meet the West on its own terms, why not they? In Persia, where England and Russia were jockeying for position, the native people rose up against both; in Turkey a group of military officers revolted against the Sultan, who was allowing his once-vast empire to crumble away as the Western powers bit off piece after piece. In India a class of educated Indians, who under English tutelage had absorbed everything Western from Christianity to Marxism, now revived Hindu tradition as well. They began to press for a share in government; after 1919 a truly mass movement emerged and eventually won independence.

The significance of the Age of Imperialism can be endlessly debated. For the non-Western peoples of the world the impact of Western civilization was harsh and brutal. The West disrupted the customs of tribes in Africa and the sophisticated civilizations of Japan and China, confounding foreign peoples who could not withstand the intrusion. The West grasped at the raw materials of these areas, and the colonial peoples found themselves producing for a world market, subject to the fluctuations of prices in distant places and dependent on the prosperity of Western capitalism.

But one fact is incontrovertible. Before the Age of Imperialism, the world consisted of disparate entities—Europe and the Americas, the world of Islam, sub-Saharan Africa, the exotic and mysterious Orient. By 1914 these civilizations were all interconnected and interdependent. The Europeans, by carrying their science, their industry and their political organization to all parts of the world, created an irreversible trend toward a unified civilization. The non-Western peoples learned the lesson that science, industry, technology and political organization meant power. Before long they were to insist on sharing in this civilization, and at the same time on winning their independence from Western control and asserting the values of their own cultures, too.

The European powers, for their part, had troubles among themselves as the Age of Imperialism drew to a close. They had already quarreled frequently over rights in Egypt, Sudan, Morocco, the Turkish Empire and elsewhere, settling their disputes by compromise arrangements that often left all concerned dissatisfied. Fearing for their security, they forged alliances. By the first decade of the 20th Century, two massive blocs confronted each other—England, France and Russia in the Triple Entente, and Germany, Austria-Hungary and Italy in the Triple Alliance. And these blocs were no mere paper tigers, for the most formidable product of industrialization was armament and all the industrial nations were building weapons and the armies to wield them. All stood ready to strike if the occasion arose. Few had the vision to see it then, but by the second decade of the 20th Century Europe was heading for disaster.

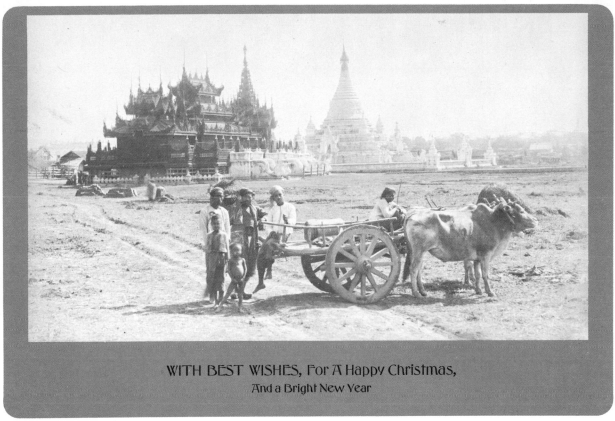

WITH BEST WISHES, For A Happy Christmas,
And a Bright New Year

A BURMESE FAMILY, *posed in front of a pagoda, decorates a Christmas card sent from Mandalay to England in 1886.*

A COLONIAL SCRAPBOOK

With restraint at first, but with greater and greater abandon, 19th Century Europeans explored, then exploited, Africa and the East. Rich in spices and the profits of trade, the East Indies in particular lured thousands of adventurers, who competed lustily for commercial markets as well as international prestige. At the height of the colonial period, 85 per cent of Southeast Asia—including Burma, Laos, Vietnam, Cambodia, Sumatra, Malaya and Java—was either administered or controlled by the French, Dutch or British. In 1885 alone, the Dutch extracted $70 million from their Indonesian colonies.

Although their economic and political methods differed, all Europeans shared one aspect of the colonial experience: they were avid recorders of life overseas. With cameras and pens, in letters and scrapbooks, the colonials unwittingly wrote their own history. As empires grew, photographs of natives in exotic landscapes (*above*) gave way to views of railroad construction and military campaigns (*pages 28-31*). Books and letters, which earlier rhapsodized on the discovery of monuments, later described the taking of capitals and the uneasy truce between European and native. Together these words and pictures reveal colonialism's classic pattern, as seen by the colonials themselves.

First impressions of the natives

The Bataks are not a bad people, and I still think so, not withstanding they eat one another, and relish the flesh of a man better than that of an ox or pig. You must merely consider that I am giving you an account of a novel state of society. The Bataks are not savages, for they write and read, and think full as much, and more than those who are brought up at our Lancastrian and National Schools.

Sir Thomas Stamford Raffles,
British Governor of Java, 1820

A BATAK TRIBESMAN POSES FOR A PHOTOGRAPHER, SUMATRA, 1880s.

On the Tropic Frontier

The neighborhood is lovely. Numbers of rustic bridges, of simple construction, are thrown across the river, and are supported by bamboo poles and fern trees in quite a primitive method. Nature has blessed Java with a healthy climate, genial

temperature, and a fertile soil.
As he gazes on the rich earth,
a Dutchman may well be
proud of his colony.

William Barrington d'Almeida
chronicler of life in Java, 1864

TWO DUTCH PLANTERS AND THEIR SERVANTS RELAX NEAR A JUNGLE BRIDGE, SOUTHERN JAVA, 1883.

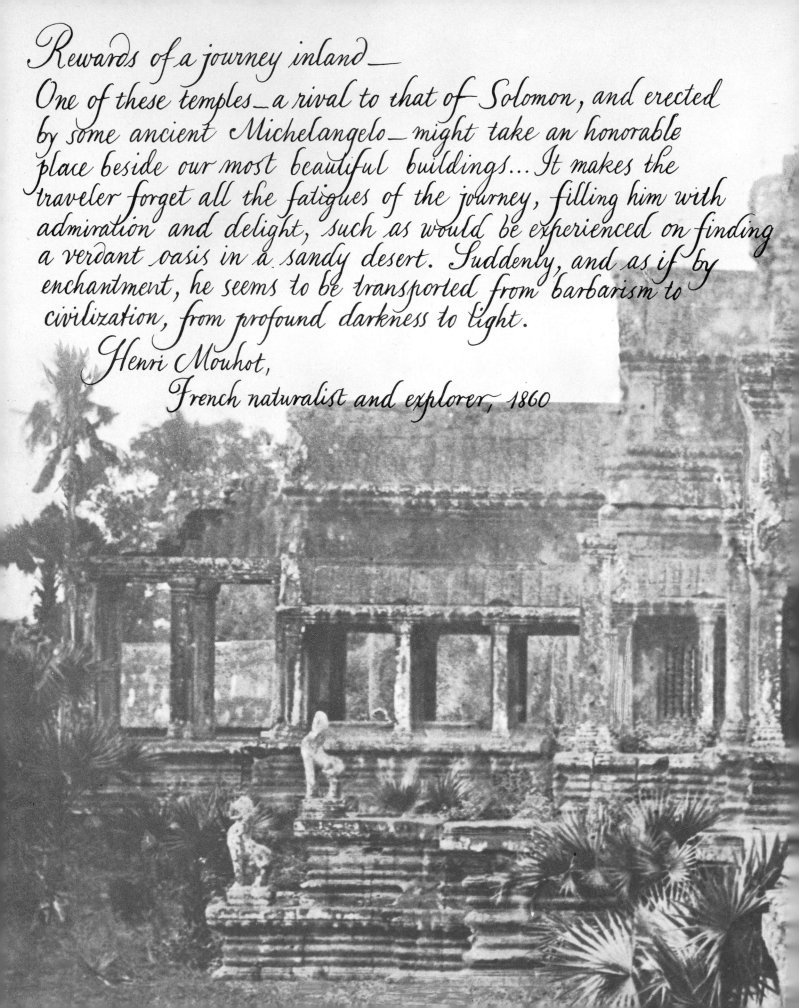

Rewards of a journey inland—
One of these temples—a rival to that of Solomon, and erected by some ancient Michelangelo—might take an honorable place beside our most beautiful buildings... It makes the traveler forget all the fatigues of the journey, filling him with admiration and delight, such as would be experienced on finding a verdant oasis in a sandy desert. Suddenly, and as if by enchantment, he seems to be transported from barbarism to civilization, from profound darkness to light.

Henri Mouhot,
French naturalist and explorer, 1860

ANGKOR WAT, CAMBODIA, PHOTOGRAPHED BY THE SCOTTISH EXPLORER JOHN THOMSON, 1866.

Thoughts of an Empire-Builder

Means of communication at present
leave much to be desired. The
construction of a railway in
the Padang Highlands
makes it possible
to send coal
from the pits
of Ombilin to
the port of
Emmahaven, whose
fortune is being made
by this trade in coal. So soon
as further railways make transport
an easy matter, Sumatra will be
able to rival Java in wealth.

Antoine Cabaton,
historian of the Dutch East Indies, 1911

DUTCH ENGINEERS AND CHINESE LABORERS CONSTRUCT A RAILROAD TUNNEL, WESTERN SUMATRA, 1892.

On the taking
of Hanoi —

All right! With a mere
two hundred I have taken
Hanoi. For us, not a scratch.
The surprise was complete and
succeeded beyond my wildest
dreams. Our gunboat cannon
stunned the poor brutes, who
had never seen an exploding
shell. It has been a model
operation. If I am
supported soon all
Indo-China is French.

Francis Garnier,
French naval officer,
explorer and author, 1873

A VIETNAMESE MEMBER OF THE FRENCH EXPEDITIONARY FORCES GUARDS A REBEL PIRATE, VIETNAM, 1882.

Comforts of a new life —
The Dutchman profits as far as possible, in matters of clothing, by the instinct and experience of the native. In the East Indian home the man is always clothed in pyjama trousers and a tunic of white cotton, his feet being bare in heel-less slippers. From the esthetic point of view the effect is disastrous, but the costume is relatively cool.

Antoine Cabaton, historian of Dutch East Indies, 1911

A COLONIAL FAMILY RELAXES ON ITS PLANTATION VERANDA, SUMATRA, 1897

2

THE LIGHTS GO OUT

In the summer of 1914, at the height of its wealth, power and global ascendancy, Europe fell into disaster. War broke out in July of that year. It became the first world war in history, and an event of profound importance in shaping 20th Century events. The frightful four-year ordeal of bloodletting so weakened Europe that the Continent lost its supremacy over the world. The War overthrew four dynastic empires and it inspired the Communist Revolution in Russia. It heralded the end of the Age of Imperialism and carried the peoples of Asia and Africa directly into the arena of world affairs.

The quarrels that had developed among the European powers during the Age of Imperialism had stretched Europe's nerves taut. The rivalry between England and France over Egypt and the Sudan, between France and Germany over Morocco, between England and Russia over Persia; the race for spheres of influence in China and the pressures involved in the partition of Africa—all these had been settled by 1914 through compromise. Repeated compromise left tensions—in Germany, which had acquired little colonial territory and craved what it thought to be its "place in the sun," and in England, France and Russia, which shuddered at every step that Germany took toward achieving hegemony over Europe. One result was the alliance system, by which each of the great European powers had garnered allies over the years in the interests of national security.

By 1914 two rival alliances confronted each other in Europe: the Triple Alliance of Germany, Austria-Hungary and Italy, and the Triple Entente of England, France and Russia. No international polity had developed commensurate with the world economy that had come into being; no organ existed to mediate international quarrels. The alliance system made it probable that a local quarrel would become a European war. And the interdependence of countries all over the world made it inevitable that a European war would be a world war.

The fateful clash came, as Count Otto von Bismarck, former Chancellor of Germany, had predicted it would, over "some damned foolish thing in the Balkans." The Balkan region was an

VICTIMS OF POISON GAS, *being herded into an aid station toward the end of World War I, were painted by the portraitist John Singer Sargent. The War, more dreadful than anyone foresaw, also brought forth such mechanized horrors as tank assaults and bombing raids on defenseless cities.*

anomaly in contemporary Europe—a region with practically no industry and with only the semblance of democratic institutions. The people carried a host of ethnic strains; they were Bulgars, Croats, Czechs, Poles, Ruthenians, Slovaks and Serbs—all of Slavic origin, like the Russians.

Some of the Balkan territory was ruled, as it had been for 600 years, by the Ottoman Empire; some of it was divided into independent kingdoms; another part, the territories of Bosnia and Herzegovina, had been snatched from the Ottoman Empire by Austria-Hungary in 1908. The Balkan peoples clamored for independence and national recognition and looked for aid to their giant sister to the north, Imperial Russia. Thwarted in every effort they made toward self-determination, the Balkan countries were rife with secret societies plotting for independence.

Few men in Austria paid any attention to Balkan demands, but there was one who did—the Archduke Franz Ferdinand, heir to the Habsburg throne. Franz Ferdinand was known to have planned reforms that he meant to carry out on his accession to the Austrian throne.

On June 28, 1914, the Archduke paid an ill-fated state visit to Sarajevo, the capital of Bosnia. Nothing is less palatable to a radical than a reformer, and Franz Ferdinand was poorly regarded by the Slavs. When his visit was announced, a cry of rage echoed across the Slavic world. One secret Serbian society, called variously "Union or Death" and the "Black Hand," sent three youths to Sarajevo for the occasion. On Sunday morning one of these boys, Gavril Princip, stationed himself on the narrow street along which the Archduke was to drive in an open car. The car came through as scheduled, and when it paused to shift gears—right in front of Gavril Princip—the 19-year-old boy fired two shots. In a few minutes the Archduke and his wife were dead.

In a paroxysm of outrage, the Austrian government resolved to end Slavic agitation in the Empire once and for all. But the officials dickered for almost four weeks over a course of action. Then, on July 23, having obtained assurance from Germany that they could count on "faithful support" for whatever they did, the Austrians delivered an ultimatum to Serbia, making several harsh demands and requiring an answer in 48 hours. The Serbs replied on time and politely, accepting most of the Austrian stipulations, but rejecting the demand that Austrian officials move onto Serbian soil to investigate the crime. The German Kaiser, who had had second thoughts about his rash offer to Austria, declared that the note "dissipates every reason for war." But the Austrians were too inflamed for appeasement. On July 28 they declared war on Serbia, then bombarded Belgrade.

The alliance system came fatefully into play. Germany had to stand by Austria. Russia could not desert Serbia. France could not risk abandoning Russia. The military leaders in each nation, moreover, had rigid mobilization plans and feared to allow a potential enemy to mobilize in advance.

The Russians, aware that their military apparatus was cumbersome, moved the fastest. Russian soldiers had to travel an average of 700 miles to reach the theater of war, and the Russian railroads were scarcely equal to the task of transporting an army so far in haste. In addition, the Russian munitions factories were turning out less than half the rifle cartridges needed for the 800,000 soldiers Russia had pledged to send. Indeed, the Russian Army was lucky to have firearms at all. The Minister of War, a corpulent general by the name of Vladimir Sukhomlinov, was hard put to imagine why anyone would discard the glorious saber for new-fangled firearms. Only a year before, he had discharged five instructors from the war college for teaching the virtues of fire

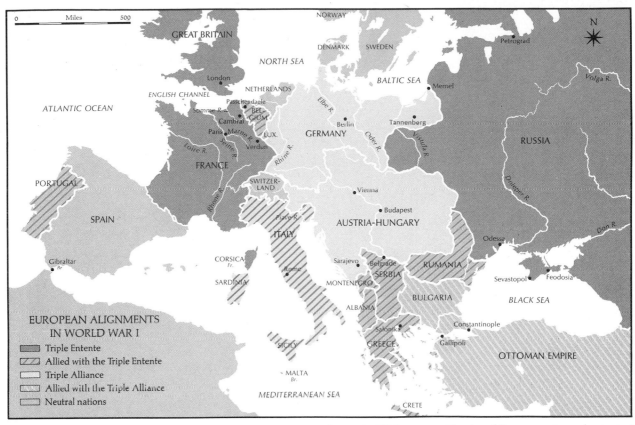

ON THE EVE OF WAR, *Europe in 1914 was an attic of rankling memories and a nest of new troubles. France was embittered by her defeat in the Franco-Prussian War of 1870; most of the European nations had joined either of two opposed defensive camps, the Triple Entente and the Triple Alliance. Only Italy hedged her bets, but she was at length won over by the Entente with the promise of foreign territories.*

power. "All these things," Sukhomlinov proclaimed, "are merely vicious innovations."

Nevertheless, there were other men in Russia who knew that mobilization was a complicated business and that there was not a moment to lose. When Austria bombarded Serbia, the Czar signed a mobilization decree. Germany declared war on Russia on the evening of August 1, and two days later on France, which was standing by Russia. England, despite commitments to the French, would have preferred neutrality. The Germans facilitated the British decision when they wantonly marched through Belgium, violating a 75-year-old treaty guaranteeing Belgian neutrality. England declared war.

By August 5 the five major European powers were in combat, and the conflict was yet to spread farther afield. Japan, faithful to an alliance that it had formed with Britain in 1902, and seeing in the War an opportunity to take over the German colonial possessions in the Far East, declared war on Germany on August 23. The British Dominions—Canada, Australia, New Zealand and the Union of South Africa—responded quickly to the crisis and mobilized; so did the French possessions in Africa. British India also entered the war effort, although the Indians themselves had no voice in the decision. By 1915 Turkey and Bulgaria had joined Germany and Austria; and Italy, which had reneged on its bargain with the Triple Alliance, joined the Allies. Before the War was over, 30 nations, with a combined population of 1.4 billion peoples, spread over six continents, were to be drawn into the conflict.

To Woodrow Wilson, President of the United States, the War seemed remote at first; it looked like another of the age-old European quarrels arising out of nationalist rivalry and greed. Although the Americans had close cultural ties with the English and the French and were generally out of sympathy with the militaristic Germans, the dominant sentiment in the United States went against involvement. Wilson spoke the feelings of his countrymen when he appealed in August 1914 for neutrality "in fact as well as in name during these days that are to try men's souls."

The "days" that Wilson spoke of turned into weeks, months and years. Yet everyone had looked forward to a brief war and no one expected the ordeal that materialized. "You will be home before the leaves have fallen from the trees," the Kaiser boasted to his troops in August 1914.

Both sides put their trust in the strategy of quick offensive. This was one reason why quick mobilization was so important. The German Schlieffen Plan, conceived by Count Alfred von Schlieffen, the former German chief of staff, was designed to knock out the French in six weeks and then turn on the Russians, thus avoiding the dread necessity of a two-front war. The French, for their part, planned to invade Alsace-Lorraine in a powerful offensive. The German armies moved first, rolling through Belgium and northern France. By early September they had reached the Marne River, threatened Paris and stood, they believed, on the verge of a quick victory. But their rapid advance created many problems; communications with headquarters at the rear were disrupted, and the soldiers were exhausted from the drive.

The French rallied and checked the Germans in the Battle of the Marne, a conflict that historians, with the benefit of hindsight, see as the most important engagement of the War. It kept the Germans from Paris and upset the Schlieffen Plan, thereby thrusting upon the Germans the dreaded two-front war, for Russia was by now advancing in the direction of Prussia. The Battle of the Marne also set the course for the rest of the War—a course in which one vast army would hurl itself against another and gain a few square yards of land at the cost of thousands of lives.

In the next few weeks the Germans tried desperately to take the Channel ports. But they failed, and the broad highway of the ocean remained open to the Allies. The British made use of that fact by blockading the enemy—a deadly maneuver, for Germany did not grow sufficient food and relied on imports. Ultimately the Germans faced the threat of starvation.

Though the French won the Battle of the Marne and the British saved the Channel, the War from that point onward was a stalemate. The strategy of lightning movement gave way to a jockeying for position. Huge armies that balanced each other in size arranged themselves in trenches that eventually zigzagged for 300 miles from the North Sea to the Swiss frontier. Everywhere the murderous firepower of the machine gun gave the advantage to the defenders. In the next four years the costliest battles in all human history netted only the smallest gains for each side. At the Somme in 1916, the British captured 120 square miles—about a tenth of the size of Rhode Island—at a cost of 400,000 men; at Passchendaele the next year they lost 240,000 men to gain 50 square miles.

For the next two years the battle lines swayed by no more than 10 miles back and forth on the entire Western Front. Each side made repeated efforts to break through the other's lines. After artillery had prepared the way, the infantry would go "over the top" with bayonets and hand grenades in readiness, only to be felled by the machine guns or trapped in barbed-wire entanglements.

The cause for which the soldiers died came to seem increasingly obscure. The unbearable life in the trenches meant mud, vermin, dread of bombardment. No other fact of the War did more to shatter the optimism of the pre-1914 world; how could anyone dream of nationalism, progress, humanitarianism, culture, in the midst of such bloodletting?

When it was clear that there would be no quick decision, each belligerent turned its attention to the home front. Entire populations had to be mobilized to support the stupendous military undertakings. Governments marshaled people and resources for the war effort as never before. They allocated raw materials, rationed food, managed their economies by fixing prices and wages, and controlled manpower. In Germany all males between the ages of 17 and 60 who were not at the front had to work in factory, office or farm, as the government directed them, to maintain production of food and war matériel.

Faced with the rigors of the British blockade and thus cut off from vital materials, Germany pioneered in economic control, establishing a war economy, or "war socialism," as it was sometimes called. The system of private enterprise and competitive capitalism had operated well enough in peacetime, but it could not make the most of the nation's resources in war. Germany had a management genius in Walter Rathenau, an industrialist and philosopher who was one of the first to foresee a long war. Under his inspiration the government organized the major firms of all important industries into giant wartime cartels, companies that coordinated production under government supervision.

Science, too, entered the service of the War. Scientists were directed to develop synthetics to make up for natural products that were in short supply. In one of the most remarkable achievements, Fritz Haber, a physical chemist, succeeded in extracting nitrates from the air, thereby making possible the production of the explosives and the fertilizers that Germany so vitally needed. Even so, the population ate less, suffered dietary deficiencies, and turned to substitute foods, eating potato bread (war bread) and in some cases having to subsist on turnips alone—a bitter irony for a country whose Kaiser had derided the Czar of Russia as "only fit to live in a country house and grow turnips."

Because of the crippling effects of the blockade, the Germans were forced to pursue their war economy more thoroughly than other countries, but governments everywhere regulated production and manpower in some measure. By May 1916 even the British, who alone among the great powers of Europe had staunchly resisted compulsory military service in the past 50 years, introduced conscription. Britain had a new prime minister in that year. He was David Lloyd George, a hot-headed, strong-willed Welshman and a silver-tongued orator. He gave such an impression of fearlessness that he was known as the "Big Beast of the Forest"; yet when faced with making a speech, his hands trembled and his shirt dripped perspiration.

As prime minister, Lloyd George revolutionized the government. He swept aside traditional protocol, and instituted a five-man cabinet that answered to no one but him. This cabinet, whose brains Lloyd George picked during interminable breakfast conferences, issued orders to the ministries of food and industry, then saw to it that its instructions were followed. In this way Lloyd George established a virtual dictatorship.

The French went even further. Georges Clemenceau, a gruff character appointed premier at the age of 76 in 1917, declared that "war is too important a matter to trust to the generals," and forthwith turned to its prosecution himself. As a former newspaper editor, he might have been expected to champion free speech and a free press; but instead the unpredictable Clemenceau censored the news, terrorized defeatists and imprisoned advocates of negotiated peace. The rigors he imposed, far from engendering resentment, bolstered the sagging morale of the French.

As the fighting dragged on, each side tried to strengthen its position outside Europe, for though the War began as a European quarrel, the stakes were global. Accordingly, the theaters of war spread to many colonial areas. The British and the French overran the German colonies of Togoland, Cameroon and German East Africa. The Germans and the Portuguese fought each other in Angola. These activities were carried on in the spirit of imperialism; no one paid the slightest heed to the Africans, who were still only pawns in the game of world politics.

In the Far East, Japan profited most from the European hostilities. Shortly after they entered the War in August 1914, the Japanese took over the German-owned Marshall, Mariana and Caroline Islands. Australia and New Zealand appropriated the German islands south of the equator. The Japanese displaced the Germans in the Chinese ports and also pressed the hapless Chinese for control of their military and domestic affairs. Had China acceded to these demands, it would have become virtually a Japanese protectorate. But China stood fast and, expecting support against Japanese encroachment, entered the War in 1917 on the Allied side. Unfortunately, little support came—an Allied failure that was to cause trouble at the postwar peace conference.

If they had no time for China, the Allies gave much attention to the Middle East. Before the War, Turkey, the center of the Ottoman Empire, had been of special concern to Germany. German capital had helped build the Turkish railroads;

MUHAMMAD VI, SULTAN OF THE OTTOMAN EMPIRE   KAISER WILHELM II OF GERMANY

German military advisers had helped remodel the Turkish Army. At the outset of the War, the Allies paid no heed to the Empire as a power—it had been called the "Sick Man of Europe" for at least a century—but Turkey lay strategically at the crossroads of East and West. For centuries Russia had coveted Constantinople because the city lay at the foot of the Black Sea, Russia's only water route to the south and west. But the Allies thought the decrepit Empire of too little account to bother with in the War—until they found that the Germans had moved in there.

The Germans were bent on blockading Russia. They steamed up to the mouth of the Dardanelles, bullied the Turks (who were vacillating over a choice of sides) and then, with Turkish acquiescence, announced to the world that they had sold their ships to the Turkish government. That done, they sailed through the Straits flying the Turkish flag, the sailors sporting fezzes on their heads—a violation of the Hague Convention, which prohibited the use of disguise. In the name of the Turks the Germans laid siege to Odessa and Sevastopol. Russia thereupon declared war on Turkey. Britain and France followed; thus another quarter of the world was drawn into the War.

In the course of the conflict, the belligerent powers engaged in a new game—psychological warfare,

EMPEROR KARL I OF AUSTRIA-HUNGARY　　CZAR NICHOLAS II OF RUSSIA

IN THE TWILIGHT OF THE GODS, *the golden years before 1914-1918, Europe was securely controlled by emperors and kings, like those at left, and by aristocratic principles that had obtained since the Middle Ages. But by the early 1920s the Ottoman Empire was no more, Germany's last Kaiser was in exile, the House of Habsburg, which had ruled Austria for almost five centuries, was extinct, and Russia was ruled by commissars rather than by czars. Aristocracy henceforth would be on the fashion pages of Europe, not in the seats of power.*

a business of inciting national discontent among the subject peoples on the enemy side. Here they were stirring up more turbulence than they reckoned on. The British and French rashly held out the promise of independence to the Czechs, Slovaks and Serbs in the Austrian Empire, and to the Arabs in the Turkish Empire—a fact that the nationalist leaders of British India and French Indochina noted attentively. The Germans supported independence movements in the Russian Empire among the Poles, Ukrainians and Baltic peoples, and in the British Empire among the Irish.

Germany fished in other troubled waters, too—and with unfortunate consequences. In January 1917, Arthur Zimmermann, the German foreign secretary, foolhardily sent a telegram to Mexico promising the acquisition of Texas, New Mexico and Arizona if Mexico would join Germany in war against the United States. Unhappily for Germany, the note was intercepted and decoded by the British, who transmitted it to Washington. The United States government released the telegram to the press, and inevitably it aroused a furor. No other incident had yet so forcefully brought the War home to Americans. Germany had carelessly given the shifting American mood a shove in the wrong direction.

The mood in the belligerent countries was changing, too. As the civilian populations endured the ordeal of privation, hunger, sacrifice and loss of loved ones, national fervor gave way to discontent. Parts of the French Army mutinied in 1917, and civilians in French Quebec and Australia rioted against compulsory military service. But these were minor episodes, with no consequences to speak of. The War was to lead to a truly earth-shaking revolution in Russia. That revolution would accomplish what many Russian revolutionaries had begun in 1914 to think impossible—the overthrow of the Russian autocracy.

The turning point of the War came in 1917, and the Russian Revolution was one of two decisive events that broke the deadlock. The other was the entry of the United States into the War.

Actually, there were two Russian revolutions that year. The first, in March, overthrew the czarist monarchy. Like the other belligerents, Russia had had to mobilize population and resources to sustain the war effort. But the cumbersome bureaucratic apparatus failed. Soldiers went into battle without rifles and sometimes had to pick up the rifles of fallen comrades before they could advance. The Czar, Nicholas II, had assumed command at the front and virtually abandoned the government of the country to the nervous and hysterical Czarina, who had fallen under the influence of various unwholesome court favorites. The most notable of these was the shadowy Gregory Rasputin, an impostor with greasy hair, filthy fingernails and, in the words of one acquaintance, "the smell of a goat." This charlatan, posing as a Holy Man, was now directing affairs of state.

As Russia's military disasters mounted, so did evidence of corruption and inefficiency. Transportation and communications, uncertain to begin with, broke down, creating a severe scarcity of food in the cities. Bread riots and street demonstrations broke out in Petrograd; soldiers sent to quell them refused to fire on the demonstrators. In December 1916, five conspirators—one a cousin and one an in-law of the Czar—murdered Rasputin. In March 1917 Nicholas II abdicated, and a coalition of liberal and democratic leaders hastily formed a Provisional Government. The Allied countries hailed the making of a new and democratic Russia. And the Provisional Government committed itself to continuing the War.

Tragically, the new government failed to grasp the true mood of the masses—the land hunger of the peasants and, above all, the overwhelming desire for peace. Thousands of men were being lost in the War every month. Soldiers were deserting in droves and marching the long road home—"voting with their feet," as the expression went. A rival power, the "soviets"—councils of workers and soldiers—grew up in several cities to challenge the Provisional Government. In the Petrograd Soviet the most extreme, militant Marxists, the Bolsheviks, gained the majority.

By tireless work and shrewd maneuvers on the part of V. I. Lenin, a fiery zealot nicknamed *Starik* (the Old Man) for his imperious manner, the Bolsheviks captured the Revolution. Before the War, despairing of reform in Russia, Lenin had exiled himself in Switzerland. In his view the War was flatly capitalist and imperialist. The capitalist powers had parceled out the world among themselves, he preached, and a dissatisfied power like Germany could seek a reapportionment of the colonial spoils only through war. The workers of the world had nothing to gain from the War, and there was no difference between the absolutism of the German Kaiser and the imperial repression practiced by the British and the French capitalists. The only path to peace and emancipation, he asserted, lay through revolution. Turn the imperialist war into a civil war, he demanded.

Lenin's ambitions for revolution in Russia appealed to the Germans; he could be used against the Provisional Government, and thus against the Allies. The German government therefore arranged Lenin's return to Russia, giving him safe passage through Germany in a sealed car.

Back in Russia, Lenin raised the slogan of "Peace, land and bread," and it fell on receptive ears. He organized the Bolsheviks in Petrograd and other cities and called for a revolutionary transfer of power to the soviets, denouncing all other parties in the government.

On November 7, 1917, the Bolsheviks arrested members of the Provisional Government and proclaimed a socialist state. It was a momentous date in world history. A small band of conspirators had successfully executed a revolution in the name of 145 million oppressed people under a banner proclaiming the cause of world revolution. The Bolshevik feat immediately won the admiration of hundreds of German, French and Italian workers, who were increasingly disenchanted with the War. By its attack upon imperialism, its denunciation of the War and its promises of peace and "democracy," the Bolshevik Revolution also held a dazzling appeal to colonial peoples.

Thus did Russia become the capital of world Communism. One of the first acts of the new regime was to pull out of World War I. The

Bolsheviks pledged to liberate the workers from capitalist exploitation and to distribute land to the peasants. They sent envoys to China to announce the surrender of the extraterritorial privileges the czarist government had enjoyed. They proclaimed the equality of all peoples in Russia. In March 1918 the Soviet government signed with an exultant Germany the Treaty of Brest-Litovsk, ceding Russian Poland and all the western provinces on the Baltic shore to Germany, promising independence to Finland and the Ukraine, and bringing peace to Russia.

The second great event of 1917 was the entry of the United States into the War. For two and a half years President Wilson had resisted committing the United States to either side. As late as November 1916 he was re-elected to office on the campaign slogan "He kept us out of war." Yet sympathies in the United States went predominantly to the Allied powers, to which heavy loans had been extended, and there was general revulsion against the German conduct of the War. Now, at the end of January 1917, the German High Command overreached itself. It prevailed upon the government to resume unrestricted submarine warfare, a practice that Wilson had persuaded Germany to suspend in 1915.

The new decision was not made easily, for the Germans were well aware that unrestricted use of the submarine might provoke the United States to war. But the German High Command saw in undersea warfare the one available tactic that could break the British blockade, open the seas to Germany and thus end the stalemate. Even if the action did arouse the United States to a declaration of war, the German High Command mistakenly reasoned, the submarine, by breaking the British blockade, could defeat the Allies in six months—less time than it would take the United States to mobilize. On January 31, the Germans announced

that they would sink all ships bound for British waters. They made the promise good; in March they sank five American vessels.

Wilson came to the conclusion that a German victory over Britain, and German domination of the Atlantic, would jeopardize United States security. For more than a century the British Navy had formed a shield behind which the United States could enjoy the luxury of isolation. In the event of German hegemony over the Continent and German domination of the high seas, who could count on the security of the United States, or on the security of any part of the Western Hemisphere, for that matter? But for Wilson the question was not solely the threat to American security; the issue had become a clear-cut case of right versus wrong.

Having come to that conclusion, Wilson addressed a joint session of Congress on the evening of April 2. The whole country was tense with expectation. Before the address was to begin, Vice President Thomas R. Marshall marched into the Hall of Representatives leading the Senators as a body, and almost everyone carried a small American flag. When Wilson arrived, the assembled Congressmen greeted him with a two-minute standing ovation; when he spoke they interrupted with frequent applause. Wilson summed up German violations of international and moral law, then asked the Congress to declare war, urging the people to fight "for the rights of nations, great and small, and the privilege of men everywhere to choose their way of life and of obedience. The world must be made safe for democracy." The Congress rose to its feet and cheered. "It was a cheer so deep and so intense and so much from the heart," wrote the correspondent of *The New York Times*, who was there, "that it sounded like a shouted prayer."

That the United States was already a world

power had been quite apparent since its intervention in the Far East in the decade 1895-1905, when it took the Philippine Islands from Spain and proclaimed the Open Door policy in China. Now the United States threw itself into the arena of world politics.

The European war, which had begun over a quarrel in the Balkans, was now truly a world war. Scarcely a segment of the world was not involved. It was also, under Wilson's leadership, a revolutionary crusade. The year 1917 was a watershed in 20th Century history. The American intervention in the War was decisive; it was also dramatic evidence of the waning strength of Europe. Europe could no longer settle its own affairs. It would henceforth be overshadowed by the presence of the two great continental powers on its flanks—the United States and Russia—and, in the East, by the mighty power of Japan.

Following Wilson's address to Congress in April, the American democracy girded for combat. As the European powers had been doing for some time now, the United States introduced economic controls it had never known. It converted peacetime industries to wartime uses, stepping up the production of food under government supervision; it sent ships to convoy the British merchant fleet through the German submarine menace, and it poured men and supplies into France.

The American intervention represented more than just an increment of strength. In Wilson the Allies had an eloquent spokesman who infused new spirit into the weary belligerents and caught the imagination of peoples all over the globe. Not only the Allies fell under his spell; in other parts of the world Wilson proved a counterpoise to the revolutionary appeal of Lenin.

The two leaders, though they represented political ideals at opposite poles, actually had much in common. Both were eloquent speakers possessed of a zeal for reform. Both held a world view that transcended local politics. Both rejected the existing international system of balance-of-power diplomacy and the principle of controlling international affairs by bartering peoples. Both envisioned a wholly new international order, and both appealed to all peoples regardless of race or color. Both emphasized the equality of all nations, great and small. Lenin spoke of the proletariat and a classless society; Wilson spoke of the common man and democracy. Between them they touched off a duel for the allegiance of the world's peoples, a duel that outlasted both their lives. By the beginning of 1918 the seeds had been sown for an ideological struggle of global implications.

The intervention of the United States, though it did not diminish his idealism, forced a change in Wilson's approach. In January 1917 he had talked of "peace without victory." As a belligerent he spoke of peace to be imposed by the Allied powers on the vanquished; of "force which shall make right the law of the world and cast every selfish dominion down in the dust." No longer was there talk of compromise or negotiated settlement; now the War was to be fought to the total collapse of the German and Austrian Empires—an eventuality that no one had foreseen in 1914.

In early 1918 the Germans, though in dire straits, were far from defeated. Relieved of the need to fight a two-front war by the defection of Russia from the Allied side, they launched a gigantic new offensive and drove deep into the Allied lines. By the end of May they stood less than 50 miles from Paris. But the offensive could not be sustained. In June American troops, who had begun pouring in at the rate of 250,000 a month, won their first victory at Château-Thierry in the Argonne Forest. In July Marshal Ferdinand Foch, who had been named commander of all the Allied armies to coordinate the military effort, organized a counterattack that succeeded with the help of nine American divisions.

By August the Germans were in retreat, and the offensive passed to the Allies. In November the British brought in a new weapon that the usually inventive Germans had failed to think of—armored tanks that could roll through gunfire, felling the enemy with a barrage of fire as they went. With 324 of these monsters in mass formation at the Battle of Cambrai, the British sent the Germans reeling back several miles.

In the autumn German morale sank. The people were suffering from hunger; mutinies disrupted the army and navy; desertions were common; revolutionary demonstrations broke out in Bavaria, which lay in the path of the advancing Allied armies. The High Command, finally at its wits' end, pressed the Kaiser to set up the democratic government that Wilson demanded before an armistice could be discussed and approached the Allies with terms for surrender. On November 9 the Kaiser abdicated his throne, and a German republic came into being by proclamation. The Austrian Empire had already disintegrated; Hungarians, Czechs and Slovaks had simply laid down their arms. At 11 a.m. on November 11, 1918, the German representatives signed an armistice on Allied terms, and the carnage ended.

The toll was staggering. Germany had lost 1,827,000 men, or 12 per cent of its men between 15 and 50; France had lost 1,400,000, or 14 per cent. Austria-Hungary had lost 1,350,000 men, Russia almost two million. Italy lost 700,000 men, Serbia 370,000. Britain and its Dominions lost 950,000. The United States left over 115,000 dead in Europe—about half of them victims of disease. For all of the combatants, the totals came to some 10 million dead, with an additional 20 million wounded. To the losses in battle had to be added the civilian casualties through invasions and blockade; epidemics of cholera, typhus and influenza; malnutrition and famine—perhaps another 10 million innocent lives. Northern France and Belgium lay in utter devastation. For France and England both, the cost in money was estimated at 30 per cent of the national wealth. Never in history had war so desolated civilization.

In one respect the War represented a victory for democracy: the last of the military monarchies perished. Four empires crumbled—the German, the Austrian, the Turkish and the Russian. Hohenzollerns, Habsburgs, Ottomans and Romanovs disappeared from the scene, and with them the princes and archdukes and all their courtly retinues. Ideas of popular sovereignty, national self-determination and self-government filled the air, advancing the political ideals of the American and French Revolutions. The colonial peoples were stirred from one side by the Bolshevik call for equality and emancipation and from the other by Wilson's call for national self-determination. They could not long be denied their aspirations.

Through the personal force of Woodrow Wilson, the United States emerged as the moral leader of the world. He was hailed as a savior of civilization, and he believed it within his power to achieve, through moral suasion, a durable settlement that would satisfy all. He advocated a just peace, world economic cooperation, an end to secret diplomacy and the right to self-determination, and toward those ends he conceived and worked to found the League of Nations. The Wilsonian credo implied that democracy and liberalism would go along inevitably with national independence and that free nations would guarantee world peace. It was a typically American credo, and it held wide appeal. The peoples of Asia were aroused by the hope that they too were included in the Wilsonian program.

A peace conference convened in Paris in January

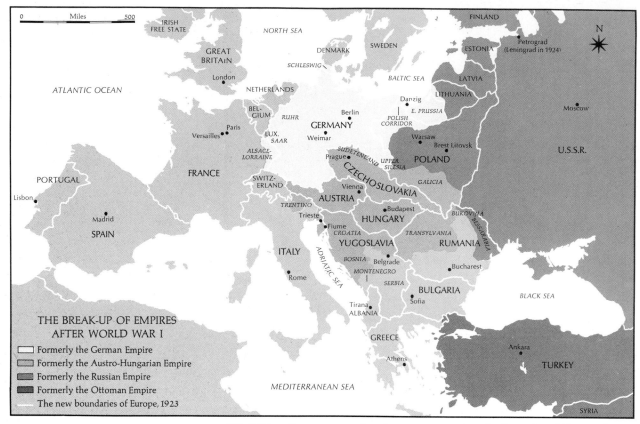

THE BREAK-UP OF EMPIRES
AFTER WORLD WAR I
☐ Formerly the German Empire
☐ Formerly the Austro-Hungarian Empire
▨ Formerly the Russian Empire
■ Formerly the Ottoman Empire
— The new boundaries of Europe, 1923

THE AFTERMATH OF WAR *produced seven new nations in Central and Eastern Europe that owed their existence to President Wilson's theories of self-determination. These proud countries, carved out of four empires, gave a certain vitality to postwar Europe— but did not constitute a permanent solution to the political ills of the Continent.*

1919. Twenty-seven nations were represented. Russia, torn by revolution, was absent. Many unofficial delegates as well came from all parts of the world. But the spokesmen for Britain, France, the United States and Italy—David Lloyd George, Georges Clemenceau, Woodrow Wilson and Vittorio Orlando—made the important decisions. The smaller nations complained that at the end of a war fought for national liberation they had little voice in the settlement. But the issues were complicated, and time pressed for more rapid decisions than open deliberations would permit.

With respect to the colonial world, the disposition of the former German and Turkish possessions corresponded to the wartime conquests, but with a significant innovation. Direct annexation by the victor powers would have been a blatant contravention of Wilson's principles. The alternative

on which the peace negotiators settled was a mandate system, under which the Allies were confirmed in the possession of the territories they had occupied during the War, but the territories were to be held in trust —as "mandates"—in behalf of the new League of Nations.

Each mandatory power was to report annually on its stewardship to the League of Nations. As part of its mandate, it had to guarantee freedom of religion, prohibit the slave trade, ban military fortifications and pledge itself not to undertake the military training of the native inhabitants. A promise of eventual self-government for the colonial peoples was made, but no one in 1919 believed they were ready for self-government. Indeed, the Covenant of the League of Nations stated that the colonial peoples were "not yet able to stand by themselves under the strenuous conditions of the modern world" and needed the guidance of "advanced nations." Besides, to grant them independence would raise serious and embarrassing questions about the colonies of the victor powers, the British and the French.

The mandate system, avowedly a compromise, underscored the uneasy equilibrium of the colonial world. The strength of European imperialism was implicitly undermined by it. The idea of international supervision over colonial areas, protection of the peoples governed and the promise of eventual self-government presaged the passing of imperialism. In effect, the mandate system confirmed the justice of the rising colonial demands for independence, but many years and another war would ensue before such demands would be honored.

The settlement in the Far East caused other difficulties. Japan had no intention of relinquishing its wartime gains in China and the Pacific. But the Chinese, who had fought on the side of the Allies, held high hopes that the peace conference would end all foreign concessions and the unjust treatment to which their country had been subjected. Their hopes were disappointed. The Japanese occupation of Chinese ports was confirmed, and nothing was done to end the system of foreign concessions and privileges. In fury, China withdrew from the conference and refused to sign the peace treaties.

No one emerged from the conference more resentful than Germany. The new German Republic had made peace on the general basis of Wilson's statements and counted on sympathy. But their hopes too were dashed. The Allies made extravagant demands that Germany pay for the War, partly as a matter of principle, but chiefly because the Allies faced huge debts to the United States. To provide legal sanction for the payment of reparations, a "war-guilt" clause was written into the treaty, by which Germany "accepted the responsi-

bility" for the outbreak of the War and the damages that had resulted. The War, the treaty said, had been "imposed" on the Allies by the "aggression of Germany and her allies." Nothing rankled more in the hearts of the defeated than that statement.

By other terms of the treaty Germany lost one eighth of its territory and 12 per cent of its population. Part of this land went to create the Polish Corridor, a strip of territory that, in order to give Poland access to the sea, divided the German province of East Prussia from the rest of Germany. Poland was an ancient nation now restored to statehood out of territories held by Germany and Russia in the 19th Century. The Germans had other grievances. Danzig, formerly a German city, became an international free city that was to be ruled by a High Commissioner appointed by the League of Nations. Some three million Germans were left in the new state of Czechoslovakia (created out of the old Austria-Hungary) to give that state a viable frontier. Although the victors made genuine efforts to honor the principle of self-determination, and although the new frontiers corresponded more closely to ethnographic divisions than ever before (the new states of Hungary and Yugoslavia also came out of the treaties), for various reasons a whole new set of minority problems resulted from these arrangements.

Many other decisions were compromises that satisfied no one. The French wanted to detach the Rhineland from Germany to provide themselves with a safe frontier. Wilson opposed this because such an arrangement would create a virtual Alsace-Lorraine in reverse. But he agreed to a treaty guaranteeing that the United States and Britain would come to the aid of France in the event of a future German attack—a far-sighted arrangement that the United States Senate refused to ratify, leaving the French embittered and frustrated.

The wisdom of the peace treaty, which was finally signed in June 1919, would long be debated. Germany was disarmed, deprived of territories, burdened with enormous reparations and made to suffer severe humiliation. Yet German industry was left intact, and the nation had strong recuperative powers. The peace imposed neither the harsh terms that, properly enforced, could have prevented a resurgence of German militarism nor the charitable and just terms that Wilson had hoped for. But the major drawback was that the settlement was left to be enforced by Britain and France alone, and both were too weakened to do so. Only an alliance of Britain, France, the United States and the Soviet Union could have enforced the treaties.

Nonetheless, despite all the compromise and frustrations, Wilson looked optimistically to the future. The Covenant of the League of Nations, a solemn agreement invested with an almost religious character, formed part of the treaties. Wilson had set his heart on one supreme goal, the establishment of the League, and he believed that this goal had been achieved. In his view the decisions reached in the Paris talks were less important than the newly created international machinery of the League of Nations. Through that body, he believed, economic cooperation, universal disarmament and the peaceful settlement of international differences could be achieved.

But the League turned out very different from the organization that Wilson had envisioned. Ironically, the United States never joined. Irritated by the bickering in Paris, indignant over the revelation of secret treaties and disillusioned by manifestations of nationalist greed and rivalry, Americans withdrew into a mood of isolationism. The same idealism that had made them want to save the world for democracy made them turn away from the European power game they saw at Paris. Partly out of naïve idealism and partly out of inexperience in world affairs, they returned in disgust to an old American slogan, "No entangling alliances." They signed neither the treaty concerning Germany nor the Covenant of the League of Nations. The United States was refusing to accept international responsibilities and a role in world affairs commensurate with American political and economic strength. Woodrow Wilson died a brokenhearted man.

The absence of the United States made the League a hollow mockery of Wilson's dream. As constituted, it was a body dominated by European powers, Britain and France, an arrangement that was inconsistent with the new balance of world economic and political forces. It was to prove impotent in the face of aggression.

Yet despite the flaws, there remained a symbolic and inspirational importance to the League of Nations. It brought to life the idea of a "general association of nations." Peoples of all tongues and all cultures could convene in a common assembly. Although in the end the League failed, the idea of a concert of nations was to live on in the 20th Century.

The peace proved to be a fragile one. Perhaps it did not endure because of the grievances written into the treaty, or because of the withdrawal of the United States, or because the resulting arrangements were inconsistent with the new distribution of world strength, or because of economic strains that followed in the wake of the War. No one can say. But before the ink was dry on the treaty, the decisions were being contested. Despite all the hopes of the peacemakers, the seeds of a new war had been planted. That war was to have further consequences for the wane of Europe, for the competition between democracy and Communism, for the awakening of the colonial world and for the redistribution of world power.

COME LAD
SLIP ACROSS AND HELP

A COMRADELY INVITATION *to adventure was expressed in this recruitment poster of a British soldier asking a compatriot to join the war effort.*

A CHANGING VIEW OF WAR

Diplomatic miscalculations started World War I, nightmarish military blunders bled Europe white during its four deadly years, and an unforeseen restructuring of world power was its legacy. The illusion—and gradual disillusionment—of the Allies can be clearly traced in their wartime posters. At first expecting that moral right and courage would result in a quick victory over Germany *(above)*, Britain and France were brought to the brink of despair by the pointless horrors of trench warfare *(pages 52-53)*. The entry of fresh American troops, and the exhaustion of the enemy's resources finally ended the war. German aggression was thwarted and democracy was precariously enthroned across the continent, but the glory and might of prewar Europe lay in ruins.

YOUR KING & COUNTRY NEED YOU

A CHIP OF THE OLD BLOCK.

TO MAINTAIN THE HONOUR AND GLORY
OF THE
BRITISH EMPIRE

EVERYONE SHOULD DO HIS BIT

ENLIST NOW

BRITAIN'S OPTIMISTIC VISION OF WAR

To the British, the War seemed a long way off when it first blazed up on the European mainland. Protected by the world's most powerful navy and nurtured by a sense of its own historical greatness, the island kingdom felt no deep foreboding during the early weeks of conflict. The public expected victory in a matter of months.

Recruiting posters appealed to noble concepts of "honour" and "glory" and "tradition." Most people believed that the specific aim of the War was to liberate innocent Belgium—although government leaders were more impressed by the need to prevent a German takeover of the continent, which would severely challenge British power. But the confusion and vagueness of reasons for war did nothing to dampen national optimism. When the War Minister asked for an initial 100,-000 volunteers, 175,000 signed up within a single week and 750,000 within two months. The poet Rupert Brooke, destined to die in battle, distilled the British mood in lofty verse: "Now, God be thanked Who has matched us with His hour."

APPEALS TO HONOR, *rather than to fiercer passions of war, characterized early British recruiting posters. The subdued, confident propaganda was so successful in drawing military volunteers that no conscription law was passed in Britain until 1916.*

WOMEN OF BRITAIN SAY — "GO!"

PATRIOTIC WOMEN, shown urging their men off to war, eventually served too. Nearly two million women took men's jobs during the War.

EAGER FOR COMBAT, *a confident French soldier cried, "We'll get them!" in a poster asking the public to support a war loan.*

3ᵉ EMPRUNT
DE LA DÉFENSE NATIONALE
CRÉDIT LYONNAIS
Souscrivez

THE FLAG OF LIBERTY, *planted on the bloodied map of Europe by a French soldier in this war-loan poster, reflected France's determination to drive Germans off its soil.*

FRANCE'S PASSION FOR ATTAC

A mood of "national devotion," in the words of one foreign observer, swept France after the German invasion. Stripped of the provinces of Alsace and Lorraine by the Germans in 1870, the French felt that aggressiveness would bring victory this time. Posters made a cult of courage and portrayed France as the liberator of peoples oppressed by Germany. Even the military training manual made a reckless vow: "The French Army, returning to its traditions, henceforth admits no law but the offensive."

A GENERATION DECIMATED

The military ardor of the French was short lived. During the first year of war almost half of all French families received a telegram announcing the death of a husband or son—more than 600,000 men died within six months. Yet the French generals, refusing to admit that their doctrine of aggressiveness did not work in trench warfare, continued hurling men against German machine-gun fire.

The war-loan poster at right—asking the French to hold fast "for the last quarter hour" of the War—frankly showed weary soldiers hobbling across a shell-cratered landscape, deep within invaded France. By 1917 morale had all but collapsed. Antiwar propaganda was openly spread among the troops, and one bitter regiment threatened to march on Paris. A change of commanders partially revived morale—but the deadlocked War still showed no sign of ending.

pour le dernier

LES SOUSCRIPTIONS A L'EM
BANQUE NAT

DEVAMBEZ, IMP. PARIS

...uart d'heure...,

aidez·moi!..

...RUNT NATIONAL SONT REÇUES A LA

...ONALE DE CRÉDIT

MEN OF BRITAIN!
WILL YOU STAND THIS?

Nº 2 Wykeham Street, SCARBOROUGH, after the German bombardment on Decʳ 16ᵗʰ. It was the Home of a Working Man. Four People were killed in this House including the Wife, aged 58, and Two Children, the youngest aged 5.

78 Women & Children were killed and 228 Women & Children were wounded by the German Raiders
ENLIST NOW

ZEPPELIN BOMBING OF LONDON—*the first major assault on English soil in more than two centuries—caused a great public outcry. British aces battled the slow-moving raiders and shot many down.*

A CRISIS OF CONFIDENCE

In 1915, German Zeppelins began to cross the Channel and rain bombs on London. The wartime toll, 1,117 civilians killed, was low compared to that exacted by the Battle of Britain in World War II, but profoundly shocking at the time. In 1916 the British Army, carrying out its first full-scale offensive at the Somme, suffered 400,000 casualties and gained no strategic ground. Britain's zest for war evaporated, antiwar movements sprang up, and people began to question the wisdom of their leaders. Winston Churchill, wartime Lord of the Admiralty, wrote: "Injuries were wrought to the structure of human society which a century will not efface."

NEVER AGAIN!

—THE NO MORE WAR MOVEMENT
11 DOUGHTY STREET LONDON WC1

A DEEP REVULSION for the war was expressed by a popular pacifist movement (above) and also by the Independent Labour Party.

FIRED-UP MARINES, *true to the poster above, fought so well in their first battles that the German Command reluctantly reported: "The American soldier proves himself brave, strong and skillful."*

AMERICA'S MORAL MISSION

By 1917, Europe was hopelessly bogged down in the mud and blood of battle, and the New World came to the assistance of the Old. For the first time, the United States became directly involved in European affairs. Posters re-awakened the nation's fighting traditions and announced that a great moment in history was at hand. President Woodrow Wilson, picturing America as "one of the champions of the rights of mankind," sent nearly two million fresh troops overseas and lent $10 billion to the Allies. The war was won in 18 months—and European world supremacy was forever undone.

THE NAVY NEEDS YOU! DON'T READ AMERICAN HISTORY — MAKE IT!

THE FINAL SURGE of the Allies crushed Germany—symbolized by the spike-helmeted Kaiser—by sheer numbers. In the last months of war, the Allies had

a 40 per cent manpower advantage on the Western Front. In November of 1918, the Kaiser fled and the newly formed German Republic sued for peace.

3

SCOURGE OF
THE DEPRESSION

For a decade after the close of the War, the world appeared to be returning to stability and peace. Science and technology continued to make rapid advances—the 1920s were the years in which cellophane, commercial airlines, talking movies and the household radio came into use. Europe recovered from the physical destruction of the four-year holocaust. American capitalism enjoyed a booming prosperity; so did the economies of other countries, including defeated Germany. Constitutional republics and monarchies rose in the new small European states that had been created at the Paris peace conferences in 1919.

In the colonial world the mandate system was bringing about a modification of the old forms of colonial rule, and independence movements were appearing everywhere. In 1928 representatives of 15 nations gathered in Paris to sign the Kellogg-Briand Pact, which renounced war. More than 60 nations eventually endorsed the Pact, and although as an instrument of peace it proved in the end to be fruitless, it was a mark, nevertheless, of international sentiment in the decade following the devastation of World War I.

The belief prevailed that life would return to the way of the pre-1914 world—but that belief was illusory. Many people failed to understand that Europe had lost its pre-eminence and that the United States had emerged as the leading industrial and financial power of the world. The implications of the dynamism of Russia, the growing importance of Asia and the swelling tide of colonial nationalism were also overlooked by the West, which was dazzled by the booming prosperity and the appearance of political stability.

The good times also obscured two other ominous facts. One was that the postwar prosperity was fragile; it was soon to shatter, leaving the world in a financial shambles. The other was that aggression was on the march, driving the world to another global war.

For all its ebullience, the new economy of the 1920s was quite different from that of the prewar world, and it rested on a different basis. To begin with, Britain was no longer the world's banker. In buying war matériel and food without being able to sell in exchange, Britain had used up its foreign investments and gold reserve, contracted debts and lost to the United States its place as a source of capital. France, too, had contracted debts; it had also lost its heavy investments in czarist Russia. Germany, the vanquished, had lost all its foreign capital and came out of the War saddled with large reparations to the Allies.

The American economy, on the other hand, had been stimulated by the War. The value of United States exports, agricultural and industrial, tripled between 1914 and 1918. At the start of the War the United States had owed Europe some $4 billion; at the end it emerged the principal creditor of the world, owed some $10 billion by the European countries.

Other countries outside Europe had benefited from the War, too. Japan had sold large quantities of munitions to Russia and displaced European traders in China and India. In Latin America at least two nations, Argentina and Brazil, turned to manufacturing when they found themselves cut off from British products. In India a family textile enterprise developed into a giant iron and steel industrial network. Even China, temporarily free of foreign domination, took hesitant steps toward industrialization. As a result of these developments during the War, Europe by 1918 had ceased to be the workshop of the world.

Despite the fact that Europe lost its former preeminence, world commerce revived. By 1925 the world output of food and raw materials was 16 per cent higher than that of the prewar level (the population was only 6 per cent greater), and the output of manufactured goods was 20 per cent higher than before. The United States retained the lead it had taken during the War; by 1928 it was producing over two fifths of the world's manufactured goods. In new industries—motor vehicles, for instance—the United States was turning out four fifths of the world's production.

The United States was the leading exporter of capital as well. The loans and investments of American banks and private citizens made possible the revival of Europe. Even Germany, now a republic, experienced a brisk prosperity that crowded out the bitter memories of defeat. Germany's building industries—ship construction and civil aviation—burgeoned with the backing of Americans, who invested over $1 billion in German business in the 1920s. Total American investments abroad rose to more than $3.5 billion during that decade.

Such facts gave people, Americans particularly, a belief that all was well with the world. President Herbert Hoover, when he was inaugurated in March 1929, spoke as though nothing could bar the way to indefinite progress. "We have reached a higher degree of comfort and security than has ever existed before in the history of the world," he declared. "Through liberation from widespread poverty we have reached a higher degree of individual freedom than ever before. . . . We are steadily building up a new race, and a new civilization, great in its own attainments." In many parts of the world the hope prevailed that what science, technology and industrial enterprise had achieved in America could one day be accomplished in the rest of the world.

There were, however, flaws in the economic fabric, flaws so serious that the world economy was to be rent asunder. For one thing, American export of capital was not so steady as Britain's had been before 1914, and more of the loans were of a short-term nature, which meant that renewed loans would be dependent on continued American prosperity. For another, the role of the United States in trade was different from that of prewar Britain. Before 1914 Britain had imported heavily, stabilizing the world balance of payments by accepting foods and raw materials in exchange for British exports of capital and machinery. But by

THE CAREFREE FLAPPER, *sketched by John Held Jr., became the symbol of the "Roaring Twenties," an era of speakeasies, scanty clothes and frantic dances that ended with the 1929 Crash.*

the European countries could not pay their debts except with money they collected from Germany as war reparations, and the Germans could pay reparations only with American loans, world finance was caught in a vicious circle.

Farmers as well as businessmen faced serious difficulties all over the world. During the War wheat production in Europe had fallen off by a fifth. At the same time the War had increased the demand for wheat; prices rose, and farmers outside of Europe therefore had an incentive to increase their output. They were able to do so because the substitution of tractors for horses and the use of the harvester-thresher combine increased the acreage the farmers could till, and the introduction of scientific farming increased their yield per acre. Wheat growers in the United States, Canada and Argentina saw profits to be made out of expansion, and many of them borrowed heavily to acquire more land and equipment.

After the War the farmers sustained their high production. In the early 1920s grain production in the United States and Canada was one sixth greater than before the War; by the latter part of the decade, it had become one third greater than before the War. Grain exports had doubled. But Europe quickly resumed its own wheat production. And the demand also slackened—Europeans were eating more dairy products, meat and fruits than before, and less bread. Stocks of unsold wheat rose to 15.9 million tons in 1929, and wheat growers everywhere faced ruin.

Growers of other crops had trouble as well. The output of cotton, wool, corn, cocoa and coffee had risen. The development of large plantations in the East Indies had increased rubber output; scientific cultivation in Java had resulted in much larger yields of sugar. Farmers in Australia, New Zealand, Africa and the Americas faced a new problem: the wonders of modern science had

the end of the War the United States had become practically self-sufficient. It grew its own crops for food consumption and mined the metals it needed for its manufactures. Therefore it set up high tariffs to protect its domestic market. Unlike the Britain of former times, the United States demanded money in return for its exports.

In addition, the value of the dollar was very high. And the cost grew ever higher, for the United States, in accumulating a large gold reserve through wartime sales to Europe, had acquired a firm currency; other countries, lacking gold, suffered crippling inflation and instability. Because brought about overproduction and falling prices. For them the adoption of scientific agriculture seemed to be spelling doom, not progress. They could not meet their debts or mortgage payments, and they could not buy the cars, radios and other consumer products with whose industries their own prosperity was now linked.

Of the many flaws in the world economy, the gravest existed in the most prosperous nation of all—the United States. On Wall Street in New York stood the very symbol of American capitalism, the New York Stock Exchange. As industry expanded and profits rose, investment in stocks offered attractive prospects for those who wished to share in American industrial growth. In the middle of the 1920s stock buying became a passion, indeed a fever. The practice was indulged in by people in all walks of life. As the passion for investing gained momentum in the latter part of the decade, the average price of stocks on the New York Stock Exchange rose by 25 per cent in 1928, and then again by 35 per cent in the first months of 1929.

The volume of trading rose correspondingly. It reached three and a half million shares per day in March 1928, and throughout the spring, conversation revolved around the question of whether trading would reach the five-million mark. In June it did. Five months later, on November 16, 1928, an unprecedented six and a half million shares of stock changed hands in a single day.

By that time, investment had become dangerously speculative. The stock market was virtually unregulated; what made matters even more dangerous was the excessively easy system for buying stock on credit, a practice that was called buying on margin. A speculator could buy large quantities of stock by making only a small cash payment, 10 per cent of the stock value, and borrowing the rest from a broker or a bank. The collateral for this loan was the market value of the stock; if the stock value dropped, the loan would no longer be covered by sufficient collateral, and the man who had bought on margin would have to supply more money—in cash. But stocks kept going up, not down, and nobody worried about such a contingency.

A day of reckoning was due, however. The fundamental causes of the disaster that came are still being debated. But several signs of danger that appeared at least as early as the spring of 1929, if not before, are easy to see with hindsight. For one thing, although more wealth was being produced than ever before, it was unevenly distributed. The working classes received far less of a share in the national income than was healthy for the economy; their purchasing power was inadequate to sustain the currently high level of production. Indeed, though the fact was scarcely noted at the time, industrial production fell in June 1929, and continued to decline thereafter.

But while production fell off, the stock market catapulted ahead by leaps and bounds. Ordinarily the stock market becomes somnolent in the summer, but not in 1929. The *New York Times* index of stock prices rose 110 points in three months; in 1928, a good year, it had risen a then unprecedented 86.5 points in 12 months. In the summer of 1929 the volume of trading hovered between four and five million shares a day, sometimes surpassing that figure. Brokers' loans for buying on margin jumped at the rate of $400 million a month, and by the end of the summer reached a total of more than $7 billion—some of that total having been lent at 15 per cent interest.

On October 24, 1929, "Black Thursday," the great crash came. The morning began inauspiciously; it ended with an avalanche of orders to sell stock at any price. Why the panic started, nobody knows, but in the stampede that occurred, prices fell and speculators who had bought on margin had to sell one stock after another to cover the money they had borrowed to buy the stocks in the first place. Almost 13 million shares were sold before the day was out. Values fell precipitously; some stocks dropped as much as 75 points, which meant a loss of $75,000 for someone holding 1,000 shares, $750 for the small investor with 10. More drastic drops followed on October 28; General Electric fell $130 a share, Westinghouse $194, the First National Bank $500. By the end of October investors had lost over $40 billion; by November 13 the index of industrial stocks had fallen from 469 to 220, more than half.

Even worse reverses lay ahead. With the exception of a brief market rally in the first three months of 1930, prices went steadily down until the summer of 1932. By that time the average value of 50 typical industrial stocks had dropped from 252 to 61. Some dropped even more. The common stock of the United States Steel Corporation, for instance, which on the day after Labor Day in 1929 had sold for $262 a share, went for $22 a share in July 1932. Some stocks that had been over $100 went for about 50 cents.

The Wall Street crash in the autumn of 1929 was the harbinger of a crisis in American industry and the Great Depression. As faith in the economy disappeared, investors ceased pouring money into business expansion. As their incomes fell, consumers ceased buying. As sales slowed down, production orders were suspended and inventories began to accumulate. Some factories cut back production; others shut down entirely. The Ford Motor Company cut its work week from six days to five in the spring of 1930 and to three in August of that year. General Motors sold five and a half million cars in 1929, only two and a half million in 1931. Industrial production fell by more than half between 1929 and 1933, national income

by three quarters, wholesale prices by about a third. Unemployment rose from 1.5 million in 1929 to more than 12 million in 1932, or almost 25 per cent of the working population—an appalling figure, when it is remembered that an unemployment figure of 5 per cent is considered dangerous today.

The crisis undermined confidence in the banks, too. Depositors rushed to withdraw their savings, but many of the banks could not meet the demands of their customers because they had engaged in speculation themselves. The result was that in three years 5,000 American banks went bankrupt. When many of the banks in Detroit closed their doors, workers in that city could not cash their pay checks; in Boston the police were not paid at all for a time. In the Middle West farmers had no money to buy feed for their animals, and the cows stopped giving milk; elsewhere, vegetables rotted for want of customers.

The crisis did not end with the boundaries of the United States; it spread over the world. American bankers withdrew their funds abroad, thus pulling out the props from German and Eastern European prosperity. As in the United States, there was a run on the banks in Europe and a cycle of bank failures followed. In May 1931 the Vienna Creditanstalt, the leading bank in the Danube basin, became insolvent, a collapse that shook the financial centers of Europe. The following July one of the four leading German banks declared itself bankrupt. The Berlin Stock Exchange closed down for two months.

At the outset of the crisis, British investors took losses in the United States and in Central Europe; later, markets for British exports disappeared. In 1931 the British government suffered a deficit of £1 million per week because so many Britons were drawing unemployment insurance. And for eigners, lacking confidence in the pound, withdrew their investments in London and exchanged sterling for gold or francs or dollars. By midsummer of 1931 the Bank of England was losing gold through withdrawals at the rate of £2.5 million a day. On September 21, 1931, the British abandoned the gold standard, the system by which, for most of the preceding century, the pound had been convertible on demand into 113 grains of fine gold. As long as that system had obtained, the pound had been the most stable and the most respected currency in all the world.

No sooner had the British discarded the gold standard than the pound dropped by about 30 per cent of its prewar value—from $4.86 to $3.40. For over a century the British pound had seemed unassailable, and the free conversion of currency into gold upon request had been an article of faith in the capitalist economy. Now an age had come to an end.

The cheaper pound was intended to stimulate foreign purchases of British goods, but instead it dealt another blow to international trade. In less than a year, more than a dozen other countries had devalued and abandoned the gold standard, too, among them Portugal, Siam, Egypt, Bolivia, Japan and the Scandinavian countries. The United States followed in 1934 and the French did the same in 1936. By then the gold standard was gone and trade was coming to a standstill.

The success story of capitalism was suddenly told in reverse. Everywhere in the Western world, men and machines lay idle. The great industrial economy came to a grinding halt. In the cities men tramped the streets to find any kind of employment that would keep themselves and their families alive. They queued up at soup kitchens, took shelter in municipal lodging houses. Professional men—lawyers, engineers, architects, teachers —shoveled snow and dug ditches. Men sold apples on street corners, or drew pictures on the sidewalks

THE NOT-QUITE-ALMIGHTY DOLLAR.

Pound Note (*to Dollar Bill*). "I KNOW THAT SINKING FEELING. GLAD YOU'RE GOING TO TAKE THE SAME STUFF AS I TOOK. PICKED ME UP A LOT."

ECONOMIC MEDICINE *is prescribed in a 1932 English cartoon, which pictures a healthy British pound encouraging an ailing American dollar to follow its example by drinking "Budget Balance Tonic." The cartoonist's confidence in the British economy proved to be unwarranted; although the British tried to balance their budget in 1932, they failed. The dollar, shaky as it might have been during the Depression, continued to be more stable than the pound.*

to collect a few pennies from passersby. Young people, seeing only a bleak and dismal future ahead, became demoralized; men in the prime of life turned bitter; self-respect collapsed as people were forced to survive on charity, handouts from relatives and government doles. No one who lived through the Depression could ever forget the despair, the anxiety, the hopelessness; on an entire generation it left a scar.

In the interdependent world economy of the 20th Century, no people escaped the economic blizzard. Industrialized nations were the hardest hit, but even agricultural economies were severely affected, for prices dropped precipitously and in some instances export markets disappeared. In 1933 wheat and rice farmers were selling their products at two fifths of 1929 prices. In Brazil coffee dropped from 23 cents a pound to eight. Much the same doleful tale was true of sugar farmers in Central America, rubber producers in Indonesia, cotton and silk growers in Egypt and Japan, wool producers in Australia—in short, of farmers in every part of the world.

Of the several great casualties of the Depression, one was international cooperation. By shattering the world economy, the Depression encouraged isolationism. All countries turned inward, seeking to shelter their economies. They placed quotas on imports, they licensed and regulated trade. They entered into bilateral pacts with other countries, "dumped" products abroad at lower prices than they sold them for at home and raised tariffs. In 1930 the United States introduced the highest tariff in its history. Other countries retaliated promptly, among them France, Canada, Italy and Spain, and the next year, India, Argentina, Brazil and China. Even England, the classic land of free trade, fell in line, adopting protective tariffs and making special arrangements with Canada, Australia and New Zealand to trade with one another

under more favorable terms than with outsiders. Every country did what it could to hold or capture export markets.

The crisis affected every aspect of finance. Although the gold standard was gone and no country had to back its currency with a fixed percentage of gold bullion, gold nevertheless remained a problem. The currencies of Japan, Germany and Italy were unstable and inflated, and consequently unwanted in world trade. The United States therefore demanded gold instead of German, Italian and Japanese currencies in payment of sales. Those countries were hardly able to pay in gold, however, and so they made intensive efforts to become self-sufficient. Germany, for instance, entered into regional barter agreements with Bulgaria, Hungary, Rumania and Yugoslavia, making those countries virtually economic dependencies to which Germany sent manufactured products and from which it took agricultural products in return. Japan, to protect its own interests, made similar arrangements with China, India and Iraq.

Prior to the Depression, trade had been multilateral—literally "many-sided." In multilateral trade one entrepreneur in Chile, for example, could sell nitrates to Britain, while other Chileans might buy precision instruments from Germany or perfumes from France. It did not matter if Chileans bought little from Britain or sold little to Germany and France. Sales to one country balanced purchases from another. Pounds, dollars, francs, marks and pesos were all easily interchangeable, and at stable exchange rates.

Now regional specialization and free exchange among buyers and sellers were disappearing, and trade was becoming increasingly bilateral. An importer was permitted to purchase only from countries to which his own country had already shipped sufficient exports. The contrast to the pre-1914 pattern, when international commerce had bound all the parts of the world together, could scarcely be more striking. Governments controlled trade as never before in peacetime. The result of all the nationalistic policies was that practically all countries worked at cross-purposes, making it almost impossible to restore international trade.

No solution to the problem was readily apparent. A few economists held the belief that the Depression was part of a self-regulating business cycle and that if left to its own devices the economy would recover. President Herbert Hoover shared this view and asserted that "Prosperity is just around the corner." He and many others held that the capitalist economy operated according to "natural laws" and that interference would cause positive harm. According to this view, the role of government was chiefly to set an example of retrenchment and economy, and thereby inspire in business circles the confidence that could alone bring recovery. But this attitude required faith and patience, which could not be expected of many in the circumstances.

When the situation looked the blackest, Franklin Delano Roosevelt was elected President of the United States in a landslide vote. In stark contrast to the glowing tones of his predecessor, Roosevelt sounded a somber keynote in his inaugural address on March 4, 1933. "Values have sunk to fantastic levels; our factories are without orders," he said. "The withered leaves of our industrial enterprise lie on every side; farmers find no markets for their produce; and the savings of many years in thousands of families are gone. More important, a host of unemployed citizens face the grim problem of existence, and an equally great number toil with little return."

At the same time, Roosevelt sounded a note of hope. "Our greatest primary task is to put people to work," he said. "This is no unsolvable problem if we face it wisely and courageously. It can be accomplished in part by direct recruiting by the government itself, treating the task as we would treat the emergency of a war, but at the same time, through this employment, accomplishing greatly needed projects to stimulate and reorganize the use of our natural resources."

Roosevelt promptly launched his celebrated New Deal. Under his administration, the Federal Government subsidized public works projects, conservation programs and public housing. It created jobs and gave relief payments to the unemployed. It extended financial aid to threatened business firms. It developed power and irrigation systems, such as the Tennessee Valley Authority, that changed the life of whole regions—and that later served as models for reclamation in underdeveloped countries all over the world.

It adopted legislation to supervise the banking system and to police the stock exchanges so that the crash of 1929 could not be repeated. It encouraged trade union growth and collective bargaining as a means of insuring higher purchasing power for the working classes. It enacted laws establishing minimum wages and maximum hours for the work week. Following the example that had been set earlier by Germany, England and the Scandinavian countries, the United States adopted social security legislation, providing payments to the unemployed, the aged and the disabled. It gave subsidies to farmers to encourage the substitution of soil-conserving crops, and it underwrote low-cost mortgages.

A major innovation of all these programs was that the government managed them by deficit financing—that is, by spending beyond its means. Governments in the 1930s undertook programs that their treasuries did not have revenues to pay for. Prior to the Depression such spending was anathema in private, academic and public circles. After the Depression it gained respectability.

Out of the bold steps taken to cope with the Depression, the 20th Century welfare state emerged—a state in which capitalism was reformed. As a result of the measures adopted during the Depression, the United States underwent a social and economic transformation that has remained in effect to the present day.

Another result of the Depression was a formal revamping of orthodox economic theory as well as practice. In 1936, while the United States and other governments were groping for a means to deal with the Depression, the British economist John Maynard Keynes published *The General Theory of Employment, Interest and Money*, a book that redefined the traditional relationships between government and economy. The ideas that Keynes put forward were to grow in influence to match Adam Smith's *Wealth of Nations*, published in 1776, the bible of the older theory of capitalistic economics. Keynes justified and elaborated on the principles of deficit financing, public works programs and fluctuating rates of interest and taxation, depending on the changing economic needs of the nation. He recognized the close ties between national economies and international trade. He challenged the traditional economic view, which held that in the long run natural laws would bring about recovery. "In the long run," Keynes wrote, "we are all dead."

In sharp contrast to the rest of the world, Communist Russia escaped the business slump and unemployment of the Depression. Russia had been cut off from world trade since the Revolution. Ironically, it emerged an industrial giant in the very years when Western industry lay crippled.

During this period Russia was ruled with an iron fist by Joseph Stalin, a former theological student who had been expelled from school for insubordination. He had since become a Marxist and a professional revolutionary. When Lenin died in 1924, a power struggle ensued in the Communist Party Politburo, and Stalin won out. In 1928, having taken over control of the government, he launched a program of building "socialism in one country"—putting aside the Marxist principle of world revolution. He established an elaborate central planning apparatus with an enormous bureaucracy. Instituting the first of several Five Year Plans by which he aimed to industrialize Russia, he pushed the country to surpass the capitalist countries of the world.

In 1929 Stalin stated: "We are advancing full steam ahead along the path of industrialization to Socialism, leaving behind the agelong Russian 'backwardness.' We are becoming a country of metal, a country of automobiles, a country of tractors. And when we have put the Soviet Union in a motor car and the peasant in a tractor . . . we shall see which countries may then be classified as backward and which as advanced."

Stalin's Five Year Plan set ambitious goals. The object was to transform the economic and social character of the country without foreign help, and this was to be done by strict government supervision of industry and agriculture. The people of Russia were to work hard at low wages and to look to the future for their reward. Collective farms were set up to be tilled jointly by the peasants who lived on them, with farm machinery provided by the state. In the cities the government created and maintained new industries, into which it absorbed hosts of new workers. Between 1926 and 1939, 20 million people moved from the country to the towns to take industrial jobs. Workers were paid according to their output. Wages varied according to the job, but there were no paupers and no very rich. The first Five Year Plan was followed by a second in 1933. Together the plans pushed Russia into the industrial age and created an exhilarating feeling that all were working in concert to build a glorious socialist state.

But the costs in human life, freedom and well-being were staggering. In the relentless drive to build an industrial state overnight, Russian workers labored long hours for poor pay, lived in cramped, unheated quarters and had to forego things that Westerners take for granted—shoes, radios, even food. They had to live with the system whether they liked it or not.

To protest was futile. Stalin and his henchmen brutally repressed whatever real or imagined opposition they encountered. Factories and farms were given production quotas they had to meet. The Party rulers laid at the door of "wreckers," "foreign spies" and "imperialist agents" the failure of a factory to produce its quota of ball bearings, or of a farm to grow its quota of wheat. The failure often cost the plant or farm manager his job—and sometimes his life. Land-owning peasants who resisted the taking over of their farms were herded into concentration camps; within five years one million of these *kulaks* were put to death or sent to labor camps in Siberia, together with four million members of their families.

Stalin dealt even more fiendishly with political opposition. In 1936, charging that treason had been uncovered, he set in motion a series of notorious purge trials. After publicizing the luckless men's "confessions," Stalin had them put to death. In the army alone he liquidated some 400 officers from colonel upward—more than half the officers of the army. Among them were three of the five army marshals, 13 out of 15 army commanders and 30 out of 58 corps commanders.

More purges followed in 1937 and 1938, in which teachers, former government officials and two chiefs of police (who had themselves supplied "evidence" at the earlier trials) fell victim to the same treatment. Possibly a real revolution was brewing—many of those executed were Old Bol-

sheviks, men who had staged the Revolution of 1917. Stalin was taking no chances. By such methods he surrounded himself with yes-men who could be counted on to do his bidding.

Thanks to Stalin's reign of terror, the Five Year Plans succeeded in their tremendous undertaking—insofar as their objective was to industrialize the nation. Though food, shoes and housing remained in short supply, the plans gave airplanes, railroads, tractors and army tanks to Russia in an abundance that staggered those who could remember Russia prior to Stalin's advent. In the 10 years of the first two Five Year Plans, Russia had the fastest industrial growth of any country in the world at that time.

Iron and steel production were expanded fourfold; coal, three and a half times. In 1938 four fifths of Russian industrial output came from plants newly built or reconstructed during the Five Year Plans. The new metallurgical plants at Magnitogorsk and Stalinsk were producing as much iron and steel as the whole czarist empire had produced in 1914. New industrial cities were laid out and built beyond the Urals. Industrial projects sprouted everywhere—coal mines at Kuznetsk, oil wells and refineries in the Caucasus, a great hydroelectric power plant at Dnepropetrovsk, tractor factories at Chelyabinsk and Stalingrad. Areas that had once been vast spaces dotted with sleepy towns and quaint bazaars now felt the impact of modern industry and urbanization.

By 1939 the Soviet Union had become a powerful industrial state surpassed in production only by the United States and Germany. It had industrialized by its own efforts, without dependence on private enterprise and without foreign capital. Total economic planning, never explicit in the doctrines of Karl Marx, was put into practice by the Russian Communists. In 1933 Turkey modeled a Five Year Plan on Russia's; Mexico adopted a Six

A REWARD FOR PRODUCTIVITY, *this medal, called the Red Banner of Labor, was given by the Russian government from 1920 on to workers who had surpassed their quotas. The inscription around the border is the slogan: "Workers of the World, Unite!"*

Year Plan in 1934; several Asian and African countries emulated the Soviet plans when they gained independence after the Second World War.

In addition to industrializing, the Soviet Union made great strides in education under the Five Year Plans, so that by 1941, 85 per cent of the country was literate. Russia is a land of many tongues and many nationalities, both European and Asian. Until recent times it was a world virtually unto itself. It covers one sixth of the surface of the earth, stretching from the border of Poland in the west to the Pacific in the east, from the Arctic in the north to the borders of China and Persia in the south.

The czars had followed a policy of "Russification," by which they meant to make all their subjects over in their own image, regardless of the vast cultural and linguistic differences that existed among the people. Toward that end the czars had forced the Russian language and culture on virtually everybody in the Empire from Finland to Siberia. The Communist rulers, on the other hand, fostered cultural autonomy, encouraging the preservation of folk song and dance, writing down languages that had never been put in writing before. Even politically the government was organized along federal lines divided according to nationalities.

Russian accomplishments in the face of an otherwise worldwide depression enhanced the prestige of the Soviet Union. Many who did not like its methods envied the results. Even in the United States and Western Europe, the attractions of Communism seemed strong to those who suffered disillusion in the Depression. The future Prime Minister of India, Jawaharlal Nehru, who was educated in the Western liberal tradition, later testified to its effect on Asians. "While the rest of the world was in the grip of the Depression and going backward in some ways," Nehru wrote of the 1930s, "in the Soviet country a great new world was being built up before our eyes."

The Indian leader was too closely tied to liberal democratic traditions to adopt the methods of Communism, but elsewhere the "new civilization" won many adherents. Anticapitalism and anti-imperialism, and respect for Russian accomplishments in the very years of Western difficulties, went hand in hand. The Communists, in turn, encouraged independence movements in the hope of attacking European capitalism on its flank.

The Depression seemed to lay bare the weaknesses of the Western civilization that had dominated the world in the years before 1914. The West seemed unable to understand or control the inner workings of its own capitalism. Communists found a vindication of Marxism in the instability of the capitalist system.

In Germany, where unemployment reached six million in a nation of only about 18 million workers, the Depression had dire consequences. The people cried for action, and responded to the harangues of Adolf Hitler, a mad genius from Austria who rose up promising to repudiate the crippling treaties and unendurable humiliation that ended World War I, to cease paying reparations to the Allies, and to raise the German folk to the eminence they deserved. Voted into power, Hitler coordinated all German institutions into the totalitarian, racist and militarist Third Reich, made scapegoats of the Jews, put youths in uniform and the unemployed in factories, where they set to work producing arms. Soon he embarked on a path of aggression that made the renewal of conflict inevitable.

In Japan the Depression provided an excuse for imperialist adventures. Japanese industry depended heavily on foreign trade, particularly on trade with the United States. Some 90 per cent of all Japanese silk went to the United States, and silk comprised two fifths of the total value of all Japanese exports. But there was little use for silk in the United States in the 1930s, and the Depression therefore cost Japan its most important foreign market. As the Depression got underway, trade fell by one third and unemployment mounted. In the 1920s a clique of militarists gradually gained control of the government; in 1931 these men launched an invasion of Manchuria, planning to carve out of China an empire that would provide Japan with coal, oil, soya and wheat, and serve as an outlet for Japanese manufactures.

The Depression was an economic catastrophe of a scope never before experienced in history; everywhere in the world it evoked demands for action. The solutions to the crisis, though they might be humanitarian, as in the United States, or maleficent, as in Germany, were everywhere radical. And ironically, Adolf Hitler and his evil policies indirectly helped to bring an end to the Depression, for when the West finally rose to challenge him, the inauguration of vast armaments programs and the coming of war finally liquidated the crisis and provided full employment in the industrial countries. Faced with the catastrophe of another world war, governments acted with the instinct of self-preservation. Almost in spite of themselves, they undertook programs on a scale that would have staggered the imagination in earlier years, spending money they did not have, putting to work men who had lain idle for the better part of 10 years, cranking into motion industry that had slumbered just as long. Once so geared up, Western industry kept going after the War was over, and prosperity followed.

Thus the scourge of the Depression merged with the even greater scourge of war. When the nightmares were over, the changes that had been eroding the old world order since the opening of the 20th Century were to be accelerated still again.

"Lindbergh Is In Paris!"

"We" was the way Lindbergh always referred to himself and his plane, the "Spirit of St. Louis" (above). It was a rare partnership between man and machine. "It seems to form an extension of my own body," wrote the young hero, "ready to follow my wish . . . without [my hand's] commanding."

Lindbergh stands in front of his plane before taking off from Long Island's Roosevelt Field. The resolve to attempt the nonstop flight to Paris, for which a $25,000 prize had been offered, came one moonlit night when Lindbergh, not yet 25 years old, was flying his mail route over Illinois.

Excited French throngs gathered long before Lindbergh completed his flight, causing monumental traffic jams as they shouted their welcome at the airport and all the way along the route to Paris.

In the prosperous, headline-happy year of 1927, Tunney beat Dempsey in the "Fight of the Century" and Babe Ruth hit 60 home runs. But for 33½ hours on May 20-21, the event that eclipsed all others was the spectacle of one man in a single-engine airplane, fighting sleet and fatigue across a stormy Atlantic Ocean. When Charles Lindbergh set his "Spirit of St. Louis" down outside Paris, the press sang out the stunning news. That anyone could fly a small, rickety-looking contraption 3,600 miles without falling in the water seemed a miracle; that a gangling, 25-year-old Midwesterner with the nickname "Slim" did it set Americans delirious. It was the ultimate triumph in an era that craved ultimate heroes—and the first global victory of the air age.

PREPARATIONS: THE DEADLY BATTLE AGAINST WEIGHT

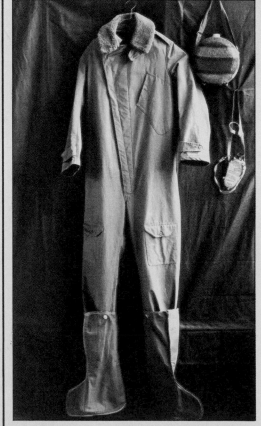

In cutting pounds Lindbergh even replaced the flying boots he wore as a mail pilot (above) with light canvas ones (below).

The "Spirit of St. Louis," in a picture autographed by Lindbergh. The craft, 27 feet long, with a top speed of 129 m.p.h., was a small airplane even in its own era.

Convinced that weight would be his chief opponent on the long flight, Lindbergh shopped for a company that would build him a light, uncomplicated plane with a single engine. He ended up at San Diego's Ryan Airlines factory, a ramshackle waterfront building within the perfumed reach of a fish cannery. There he collaborated with Ryan's chief engineer, Donald Hall. To conserve weight, they eliminated the customary navigator and his second cockpit and even dispensed with such standard but heavy equipment as a radio. To permit installation of an oversized 451-gallon gas tank, they moved the plane's engine forward and the pilot's space down behind it. In what seemed pathetic contrast to other planes attempting the flight—one of which, the "American Legion," carried 9,000 pounds in gas alone—the "Spirit of St. Louis," fully loaded, weighed only 5,250 pounds.

A contender for the Transatlantic prize, the heavy, three-engine "American Legion" (above) crashed at take-off, killing its copilots. All told, six men died and three were seriously hurt in the competition Lindbergh finally won.

Relying on his single engine, a 223 h.p. Wright Whirlwind, Lindbergh (above) personally checked every nut and bolt before take-offs. Like most planes of the day, the motor had no automatic starter; an assistant spun the propeller by hand (left). Even with weight pared to a minimum, the plane cleared telephone wires at the end of the runway by a bare 20 feet.

The Flight: On Target

Ready for take-off, the young aviator had with him one quart of water and five sandwiches for in-flight rations. "If I get to Paris I won't need any more," he said. "If I don't—well, I won't need any more either."

Of all the nicknames Lindbergh later endured, none was less apt than "The Flyin' Fool." After five years as a mail pilot, barnstormer and Army Air Service pilot, he was, at 25, one of the country's best aviators, and he executed his Transatlantic flight with all the instincts of a master. To avoid a storm, to fight fog and catch glimpses of the sun, he varied altitudes, sometimes riding at 10,000 feet, sometimes skimming the waves at 10. Twenty-seven hours out, he spotted fishing boats. Diving within 50 feet of them, he noticed a man peering from a cabin. "Which way is Ireland?" Lindbergh called. No answer came; apparently he was not heard. Lindy flew on. An hour later, he saw Ireland.

Lindbergh's instrument board (below)— located directly behind the huge gasoline tank—completely blocked his forward vision. It included a periscope (small window, left) and a new, electrically operated compass.

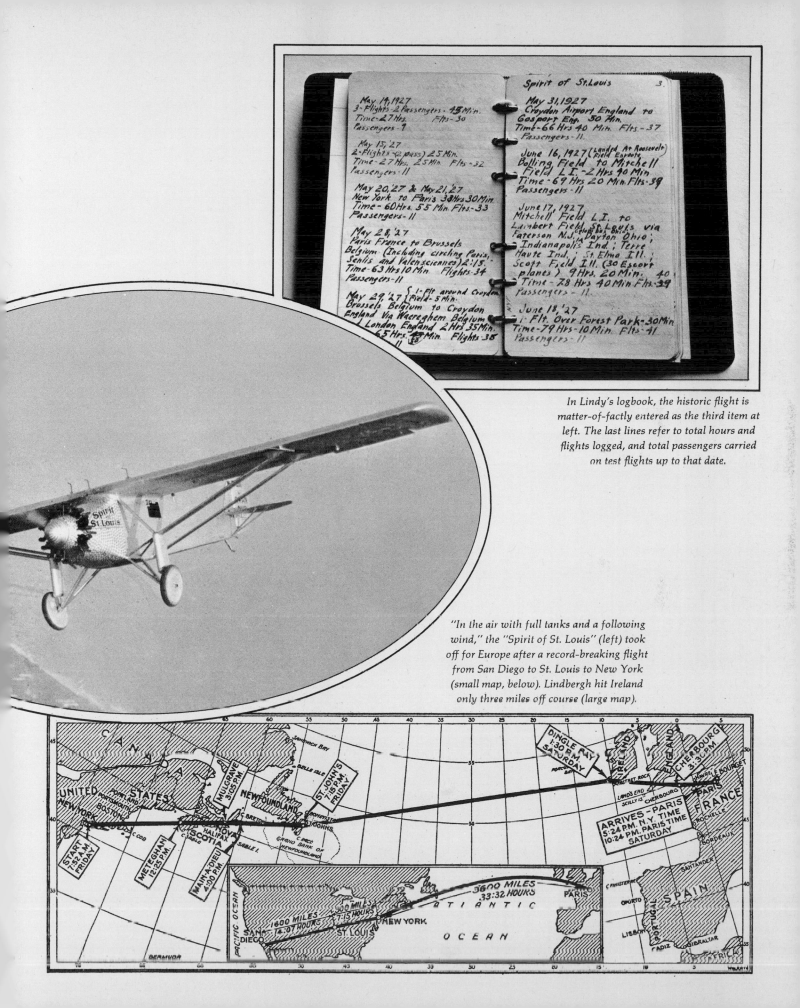

In Lindy's logbook, the historic flight is matter-of-factly entered as the third item at left. The last lines refer to total hours and flights logged, and total passengers carried on test flights up to that date.

"In the air with full tanks and a following wind," the "Spirit of St. Louis" (left) took off for Europe after a record-breaking flight from San Diego to St. Louis to New York (small map, below). Lindbergh hit Ireland only three miles off course (large map).

Gendarmes with bicycles (left) stood guard on crowds awaiting the hero at the Paris airport. But they were swept away the moment the plane landed, as tens of thousands of people swarmed onto the field. On his triumphant way through Paris Lindbergh (below) was mobbed again.

At a window of the Aero Club of France, Lindbergh appeared with U.S. Ambassador Herrick (at right, below) and club president, P. E. Flandrin. Lindbergh, read one account, "blushed like a girl. [Yet] a manlier . . . simpler character no idol of the multitude ever displayed."

The American hero seldom lost his cool manner but broke into a grin when he received congratulations—and the customary buss on the cheek— from France's pioneer aviator Louis Blériot.

A Wild Welcome For The Hero Of The Sky

Tidal waves of humanity engulfed the "Spirit of St. Louis" the instant it rolled to a stop at Le Bourget airport. When Lindbergh started to step from the plane, he was scooped up by scores of hands and could not touch ground for a half hour. Planned ceremonies went askew: the U.S. Ambassador Myron Herrick proffered roses to a young man wearing Lindbergh's helmet who was thrust by the crowd into the receiving pavilion through a smashed window. The young man was not the hero. Two French aviators had rescued Lindbergh by tossing away his helmet to divert the mob and hiding him in a darkened hangar.

The joyous assault continued unabating during the days Lindbergh remained in Europe. The King of Belgium received him when he flew into Brussels from Paris. At London's Croydon Airport, 150,000 people overwhelmed police lines. Afraid his propellers might kill someone in the crowd, Lindbergh touched ground but immediately took to the air again, circling a full five minutes before he could come down safely.

Seeking landing space, Lindbergh hovered over London's jammed airport (above). Once on the ground, he slipped the crowds to meet King George V, who decorated him with the Royal Air Force Cross.

English reserve collapsed in excitement over the feat. "The more drab the world becomes, the more gladly we welcome such a fine achievement as his," said Secretary for Air Sir Samuel Hoare. Mobs at the airport (left) battered the plane.

A Triumphant Homecoming

The hero's reception included sign-bearing tugboats shrieking their welcome to New York (above); later, President Coolidge presented him with the Congressional Medal of Honor (right).

Back in his own country, Lindbergh received a tumultuous tribute of affection. President Calvin Coolidge had dispatched the U.S. cruiser *Memphis* to bring the aviator home to Washington, and as they steamed up the Potomac, convoyed by destroyers, blimps and planes, they were greeted by a din of whistles, church bells and ceremonial guns. The welcome in New York *(above and right)* was hardly less spectacular. In the years to follow, a gradual alienation of hero and worshipers and the tragic kidnaping of a son were to tarnish the legend. But in that bright moment Lindbergh's feat, firing the imagination of people everywhere, had given commercial aviation an unparalleled boost. A hit song summed up the sentiments of the time: "Others may make that trip across the sea/ Upon some future day/ But take your hats off to plucky Charlie Lindbergh/The Eagle of the U.S.A."

After sailing up New York's flag-decked harbor in the mayor's yacht, "Our Lindy" switched to an open-topped limousine to start the march up lower Broadway and Fifth Avenue.

Four million joyous New Yorkers showered 1,800 tons of confetti and ticker tape on Lindbergh, who was honored in the noisiest parade in the city's history.

4
A WORLD AT WAR

World War II was the most devastating conflict in human history. Some 70 million men fought in it and at least 30 million soldiers and civilians died in it. If the number of missing people is included—as well as the victims of the bombings, the mass extermination programs, the forced deportations, the postwar famines and epidemics—a total death count of close to 40 million is believed more accurate. Germany lost roughly 8 per cent of its population; although no reliable statistics exist for the Soviet Union, historians conclude that one of every 10 Russians died in the War.

In every way World War II was more truly global than World War I. In the first conflict the United States had fought for only a year and a half and Japan had played a limited role; in World War II both countries were heavily engaged. Most of the battles of the first war took place on the mainland of Europe in territories that had been evacuated by civilians; in the second war the entire world was in flames. Navies clashed in the Pacific, land forces vied with one another on the plains of Russia and in the deserts of North Africa. The airplane, which became a major weapon only in World War II, was used to shower bombs on cities, causing civilians at home to suffer nearly as much as soldiers in the field.

World War II also resulted in a worldwide political shakeup. It brought on the collapse of a world order that the first war had only jarred. It toppled European colonial empires in Southeast Asia and hastened colonial independence movements elsewhere in Asia and Africa. Furthermore, the War confirmed the Soviet Union as a leader in international affairs and led to the spread of Communism in Europe and Asia. The world's peoples, their traditional societies disrupted, were soon caught up in a rivalry between two superpowers, the United States and the Soviet Union.

The War, which ended with the virtual collapse of the power system through which Western Europe bound the world in the 1920s and 1930s, was triggered by the expansionist ambitions of Germany, Italy and Japan. These three aggressors, which became allies during World War II, all thought of themselves as "have not" nations that could achieve prosperity only through large-scale military conquests. They came to be known as the "Axis" powers because Italy and Germany supposedly formed the ends of an axis, or axle, around which all of Europe would eventually revolve; later the term was broadened to include Japan as well, and the coalition harbored schemes for ruling the world.

Germany and Italy subscribed to a political ideology known as Fascism. As a political movement, Fascism (a name derived from the Latin *fasces*, the bundle of rods carried in front of Roman magistrates as a symbol of authority) had gotten its start (and name) in Italy soon after World War I. Although Italy fought on the winning side in that War, a postwar economic slump caused inflation, social unrest and widespread unemployment. Industrial workers staged sit-down strikes, peasants seized land and middle-class industrialists and landowners became terrified of a Communist revolution. Backed up by the fearful middle class, bands of ruffians roamed the streets engaging in hand-to-hand battles with leftists and workers; these ruffians were known as the *fasci di combattimento* ("groups for combat").

The leader of the Fascists was Benito Mussolini, a spirited opportunist who had begun his career as a revolutionary Socialist but then turned to a superpatriotic support of nationalism and even the monarchy. He was consistent, as one historian has put it, in only two things: "He always hated parliaments and he always loved violence." Inflamed by his impassioned oratory, the Fascists became so numerous and powerful that Mussolini was able to march on Rome with his followers in 1922, threaten a coup and form a new government.

Mussolini's attitudes were characteristic of the dictatorships that later sprang up in Germany, Austria, Hungary, Poland, Romania, Bulgaria and Greece. Fascists everywhere were primarily interested in gaining power and keeping it. They worshiped war and military discipline; in fact, Mussolini once declared: "War is to the man what motherhood is to the woman. I do not believe in perpetual peace; not only do I not believe in it, but I find it depressing and a negation of all the fundamental virtues of man."

A virtuous man, as defined by the Fascists, despised all ethical considerations that might weaken his will to power. A basic Fascist tenet held that certain men and nations were inherently stronger than others, and that to object to this "law of nature" was sentimental nonsense. The individual's right to dissent on any subject was rescinded and all political action was subordinated to the interests of the state. The state became all-important, a mystical entity with a destiny of its own. Italy's destiny, Mussolini believed, was to establish an empire that would rival ancient Rome's. Mussolini erected vast, columned buildings in neo-Roman style, renamed the Mediterranean with the Latin words, *Mare Nostrum* ("Our Sea"), and considered himself an heir to the Caesars. His fondest hope was to rule with his legions over North Africa and the Balkans. His first act of aggression occurred in 1935 when Italian forces invaded Ethiopia, one of the few countries of Africa left unconquered in the Age of Imperialism. Within a year Mussolini had conquered the nation, despite the bravery of the Ethiopian emperor, Haile Selassie, and the feeble efforts of the League of Nations to check the Italian aggression.

Adolf Hitler's rise to power closely paralleled—and was partly modeled on—Mussolini's. After World War I, Hitler, an unsuccessful Austrian painter and odd-job man who had become a corporal in the German Army, led a group known as the National Socialist German Workers' Party—the Nazis. Like the Fascists in Italy, the Nazis espoused a creed of militarism, patriotism and a hatred of the Communists—but they added a new article of faith: rabid anti-Semitism. At first Hitler found little support from the German people for his party except among a few soldiers and students, but when the Depression hit Germany in 1930 and 1931 his star rose. By promising to restore German prosperity and to rebuild the nation into a great military power, he won a wide following. In 1933 he was appointed chancellor and quickly transformed his office into a dictatorship.

Anti-Semitism had won Hitler widespread popularity because in a Germany that was torn with dissension, anti-Jewish sentiment was one of the few things people could agree on. Leftists loathed rich businessmen, and Rightists feared the activities of Communists; in each case Hitler identified the enemy as Jews and took away their citizenship. He forbade them to work in the professions, and prohibited their intermarriage with non-Jews. Such restrictions, however, were only a prelude to the savage racist policies that Hitler was later to pursue. Between 1939 and 1945 the Nazis killed some six million Jews—about one third of all the Jews then living in the world.

The actual beginning of the War was touched off not by Hitler's anti-Semitism but by his aggressive foreign policy. He seized most of the territories occupied by German speaking peoples, beginning with the annexation of Austria and the western sectors of Czechoslovakia. Although the British and French opposed these seizures, they hoped to appease Hitler by letting him keep his new acquisitions. Germany's hunger for territory, however, was not to be so easily satisfied—and was not confined to German lands alone. In March 1939 the Nazis annexed the rest of Czechoslovakia and, on September 1, struck at Poland. The British and French declared war.

The third major Axis power, Japan, hoped to extend its rule over all of Asia. During the 1920s Japan had cautiously experimented with parliamentary government, had given the right to vote to all men and had witnessed the growth of political parties and trade unions. But in the 1930s the government fell into the hands of a clique of military officers and aristocrats, who established a totalitarian regime somewhat like Hitler's and Mussolini's. A single ultranationalist party, the "Imperial Rule Assistance Association," replaced the older political parties, which were forced to dissolve. As in Germany and Italy, schools were ordered to inculcate students with a sense of the nation's sacred history and destiny. All male students had to undergo military training, Communism was declared a foe, and religious groups were forced to support national policies.

Japan's imperialistic schemes were quite similar to Germany's and Italy's. During World War I Japan had attempted to make China into a protectorate, but in 1922 Japan was forced by the United States and other Western powers to sign a treaty guaranteeing China's territorial integrity. Nevertheless, Japan continued to look longingly toward China, particularly toward an outlying northeastern province, Manchuria—an area rich in coal and iron, raw materials urgently needed by Japanese industries. In 1931 Japan seized Manchuria and in 1937 gained control over the coastal areas and several key Chinese cities. Soon the Japanese were casting covetous eyes southward toward French Indochina and the Netherlands East Indies.

On the eve of World War II the Japanese had already defined their master plan for Asia. The program was clearly expansionist, designed to create a great Japanese colonial empire that would provide raw materials and food for the crowded home islands and an outlet for their teeming population. It was also vehemently anti-Western. It aimed at ousting the Europeans and helping the "liberated" peoples to develop politically, culturally and economically under Japanese direction.

Most of Asia would be coordinated under what was euphemistically described as the "Greater East Asia Co-Prosperity Sphere." Although the Japanese spoke of cooperation and equality among the member states of the sphere, in actuality they considered themselves racially superior to the peoples they planned to subjugate.

In the first years of World War II the Axis powers seemed invincible. In 1939 and 1940 Hitler marched on to victory after victory in Europe, staging a blitzkrieg against Poland, quickly conquering Denmark, Norway and the Low Countries and then seizing France. With these nations overwhelmed, Britain was the only major power opposing Germany. The United States, although it supported the British with money and weapons, refused to declare war against the Axis; a large group of isolationists in America felt that the conflict should be considered strictly a European affair. Similarly, the Russians, although they despised Fascism, feared a German attack even more and had signed a mutual nonaggression pact with Hitler in 1939.

By the summer of 1942 Hitler ruled over a European empire larger than any since the time of ancient Rome. At the same time Germany and Italy were threatening to drive the British out of Egypt, to enclose the Mediterranean and to join forces in India with the Japanese.

For while Hitler conquered Europe, the Japanese were creating a great empire in the Far East. They tightened their grip on much of China and in the summer of 1941 occupied French Indochina (present-day Vietnam, Cambodia, Laos). Simultaneously, Japan's relations with the United States were growing tense. Determined to thwart Japan's imperialistic ambitions, the United States froze all of Japan's assets in America and cut off practically all trade with the Japanese. In addition, the United States lent large sums of money to Chinese

forces opposing the Japanese occupying armies. Finally, while Cordell Hull, the U.S. Secretary of State, was demanding a definition of Japanese aims in Southeast Asia, the Japanese bombed Pearl Harbor on December 7, 1941. The attack—which caused the United States to take up arms not only against Japan but against the other Axis powers as well—crippled the U.S. Pacific Fleet. In a few months the Japanese controlled Thailand and scored victories in Hong Kong, the Philippines, Malaya, Indonesia, Wake, Guam and other islands of the Pacific. Soon Japanese armies had captured Singapore, Britain's so-called "impregnable" naval base in Malaya. Burma, the Bataan peninsula and the island of Corregidor in the Philippines fell, and the Japanese were threatening India.

It was only when Hitler made a colossal mistake that Allied fortunes took a turn for the better. On June 22, 1941, Germany had broken its nonaggression pact with Stalin and Hitler's forces had invaded Russia. Although in the first few months the Germans advanced 2,300 miles into the Soviet Union, they failed to take either Moscow or Leningrad. The fighting slowed down during the winter, but resumed in the spring. The showdown between the two armies came in August 1942 at Stalingrad, a city in southwestern Russia near the mouth of the Volga River. If Hitler could win Stalingrad, he could appropriate the vital oil that was being shipped from the Caucasus up the Volga, and the river could be made the new eastern boundary of the Nazi Empire.

Hitler's forces bombarded Stalingrad so ruthlessly that three quarters of its buildings were flattened in a single day. When the German soldiers entered the city, however, they encountered unyielding resistance from the Russian troops. Day after day thousands of men died on both sides in hand-to-hand fighting amidst rotting corpses and the rubble of bombed houses and

A STRANGLEHOLD ON HITLER *was depicted in this Russian poster in 1942, after the British and the Americans had signed war pacts with the Soviets. The Western allies soon stepped up their shipments of supplies to Russia, increased bombing attacks on Germany and by 1943 had taken over all Axis-controlled territories in North Africa.*

factories. In November two additional Russian armies came to the aid of the city and trapped the Germans in Stalingrad in a pincers movement. Closing in on the city, the Russians cut off Nazi supply lines and slowly tightened their grip on the enemy. German officers begged Hitler to let them retreat, but he adamantly refused. By the end of January 1943, the Germans, their numbers greatly reduced, had no choice but to surrender. The mighty Nazi army, which had numbered more than 300,000 men when it attacked the city, was reduced to a third of its original size. The conflict, the most destructive land battle in World War II, deeply damaged German morale. After Stalingrad, Hitler was on the defensive.

Russia's victory inaugurated a radical change in Stalin's foreign policy. Until Stalingrad the Soviet Union had simply struggled to survive against the German assault, but now the Russians began to see the War as a chance not only to liberate their own land but also to greatly increase their ter-

ritory, influence and prestige in Eastern Europe.

Russia's ambitions made it an odd ally for the great democracies, Britain and the United States. The ideals of the Allies were defined in the Atlantic Charter, which Britain's prime minister, Winston Churchill, and America's wartime president, Franklin Delano Roosevelt, jointly signed in 1941. The agreement called for the international abandonment of aggression and the restoration of self-government to conquered peoples. The Charter also pledged Britain and the United States to "seek no aggrandizement, territorial or otherwise."

The American President also had strong ideas about imperialism. He told Churchill: "I can't believe that we can fight a war against Fascist slavery, and at the same time not work to free people all over the world from a backward colonial policy. . . ." Roosevelt was voicing the United States' opposition to all colonial empires—including Britain's. Throughout the War Roosevelt let it be known that Americans would disapprove of any

European countries that attempted to re-establish control over colonies in Asia.

Roosevelt elaborated on the ideological basis for the War in his famous "Four Freedoms" speech, in which he resoundingly called for guarantees of freedom of speech, freedom of religion, freedom from fear and freedom from want. Freedom from want was a new political ideal to be added to the list of human aspirations. Inspired by haunting memories of the recent Depression decade, the pledge proved to be a dynamic encouragement to the poor in all parts of the world.

After the summer of 1942, when the Battle of Stalingrad began, other key triumphs quickly followed for the Russians and their Western allies. The British crushed German and Italian armies at El Alamein in North Africa, and Axis forces were defeated in Tunisia and Sicily. The Allies staged a massive air offensive against German cities. In the Pacific the Americans won great naval victories at Coral Sea and Midway and chased the Japanese from Guadalcanal, the Solomons, the Gilbert and Marshall Islands, and the Marianas.

The main Allied effort, however, was concentrated on defeating Germany. On June 6, 1944, the greatest armada ever assembled, under the American General Dwight D. Eisenhower, launched the invasion of Normandy to liberate the Continent from German rule. More than 130,000 Britons, Canadians and Americans landed the first day, more than 300,000 within a week, a million within a month. In August, Paris was liberated after its citizens rose against the German occupying force; the recapture of the city gave Allied morale an exhilarating boost. In March 1945 the Allies crossed the Rhine and in April reached the Elbe, where they met the Russians, who had been advancing westward ever since the Battle of Stalingrad. Hitler committed suicide in Berlin. Mussolini was captured and shot in northern Italy by Italian partisans. On May 8, 1945, the War in Europe finally came to an end with the eastern half of the continent held by the Russian armies and the rest by the Western Allies.

That spring and summer British and American troops were shifted to the Far East. Slowly and painfully islands that had been overrun by the Japanese were recaptured. From aircraft carriers and from land bases in Saipan, Guam, Iwo Jima and Okinawa, the Allies launched a powerful air offensive that shattered Japanese industry. But the Japanese refused to yield until, on August 6, 1945, an atomic bomb, secretly prepared by scientists in the United States, was dropped on Hiroshima. A single explosion equivalent to 20,000 tons of TNT—2,000 times more powerful than any previous bomb—destroyed most of the city, resulted in the loss of some 68,000 lives and created a radioactive atmosphere that endangered thousands more. After a second bomb was dropped on Nagasaki, a major Japanese port city, killing about 30,000, the Japanese surrendered on September 2, 1945. The atomic bomb had opened a new era in warfare—indeed, in human history—and cast a dark shadow over the postwar world.

The War ended with the defeat of Fascism in Europe and militarism in Asia, but it gave birth to a new ideological struggle as the Soviet Union and the United States competed for the allegiance of emerging nations all over the world. While the War itself was still being fought, few people had foreseen the "Cold War" that would follow. In fact, even before the War had ended, 50 nations that had sided with the Allies against the Axis hopefully banded together to form the United Nations, the successor to the League of Nations. The creation of the United Nations was largely predicated on the belief that the Allies would continue to cooperate closely during times of peace.

This illusion was quickly shattered. During the

War, leaders of the Allied nations had met several times and discussed plans for administering the postwar world. Germany was to be temporarily divided into occupation zones, each zone controlled by one of the Allies; Austria, part of the Nazi empire, was to become free and independent, as was the Japanese-dominated country of Korea; finally, the Balkan states and Poland were to become "democratic" nations.

When the War was over and the Allies no longer shared a common cause, discords sprang up that eventually produced the Cold War. The first area of disagreement concerned the Balkans. Although the British, Americans and Russians had agreed that the Balkans should be democratic, they had different notions about what that meant. The Russians, who were in military control of the region, were determined that Communist regimes should be established in Romania, Hungary and Bulgaria. They knew that if these countries were allowed to have genuinely free elections, as the United States insisted, they would probably elect governments that were hostile toward Russia. Tension in the area increased when the United States decided to give massive financial aid to Turkey and to those Greeks who were carrying on a civil war against Greek Communists; the anti Communists triumphed with American aid, and a pro-Western Greece and Turkey, capable of containing Russia's Eastern European satellites, had been set firmly on their feet.

American-Soviet relations continued to deteriorate when the United States proposed in June, 1947 the Marshall Plan, a program for helping Western Europe and England recover economically from the devastating effects of the War. This help was acutely needed. Postwar Western European industry was down one third from its 1939 level, Britain was burdened with a $15 billion debt that had wrecked its economy, and

large Communist parties in France and Italy threatened to take over the governments of those nations. Natural disasters compounded these miseries during the winter of 1946-1947; severe blizzards destroyed wheat crops all over Europe and slowed shipments of vital fuels to industrial centers. Obviously, if Europe were not to sink to a starvation level or be drawn into the Communist orbit, the United States would have to lend enormous sums of money.

By September 22, 1947, sixteen European countries had worked out a plan for economic recovery based on American aid, and the following April Congress voted to implement the plan, which was eventually to cost the United States over $13 billion. The Russians denounced the plan—it proved enormously successful—as an American plot for establishing domination over Europe.

Because of the stepped-up antagonisms between the United States and the Soviet Union, the "temporary" division of Germany into Western and Eastern sectors became permanent, as did the division of Korea. Similarly, the Allied agreement to create a "free and independent" Austria was not acted on until 1955; until that time Austria, like Germany, was divided into occupation zones. As World War II receded into history, Europe aligned itself into two camps. On one side were Western Europe and the United States; on the other were Russia and the small states of Eastern Europe and East Germany that had come under Communist domination. The Nazis, who had vowed to save Europe from Communism, had instead started a war that advanced the red flag deep into the Continent.

The War also radically changed the political structure of Asia. Despite the shattering of Japan's dream of empire, the Japanese military conquests during the War had succeeded in stirring up new and powerful political concepts in the Far East.

The fall of Bataan, the conquest of Singapore and other Japanese triumphs throughout the western Pacific had all dealt irreparable blows to the prestige of white colonial powers in Asia. Furthermore, the discovery in 1945 of the full extent of Nazi atrocities in the concentration camps produced a profound worldwide shock. To non-Western eyes the crimes of Treblinka, Buchenwald, Dachau and Auschwitz were clear evidence of how rapidly the veneer of Western civilization could be stripped away to reveal a terrifying brutality. The myth of European invincibility was also destroyed. Captured Western soldiers and airmen had been paraded through Asian cities. The Japanese had displaced the Europeans and had for a time dominated an empire of some 450 million people that stretched south from Manchuria and east to New Guinea.

For the colonial peoples of Indochina, Indonesia, Malaya and Burma, the Japanese conquests in Southeast Asia aroused a kind of grim satisfaction; the fall of the European masters caused little mourning. In many places collaborators cooperated with the Japanese occupying authorities—at least at first. Europeans in London, Amsterdam and Paris were shocked to discover how little loyalty there was to the older colonial rule.

The economic and political programs that the Japanese had inaugurated in China and Southeast Asia outlasted their ephemeral rule. Japanese economic plans promised the occupied peoples industrial development, modernization and an end to Western imperialism and colonialism—in fact, an equal share in the fruits of the empire. Actually, the Japanese indefinitely postponed all projects for industrial development and continued the colonial economy and the plantation system set up by the Europeans. The native populations were conscripted into forced labor battalions. Goods traditionally imported from the United

DOMINATING THE WORLD, *the Axis Powers controlled the nerve centers of Europe, Asia and Africa by 1942. But then the tide turned: the Royal Air Force, having won the Battle of Britain in 1940, launched a bomber offensive against Hitler's domain; the Russians prevented the Germans' eastward sweep at Stalingrad; and the United States and Australia managed to hold the "thin line of survival" stretching across the Pacific.*

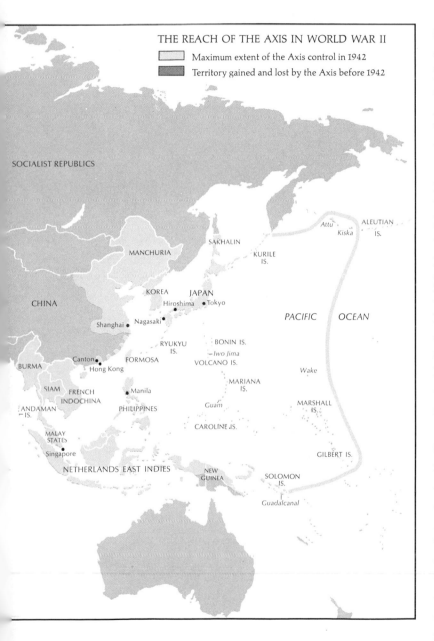

THE REACH OF THE AXIS IN WORLD WAR II

☐ Maximum extent of the Axis control in 1942

■ Territory gained and lost by the Axis before 1942

SOCIALIST REPUBLICS

SAKHALIN

MANCHURIA

KURILE IS.

Attu

Kiska

ALEUTIAN IS.

KOREA   JAPAN

Hiroshima   • Tokyo

CHINA

Shanghai •   • Nagasaki

PACIFIC   OCEAN

RYUKYU IS.

BONIN IS.

Canton •   FORMOSA

– Iwo Jima

BURMA

Hong Kong

VOLCANO IS.

Wake

MARIANA IS.

SIAM   FRENCH

• Manila

Guam

MARSHALL IS.

INDOCHINA

ANDAMAN IS.

PHILIPPINES

CAROLINE IS.

MALAY STATES

GILBERT IS.

• Singapore

NETHERLANDS EAST INDIES

NEW GUINEA

SOLOMON IS.

Guadalcanal

States and Europe were cut off. After 1943, when all of Japan's economic plans for Asia were paralyzed by Allied air and submarine attacks and by the catastrophic reverses suffered by the Japanese navy, the economy of Southeast Asia was thrown into chaos; and scarcity, inflation, privation and misery prevailed.

Politically as well as economically, Japanese promises of independence proved hollow, yet they touched off unexpected, explosive results. In releasing the peoples of Asia from European rule, the Japanese destroyed the very institutions of empire. For their own purposes they encouraged a program of independence from the West, and local people were allowed to fill key government posts, supervisory jobs in commerce and industry, and other positions that in the past had been staffed by Europeans only. In Rangoon, Kuala Lumpur, Saigon, Djakarta and Manila, Asians got the chance to help administer their own lands a chance Western rule had denied them.

Before World War II almost every country in Southeast Asia represented a crazy-quilt of rival religions, languages, cultures and races, and early independence movements had generally been unable to unite the many hostile factions. The populations of the area were heterogeneous and divided into many levels of cultural and economic development—the range of human diversity extended from the headhunters of northern Borneo to the sophisticated city dwellers of Saigon. In Indonesia, an archipelago that sprawled over 1,500 miles from Sumatra in the west to Tanimbar in the east, some 250 languages or dialects were spoken. Indochina was an artificial federation of Annam, Laos, Cambodia and other provinces. Burma and Malaya were heavily populated by unassimilated Chinese immigrants.

The common ordeal of suffering under the Japanese, however, did much to draw the people in these areas together. Certainly the Japanese occupation did not completely dissolve historic antagonisms, but it did, at least temporarily, underline the common goals and needs of each of the peoples of Southeast Asia.

More importantly, the Japanese elevated to power a new class of youthful political leaders. In Burma, for example, the Japanese set up a puppet regime to which in 1943 they nominally granted "independence." For years Burma had been subordinate both to Britain and to India. The top posts in the civil service had been filled by Indians when not filled by Englishmen, and the British Indian Army had provided for Burma's defense. During their occupation the Japanese, in contrast, appointed Burmese to key administrative and economic posts. They also trained the first Burmese military force. Having finally had a taste of "independence," the Burmese staunchly defended it—against the Japanese as well as the British. The very units that Japan had trained to fight the British turned against Japan in the last phase of the War. The Burmese Army stepped into the vacuum created by the Japanese withdrawal, appropriated the weapons abandoned by the retreating Japanese, and prepared to use force, if necessary, against the British. But the British, who had been weakened economically by the War, were in no mood to contest Burmese claims, and in 1948 they recognized Burma's independence.

In the Netherlands East Indies the Japanese set up a puppet government headed by Indonesians, trained a local army of 120,000 men and encouraged the use of modernized Malay as the one official language of this polyglot region. In August 1945, Sukarno, a leader of Indonesia's nationalist movement since 1927 who had been jailed as a subversive by the Dutch for years, proclaimed Indonesian independence immediately after the Japanese surrender. Like the Burmese, the Indonesians were armed and ready to protect their freedom against the returning Allied troops. For four years after the War the Dutch fought to regain control; but in 1949, realizing that they lacked the military means to win back the colony, they accepted the new situation. The Netherlands East Indies became the Republic of Indonesia. Despite the vast size of the island nation and the profound political and cultural differences among its people, Indonesia proclaimed its common identity.

Elsewhere the story was similar. Japanese rule catalyzed anti-Western independence movements in Malaya and Indochina (and to some extent in the Philippines), and local governments took over when the Japanese were forced to withdraw. The British sought to regain control over a Malaya that was divided into warring factions of Chinese and Malayans, and to win back Indochina the French struggled against Vietnamese troops from 1946 to 1954. But within little more than a decade after the War's end the European empires, founded in the great ages of European expansion and imperialism, had almost completely disappeared in Southeast Asia.

Asians, aroused by Western political ideals of freedom, self-determination and human rights, turned against Western rule. And the European nations, weakened by the terrible strain of the War, lacked the money and might to regain their old empires, even if they had had the moral will to do so. The Japanese conquerors, though they had not succeeded in their own objectives, accomplished more than they planned in undermining European rule. The whole vast area of Southeast Asia had been thrust into nationhood by the War. The peoples of Asia, free from European domination, were soon seeking the benefits that Western science and industry could bring to them, but at the same time they insisted on the freedom to work out their own political fate.

The Unforgettable Crime

At the end of World War II, as the horrors of Nazi anti-Semitism became widely known, people everywhere—and particularly in Asia and Africa—were forced to update their already well-grounded doubts about the merits of Western "progress" and "moral leadership." How could a civilization that had murdered six million people claim to be ethical?

Germany's savage extermination of European Jews was well documented by the prisoners themselves. Because of its wealth of surviving drawings and descriptions, perhaps the clearest picture that can be reconstructed is of Terezín (called Theresienstadt by the Germans), a camp in Czechoslovakia. It was first used by the Nazis as a ghetto for elderly Jews and later to house Jews prominent in the arts and public life.

Nevertheless, despite its privileged status, Terezín was, for most of its inmates, simply a stopping-off place on the way to the death camps. The sketch at right, which shows prisoners being herded into Terezín, was drawn by Bedrich Fritta, an inmate at the camp, who drew all the pictures on the following pages with the exception of one by Karel Fleischmann on pages 96 and 97. These reveal the miseries of camp life in all their horror. The quotations, drawn from postwar testimonies given by survivors of Terezín, grimly describe the most "humane" Nazi camp.

Photographed by Frank Lerner

Organizing the Jews

"The German Reich liked numbers, numbers meant order. . . . With a number around their necks, on their packs, on their suitcases, 50 kilograms per person, they were brought . . . to Terezín, to the ghetto." "We were . . . taken to the barracks where we had to register. . . .We were searched by the police, our luggage was examined, whereupon the SS officers and the police disappeared. We were left to ourselves, Jews among Jews, herded into a ghetto of which we had only known from history books. . . ."

"All work was done by Jews: the work of builders, locksmiths and carpenters, the work in the electricity and waterworks, road repairs and sewerage, repair work in the houses, cleaning of streets and buildings, tailoring and waste-paper collection, laundry and shoemaking. Jews kept the vital bakery and the communal kitchens going as the result of much hard work. Jewish workers laid a railway line. . . ." "We sweat and starve. We work half naked. We dig throughout the night. In the morning a fat 'Schutzpolizei' in the helmet of the Teutoburg Forest throws each of us a piece of black bread; it soars through the air and we catch it like wild cats behind iron bars, eat it avidly within a few minutes and go on digging. . . ."

Filling out forms *(above)*, a prisoner signs a document during registration at Terezín. All Jews were forced by Nazi racial laws to wear a Jewish star on their shirts. Nazi troops were kept busy filling out superfluous charts, surveys and reports on prisoners; at least 17 different files were maintained on every inmate at Terezín.

A labor force, bearing shovels *(overleaf)*, marches off to work. The Nazis used the prisoners as a source of manpower to produce goods necessary for fighting the war. Terezín prisoners manufactured uniforms and ammunition boxes for the German Army. Working parties sometimes labored in nearby mines and forests.

Life in the Barracks

"In the midst of war we lived in a concentration camp that was barbarously invented and barbarously kept going. We were packed in like cattle, slept in miserable three-tier bunks, ate our rations mostly standing, from tin utensils, relieved ourselves in stinking latrines, lived in constant fear of transports to gas chambers. But every day there was illegal education of children, every day there were theater performances, concerts, lectures, every day news came from outside and was rapidly and dependably spread further, and every day there was tenacious confidence that nothing could subdue. The hunger to take part in cultural undertakings was certainly no less abnormal than the structure of the whole ghetto society. There was something of a morose greatness in it. . . ."

"Men and women lived separate from each other in the barracks. . . . Family life was impossible, but people could see each other after the day's work was done." "Two weeks after our arrival half of my group were dead. The hunger was awful. . . . People fought for potato peelings soaked in dirt. . . . Our transportation, including garbage disposal, was done in dead-wagons. . . . People would storm these wagons for a scrap of food. . . . Those of us who worked at carting had to be severe with these people, because eating the terribly dirty scraps of food or swallowing uncooked, filthy potato peel would bring on disease—in many cases certain death."

A concertina serenade *(below)* enthralls an audience of prisoners in the barracks. In the small amount of luggage that prisoners were allowed to bring to Terezín, many people included musical scores, books and instruments, which they shared with the other inmates. As a consequence, Terezín had a thriving cultural life.

The squalid ghetto overflows with prisoners confined in dirty, crowded quarters *(overleaf)*. Before the war Terezín was a Czech fortress provided with barracks for 7,000 people; after the Germans took over Terezín in 1941 and made it into a concentration camp, the same barracks had to house as many as 85,000 prisoners.

The March to Death

"People called up for transport assembled with the last remnants of property—their bedrolls and a pack of the most necessary things." "Then they were driven—with numbers tied round their necks and carrying their packs—to the train and stuffed into . . . trains, 70 to 90 in a car. . . .

"On September 23, 1944, the SS issue an order to dispatch two transports from Terezín of 2,500 men below the age of 50 each, to be sent on war work. Dresden is given as the destination. . . . Participants in the transport are promised good treatment for their families that are remaining behind at the camp. The order specifically states that the transport is being sent to a work camp, and that it is therefore necessary to include technicians and craftsmen, members of the guard and doctors. . . .

"And on April 20, 1945, a freight train brings about 2,000 persons [back] to the Terezín camp. . . . Those who arrive at the camp from Auschwitz and other such camps no longer look like human beings. . . . The inmates of Terezín are filled with horror when they discover among the newcomers a few of those who had left the camp half a year before. . . . The replies to inquiries after other friends are all the same, though each sounds different: gas, shot, died of hunger, air-raid, typhus, electric current, scores of deaths, each in a different form."

Awaiting transports (above), prisoners assemble at a check-out point. Originally, Jewish prisoners thought of Terezín as a ghetto where they would live permanently. After 1942, however, when transports began to leave the camp, prisoners slowly came to realize Terezín was only a stopover on the road to extermination.

Leaving Terezín (over leaf), a long column of prisoners trudges toward the trains that will conduct them to the Nazi death camps. To be included in such a transport was virtually a death sentence, of the 87,000 prisoners who were deported from Terezín to other camps, only 3,100 were discovered alive in the years after the war.

5
AN AWAKENING
OF NATIONS

A NEW NATION'S PRIDE *is displayed in a national crest and flag on a car owned by Kenya's president, Jomo Kenyatta. Kenya, one of more than 60 new nations established since World War II, became independent in 1963. The word "Harambee" on the crest means "Let's all pull together."*

The drive for national independence, which took hold throughout much of Asia in the years immediately following World War II, had a particularly long history in India. Indeed, the roots of imperialism went deeper there than anywhere else. India had a great antiquity, a history of fine statecraft and a wealth of art, literature and philosophy as old as any in the world. But it suffered many invasions over the centuries and finally fell to British rule in 1763. Thereafter it remained under British domination for nearly 200 years.

Despite its history, India had little sense of unity as late as the 19th Century. The vast subcontinent spans 1.7 million square miles—19 times the size of Great Britain—and is host to a rich diversity of language, religion and ways of life. Yet unlike China, which suffered nothing but chaos under European penetration, India was given its unity by British rule. The British brought law and order and tied the Indians in with the European economy. They established English as a common language in a land where more than 700 tongues were spoken. They introduced textile machinery, railroad transportation, modern banking and commercial agriculture. They exposed upper-class Indians to English ideas of democracy and freedom. They also opened up the mysteries of India's ancient past to the world—even to the Indians themselves. All these actions were to redound in ways that few imperialists anticipated.

In their earliest years as the rulers of India, the English, like most conquerors, paid little attention to the language and customs of their subjects. But in time some of them developed an interest in Sanskrit, the language in which India's early literature was recorded. Once it began, the study of Sanskrit provided a key that unlocked the past. Archeologists and historians followed the linguists, and they brought to light a golden age of Indian culture that had flourished 2,000 years before Christ. They deciphered the inscriptions left in the Third Century B.C. by the great King Ashoka, whose scribes recorded that the King had won "safety . . . justice and happiness for all beings." They looked with new interest at the cave temples at Ajanta, where a treasury of Buddhist sculpture stood carved in the rock. As far away as the

Kansu province of China they found paintings that had clearly been influenced by Indian art. To the Indians, subjugated by imperialism, these discoveries gave a sense of history and pride that helped to unify them.

The revitalization of Indian history accomplished something else as well. It brought about a re-examination of the Hindu religion and ultimately of Hindu society and the place of India in the world. For centuries Hinduism had been associated with renunciation of the world, with a fixed social hierarchy and with serene resignation to destiny—concepts that precluded change and progress. When European and Indian scholars began to examine the sacred writings of Hinduism, they found they could rank one of them, the Bhagavad Gita, with the Christian Bible and the Muslim Koran as religious philosophy. An equally important development was the translation into English of the Hindu writings. Because Sanskrit was the language of the Scriptures it was deemed to be sacred, and it was therefore taught to hardly anyone but the brahmans, the priestly caste. After the Gita had been translated, the hitherto inaccessible writings became available to Indians of all castes for study—and study inevitably brought reinterpretation and popularization.

The new interpretations were revolutionary. One of the earliest national spiritual leaders, Bal Gangadhar Tilak, not only questioned the caste system, but even interpreted the sayings of the god Krishna as calling for the reform of society, citing the text "I shall be born in successive ages for the purpose of destroying evil-doers and re-establishing the supremacy of the moral law." Inspired with such an interpretation, Indians beginning to feel the pull of nationalism could easily put religion to work for political and social causes.

The spirit of nationalism, stirring since the 1870s, began to grow with purpose in 1885, when the Indian National Congress was founded. It began as a discussion group for Indians who wished to inquire into questions of government. By the early 20th Century it had grown into a political party. Its membership was confined to the educated, but it was bent now on securing for Indians an active share in government.

The Indian National Congress had not had much success in that direction when World War I erupted, catalyzing the development of nationalism everywhere. First, because traditional sources of manufactured goods were cut off, industry grew in importance in India, just as it did elsewhere. When it did, businessmen emerged wealthy enough to press harder for control of their own affairs. Second, the promises to guard the rights of small nations, and the slogans coined by the West to bolster the war effort—such as "Make the world safe for democracy"—incited hopes of independence. Some 1.2 million Indian troops served in the War, and they came home refusing to be satisfied with colonial inferiority.

If the slogans and the promises gave India hope, the settlement of the conflict only frustrated national movements, for the great empires retained most of their colonial holdings. The British refused to grant India such sovereignty as Canada, Australia and New Zealand enjoyed, but they did make some concessions in the hope of placating the Indians. They allowed the country to join the League of Nations, and they spoke of a "gradual development of self-governing institutions." Toward that end they created a new legislature through which the Indians were to decide on matters of education, sanitation and economic development. But the Governor-General, an Englishman appointed from London, retained a veto and, in effect, the power to rule by decree. The Indians found the meager concessions inadequate and began to demand full independence immediately.

They had to wait almost 20 years. But by 1920 they had a new champion in one of the most forceful leaders the world has ever known—the saintly Mahatma Gandhi. Under his guidance they never slackened until the goal had been achieved.

Mohandas Karamchand Gandhi—later known as "Mahatma," Great Soul—was born in 1869, in a small principality in western India. His mother, though she was a profoundly devout and orthodox Hindu, encouraged him to go to England to study law—a violation of the customs of their caste, which proscribed "crossing the black waters."

After completing his studies, Gandhi settled with an Indian community in South Africa, where he took up a struggle against the prejudice and discrimination that Indians suffered under white African rule. Among the means he chose were some he had learned in England, where he read the works of Henry David Thoreau, the originator of passive resistance. Gandhi encouraged the Indians in Africa to refuse to cooperate with official regulations—a head tax that amounted to enslaving the Indians, and a ban on traveling from state to state, which Gandhi countered with organized marches. His talent for bringing pressure to bear on the authorities and for inspiring the masses to action brought him success—and a request to return home to fight British discrimination in India.

Gandhi had a great gift for drama and publicity. One of the major grievances of Indians against the British was a government monopoly on the manufacture of salt—and a tax on the peasants for their use of it. For years Indians had quarreled with the government on that issue, but to no avail. Gandhi solved the problem with masterly dispatch. After first announcing his intentions to the Viceroy, he set out on a long march. For more than three weeks he walked barefoot over scorching roads, drawing a band of peasant followers—and reporters—that sometimes stretched

two miles behind him. After traveling nearly 200 miles, he finally reached a small town on the west coast of India. There he bent down and ladled some water out of the Arabian Sea. He set it in the sun to dry, then triumphantly held up the few grains of salt that remained.

The demonstration electrified India; the idea of producing similar homemade salt spread "like a prairie fire," the future Prime Minister Jawaharlal Nehru wrote, and people across the country took up the illegal practice. "It was really immaterial," Nehru declared, "whether the stuff was good or bad; the main thing was to commit a breach of the obnoxious salt law." After about a year the British yielded and repealed it.

Partly out of the same penchant for dramatization, partly because he believed in the simple life, Gandhi urged his people to take up the spinning wheel in defiance of the British. He practiced what he preached. He wore the peasants' simple loincloth—made out of linen he spun for himself. In the same spirit, he did without the dentures he needed because peasants could not afford the expense of dental work.

Spurred by Gandhi's forceful nature, the National Congress staged a movement of mass civil disobedience in which Western-educated lawyers, Hindu spiritual leaders, businessmen and peasants worked side by side. For their acts Gandhi and his followers spent so many months in jail that Nehru was to speak of prison as "my other home." Gandhi insisted on nonviolence, but once the cause of independence had inflamed the masses, riots and looting broke out all over India.

Still the British made only small concessions. When World War II came, the members of the Indian National Congress refused to back Britain against the Axis, insisting that they could not support a war against aggression so long as they were themselves the victims of oppression. The

British offered to let the Indians form a new Executive Council, to be composed of Indians, but refused to promise full independence until after the War ended. In July 1942 the Indians passed a resolution asserting that "British rule in India must end immediately . . . because India in bondage can play no effective part in defending herself and in affecting the fortunes of the war that is desolating humanity." The declaration came to be known as the "Quit India" resolution.

But not until the War was over did the British at long last bow to the inevitable and take steps to grant India independence. After about two years of preparation, during which the British turned over more and more offices to Indians, the nation finally became formally independent on August 15, 1947. The new Indian government, in a spirit of good will, invited the military hero Lord Mountbatten to serve as Governor General, and India voluntarily remained in the loosely organized Commonwealth of Nations.

The coming of independence brought crowds to Delhi in the millions to rejoice under the blistering August sun. But enthusiasm over the winning of independence was saddened by the loss of unity, for the land that the British had ruled split apart. The new independent nation of India included only the predominantly Hindu sections of the subcontinent, the Muslim regions forming the new nation of Pakistan. The Muslims, though once the conquerors of India, had never been absorbed into Hindu society.

The arrangement was contrived, for the areas of densest Muslim population were separated by 1,000 miles; hence Pakistan consists of two parts, West Pakistan and East Pakistan. Even the name was contrived; it is an acronym made from the names of the provinces with a Muslim majority—Punjab, Afghania, Kashmir, Sind, Baluchistan. The word *"stan"* means "country" in Persian, and

AN INDIAN IMMORTAL, *Mohandas ("Mahatma") Gandhi is enshrined in stone between two goddesses on a temple in Madras. For 40 years Gandhi sought Indian unity by peaceful means.*

"pak" means "pure"; hence Pakistanis like to think of their country as the "Land of the Pure."

The birth of the two new nations was accompanied by bloodshed. Religious tensions soon brought panic and riots. At least eight million Muslims left India; other millions of Hindus fled the territories assigned to Pakistan. Nehru, as prime minister of India, worked to create a tolerant and democratic secular state, but the leaders of Pakistan insisted that their nation be altogether Islamic, with no separation of church and state.

Pakistan's troubles lay partly in the fact that the nation was born of a negative idea to begin with—that of separation from Hindu India—and partly in the fact that the nation was no sooner founded than the leaders succumbed to divisive quarreling and intrigue. But in Pakistan and elsewhere Islam had another barrier to overcome, for Muslim dogma discourages change, and it generally rejects evaluation or criticism, even in the light of modern scholarship. The authority of the Koran, as interpreted by the religious leaders, reigns supreme in matters of law as well as religion.

The Muslim faith, which was founded in the Seventh Century A.D. by the Prophet Muhammad, spread rapidly across the world until it found its present boundaries—a territory that stretches from Morocco 10,000 miles east to Indonesia and comprises 500 million peoples: Turks, Arabs, Mongols, Black Africans, Indo-Europeans, Malayans and Indonesians. Much of that territory was conquered in the 13th Century by the Ottoman Turks, who took on the role of champions of the faith. The Turkish Sultans designated themselves the caliphs or "successors" of the Prophet, the religious leaders of all Muslims.

By the opening of the 20th Century the Ottoman Empire was still a great sprawling nation, despite the loss to European imperialism of lands in Europe and North Africa, and despite the decay of the government. During the Age of Imperialism, British, French and German capital poured into the Empire. Even so, change came slowly. Men continued to watch flocks and till fields as they had in Biblical times. Bedouins and camel caravans still roamed through the Arabian deserts.

After World War I the heterogeneous Ottoman Empire disappeared. The Allied peace treaty broke up the Empire and partitioned its lands. Despite the political changes that followed the dissolution, much of the world of Islam remained static.

One exception was Turkey—the nucleus of the fallen Ottoman Empire—where a brilliant army officer, Mustafa Kemal, rose to rally the Turkish army and force the Western powers into a more generous treaty, under which the Turks managed to hold the Anatolian peninsula and rid it of Western interference.

The man who created modern Turkey was born simply Mustafa—Turks had no surnames then—in 1881, in Salonika, a port city that teemed with foreign merchants, soldiers and diplomats and their families. Mustafa, the child of lower-middle-class Muslim parents, was a rarity among Turks; he had fair skin, light brown hair and blue eyes. Even as a child he was moody, vain and arrogant; he told his schoolmates that he was "going to be somebody." He grew up to be ambitious and dominating, proud of his shapely hands and feet, and much concerned with his dress.

At six or seven he had a mind of his own and an eye for observation. He grumbled at learning the Arabic script sitting cross-legged on the floor and balancing a tablet on his knee, and protested to his teacher that foreign children sat at desks. He also complained about the baggy pants the Turks wore and looked with envy at the neatly clad soldiers that strutted through the streets brandishing swords and looking self-important.

When he was 12 he prevailed upon his widowed mother to let him enter military school, and there he shone as a pupil; he had gone on to algebra when his classmates were still struggling with arithmetic. His teacher, who also went by the name of Mustafa, gave him another name to distinguish the child from himself; he called the boy Kemal, which loosely means "perfection." Before he was done with his studies Kemal was to acquire an avid interest in poetry and history, and to read Voltaire and Rousseau in the original.

When he finished military school at the age of 24 he was commissioned a captain and sent to a post in Damascus. He was by this time moving toward agnosticism, developing the conviction that adherence to Islam was holding his people back in the modern world. He once said to a friend that the Ottoman Empire was a place where heaven was reserved for the infidel, while Muslims endured the pains of hell.

In Damascus he founded, with some friends, a

secret society that aimed to modernize the Turkish government. Kemal's society had not made much headway when another group, one that came to be known as the Young Turks, staged a revolution in Constantinople in 1908. The Young Turks' revolution was short lived; the Sultan remained on his throne, surrounded by a corrupt bureaucracy, and the outlying parts of his Empire continued to crumble away to the West.

When World War I came and Turkey joined with Germany, Kemal distinguished himself in the field and won the awe of his men for his fearless stand under fire. He ended the War the only Turkish commander who had never lost a battle.

He returned to Constantinople to find that the Allies had taken over, and by the terms of the treaty that was being prepared, Turkey was to be carved up among the victors. The Turks were to be left only a few provinces in Anatolia, surrounded by British, French, Italian and Greek spheres of influence. British, French and Italian interference was bad enough; but the hated Greeks were demanding the whole of the Aegean coast of Asia Minor and much of the inland as well. Turkey was to be virtually deprived of its army, and what little remained was to be commanded by the Allies. Beyond that, Turkey was to surrender its finances to Allied management and the Straits of the Bosporus and the Dardanelles to international control. The Sultan, a weak man who was ill prepared for his role, looked on cynically, playing into the hands of the Allies.

He failed to reckon on the will of his people, who like so many others in the world were now burning with nationalism. No one knew that better than Mustafa Kemal. When the Greeks sent troops marching east across Anatolia, Kemal undertook to stop them, and to deal the Allies and the Sultan a blow in the bargain. Speaking eloquently of "the rights of the nation" and "the will of the people," concepts he had learned in his reading of Western literature, he whipped the army into shape, mobilized the people behind him —including women who drove carts of food and ammunition across the mountains, wearing pantaloons and carrying babies slung on their backs— and drove the invaders out. Before the war was over, the Sultan had been deposed and the caliphate, separated from the throne, was handed to another prince, who was exhorted to stick to religion and stay clear of politics.

The Turkish war for independence astounded Europe. One member of the British government observed: "It was as if a boxer, after being counted out, had risen from the ring, stunned his opponent, knocked the referee through the ropes and [run off] with the purse."

While Kemal managed affairs at home, he sent an army friend, Ismet, who later adopted the name Inonu, to Lausanne to treat with the Allies in drafting a new treaty. Out of it Turkey emerged with the entire Anatolian peninsula intact and with control of the strategic Straits. It was the only treaty dictated by one of the Central Powers, and it proved to be the only one to endure after World War II.

With the war over, Kemal proclaimed the Turkish Republic in October 1923, and soon was elected president. His new republic began by sharply separating government and religion—unheard of in Islam. After a year the caliphate was abolished. The Koran was set aside in favor of Western law codes. Compulsory education was established. New laws provided for universal suffrage. Women, traditionally held inferior under Muslim law, were encouraged to put aside their veils, to vote, even to hold office. The Gregorian calendar was adopted; so were the metric system and family surnames. Kemal took the name Ataturk, meaning "Father of the Turks."

In many of these reforms, Kemal was acting on ideas that had germinated since boyhood—his agnosticism, and his ability to learn from the ways of the foreigner. Similarly he turned his attention to the fez, the headgear that most Turks looked upon as a mark of Ottoman distinction. To Kemal the fez was as outworn as the Ottoman Empire itself, and he began to appear in public in a Panama hat. So fraught with emotion was the subject that Turkish newspapers would not use the word *shapka*, meaning hat; instead they spoke of the "protector from sunshine" or the "head cover with a brim." But pressing his fight against the hat as he had earlier against the caliphate, Kemal cajoled the Assembly into passing a bill making the fez illegal.

No reform of Kemal's was further-reaching than his substitution of the Roman (he called it Turkish) alphabet in place of the old Arabic script. As part of a campaign to wipe out illiteracy, he ordered the new alphabet taught all over the country and the newspapers to change their type. His friend Ismet observed: "Today the whole country has been transformed into a classroom, and the headmaster in that classroom is the [President] himself."

"Headmaster" was an apt term, for Kemal had blackboards installed among the marble and ormolu trappings of the palace (since becoming president he had moved into the Sultan's former quarters), and with gusto he gave instruction to all who came his way, friends, officials or household servants. Within a year of the passage of the new law, more than a million Turks—many of them former illiterates—acquired certificates attesting to their proficiency in the new script.

For all his modern and Western ideas, Kemal was too strongheaded and too zealous for quick reform to institute democracy; instead he ran a benevolent dictatorship. But by the 1930s he had made Turkey a modern nation, one that had undergone a political and cultural transformation scarcely paralleled in any other country in modern times. In the process he won the devotion of his countrymen. When he died and the steadfast Ismet Inonu became president, a Turkish woman mourned: "Turkey has lost her lover and must now settle down with her husband."

Kemal's revolution had less influence on other parts of the colonial world than might have been expected. His program frightened off reform movements in Islam because in Turkey modernization had brought about secularism and virtual rejection of the faith. These consequences were so feared that none of the other nations carved out of the old Ottoman Empire experienced Turkey's transformation. Even so, the whole Muslim world was in ferment after World War I—and particularly the part of it that belonged to the Arabs.

In Egypt, a national movement put pressure on the British until in 1922 they were compelled to end their protectorate. The British managed, however, to retain certain privileges, among them the right to station troops in the Suez Canal Zone.

The anti-Western stance in the Arab lands was intensely religious, for Islamic orthodoxy merged with nationalism to intensify the revolt against the West. Although the Arabs constituted only one fifth of all Muslims, they could boast that Arabic was the language of the Koran and that Arabian lands had been the birthplace of Islam. Common language, common historic tradition and common faith, overriding all other loyalties, provided a bond among peoples who were otherwise heterogeneous.

At the end of World War II, with the collapse of the European empires in Asia, the drive for complete independence took hold among the Arabs. The French eventually pulled out of Tunisia, Morocco and—after a seven-year war—Algeria; and

A GLOBEFUL OF NEW NATIONS

Powered by a volatile mixture of anti-European nationalism and Europe-derived idealism, some 65 nations burst forth from colonialism in the two decades following World War II. More than half of these (38) are on the continent of Africa, 20-odd in Asia, four in the Western Hemisphere (below) and three amidst the Pacific islands—Western Samoa, Nauru and Tonga (not shown). In a few cases, notably British India, independence was achieved when the mother nation peacefully hauled down the imperial flag in the face of an inevitable native takeover. But in many more cases—notably Dutch East Indies and French Indochina—the mother nations withdrew only after protracted, bloody wars. Imperialism, as practiced by the Western nations and the Japanese, became an unforgettable theme of history, leaving the new nations with a bitter common heritage and an eagerness to work together as one of the world's balancing forces.

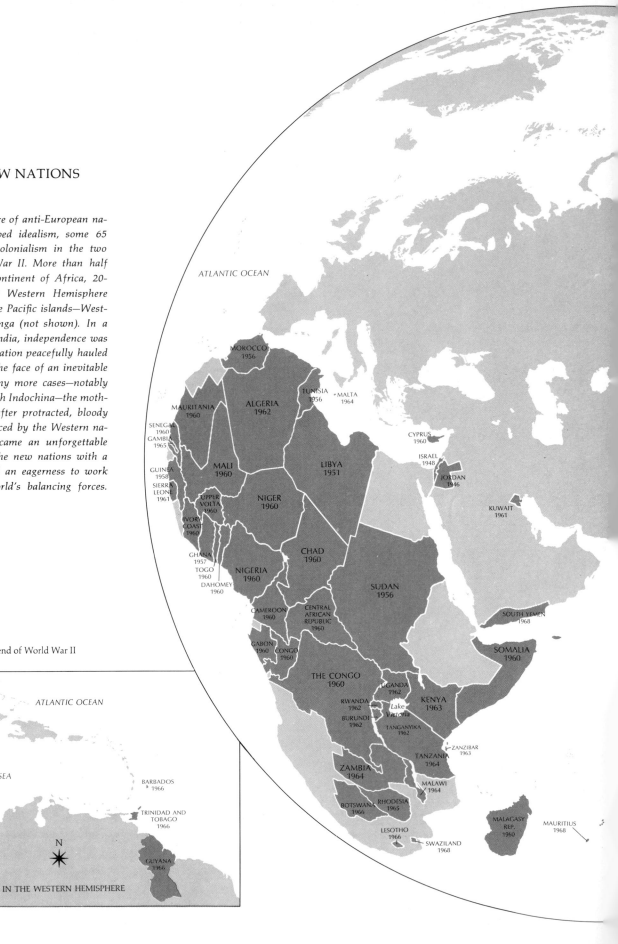

▮ Independent since the end of World War II

ATLANTIC OCEAN

MOROCCO 1956

MAURITANIA 1960

SENEGAL 1960
GAMBIA 1965

GUINEA 1958

SIERRA LEONE 1961

ALGERIA 1962

TUNISIA 1956 • MALTA 1964

CYPRUS 1960

ISRAEL 1948

JORDAN 1946

KUWAIT 1961

MALI 1960

UPPER VOLTA 1960

IVORY COAST 1960

GHANA 1957
TOGO 1960
DAHOMEY 1960

NIGER 1960

NIGERIA 1960

LIBYA 1951

CHAD 1960

SUDAN 1956

CAMEROON 1960

CENTRAL AFRICAN REPUBLIC 1960

GABON 1960   CONGO 1960

SOUTH YEMEN 1968

SOMALIA 1960

THE CONGO 1960

UGANDA 1962

RWANDA 1962
Lake Victoria
BURUNDI 1962

KENYA 1963

TANGANYIKA 1962

ZANZIBAR 1963

TANZANIA 1964

ZAMBIA 1964

MALAWI 1964

BOTSWANA 1966

RHODESIA 1965

LESOTHO 1966

SWAZILAND 1968

MALAGASY REP. 1960

MAURITIUS 1968

ATLANTIC OCEAN

JAMAICA 1962

CARIBBEAN SEA

BARBADOS 1966

TRINIDAD AND TOBAGO 1966

PACIFIC OCEAN

N

GUYANA 1966

0   Miles   500

IN THE WESTERN HEMISPHERE

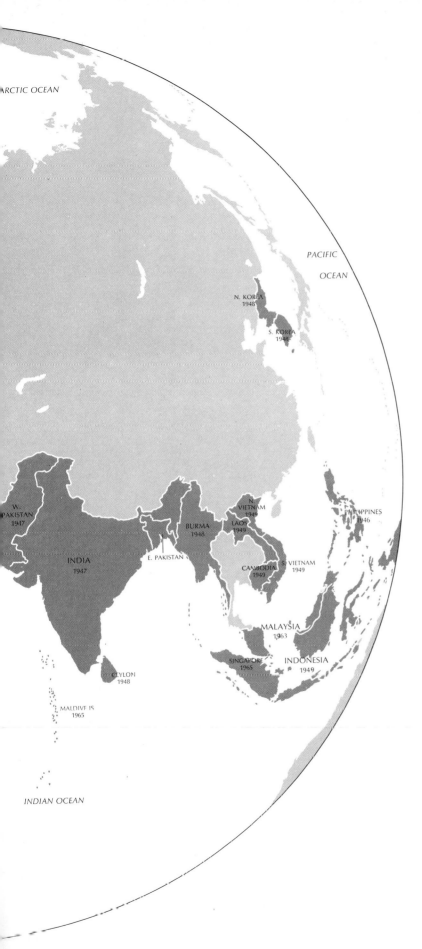

ARCTIC OCEAN

PACIFIC

OCEAN

N. KOREA
1948

S. KOREA
1948

W.
PAKISTAN
1947

N.
VIETNAM
1949

PHILIPPINES
1946

BURMA
1948

LAOS
1949

INDIA
1947

E. PAKISTAN

CAMBODIA
1949

S. VIETNAM
1949

CEYLON
1948

MALAYSIA
1963

SINGAPORE
1965

INDONESIA
1949

MALDIVE IS
1965

INDIAN OCEAN

the British withdrew their troops from Egypt. By the 1960s a dozen independent Arab countries had joined the United Nations.

The mere assertion of independence for these states was not enough to satisfy Arab nationalism. With Western political control gone, the remnants of Western influence came to seem intolerable. Arab resentment festered over a host of grievances —the British foothold in the Suez Zone, the French war in Algeria, the Western sponsorship of Israel.

Arab resentment was kept alive by an Egyptian army officer, Gamal Abdel Nasser, a strident nationalist who was hailed by his followers as a second Saladin—a reference to the 12th Century Egyptian sultan who routed the Crusaders after five years of "holy war." Nasser joined in overthrowing the Egyptian monarchy in 1952, then seized power for himself. In 1956 he seized and nationalized the vital Suez Canal. Refusing to ally himself with any single camp, he sought funds from the West and from the Soviet Union to modernize and strengthen his country.

The end of colonial empires throughout Asia, North Africa and the Middle East was perhaps to be expected, but the West was due for a surprise in the sudden demise of the European empires south of the Sahara. National independence movements that had taken decades to mature in India were telescoped in Africa into a few short years. After 1945 nationalist leaders moved rapidly from pressure for liberal reforms and a share in government to the creation of mass parties, and then to insistence on quick independence.

Rumblings of discontent had been heard in Black Africa before World War II, but economic development and urbanization had not proceeded sufficiently, nor had enough nationalist leaders appeared, to make the dissent effective. A handful of Western-educated leaders voiced protests, but as yet they reached only limited audiences.

Slowly a small Western-educated minority grew in influence. Africans, like Indians, went to the West for their schooling and absorbed Western ideas at Oxford or the Sorbonne, or Lincoln or Howard University; still others studied at Western-style universities in Nigeria, Uganda and Kenya. Like the Asian leaders, the young Africans learned to envy Western science and technology and acquired Western concepts of self-government, freedom and independence.

That was apparent when they began to work for independence. One French writer, Bertrand de Jouvenel, called the struggle in the French colonies "a battle of ideals which takes place within the context of French thought and French political vocabulary. The main rebels [are] conscious replicas of Lafayette, Mirabeau or Robespierre. They are playing a role against France which is taken from a French script." He might have added that many of the Moroccan and Algerian leaders had learned their ideas on the café terraces of the Latin Quarter in Paris; that Habib Bourguiba of Tunisia was a Paris-trained lawyer who had married a Frenchwoman; that Léopold Senghor of Senegal synthesized in his poetry and his politics the best in French culture and Black African civilization.

The African leaders not only acquired Western ideas; like the Indians, they also looked to their own past. They recalled the ancient African civilization that flourished along the Nile, the states of the Western Sudan, Ghana and Mali, a thousand years ago. Much of that proud history was new to the Westerner, who generally knew far less about Africa than he did about the ancient civilizations of India and China, the Muslim civilization of the Middle East, or the Aztec and Inca civilizations of the Americas. Kwame Nkrumah, the future leader of Ghana, often declaimed: "Long before the slave trade and the imperialistic rivalries in Africa began, the civilizations of the Ghana Empire were in existence. At that time, in the ancient city of Timbuktu, Africans versed in science, arts and learning were having their works translated into Greek and Hebrew."

World War II caused no disruption of life to Africa south of the Sahara comparable to the turmoil created in North Africa and Asia, but it initiated important economic changes and brought the colonial ferment in Africa to a head. The War led to a great demand for African products, because Africa had copper, iron ore, cotton, coffee, tea, cocoa and rubber that the world needed. Cities grew fast as shipping centers and processing areas. The new cities were not only important as centers of activity in themselves, but they also served to bind scattered areas together, creating political and economic unity, as did the improved transportation and communications that came with urbanization. Africans now recall that, in earlier times, to make a long-distance telephone call from one African city to another, the call had to go by way of a European city. There were no direct lines connecting African cities.

The new towns provided the nationalist spokesmen with a mass audience for the first time in African history. Leaders versed in Western political techniques sprang up, and they created mass organizations and political parties.

The first dramatic break came in the British West African colony, the Gold Coast, in 1947. In that year Kwame Nkrumah, a fiery orator who flirted with Communism, returned home from studying in the United States and England to throw himself into a whirlwind campaign to win independence.

Nkrumah was the son of a goldsmith in a small African mud-hut village. Like Gandhi, he acquired an education thanks to his mother, an illiterate woman who sent him to study at a missionary school in a village nearby. He did so well that his teachers urged him on to a school in Achimota, near Accra. Graduating from there at the head of his class, Nkrumah set out to teach, but a wealthy uncle, a diamond prospector, gave him the money to go to the United States.

There he entered Lincoln University in Pennsylvania, where his classmates were to vote him "Most Interesting." When he sailed out of New York harbor at the end of his course, he recalled later, he looked up at the Statue of Liberty and said to himself: "You have opened my eyes to the true meaning of liberty. I should never rest until I have carried your message to Africa."

And he did not rest. In London, where he went intending to study law, he involved himself with a Marxist group instead, then in 1947 returned to Ghana. By then, demands for independence were causing riots—and the British, to most Africans' astonishment, responded by granting the Gold Coast a constitution and the privilege of popular elections. One Gold Coast leader crowed: "It took India 25 years to gain what we are about to gain in less than two years."

Nkrumah was not so easily satisfied. He loudly denounced the constitution as a "fraud" and organized nonviolent strikes for immediate independence. "Youth of our country," he declaimed, "wake up for redemption. . . to make the Gold Coast a paradise so that when the gates are opened by Peter, we shall sit in heaven and see our children driving their airplanes, commanding their own armies."

Calling himself "a nondenominational Christian" and a "Marxian Socialist," Nkrumah wrote articles inflaming anti-Western sentiments. He put together a new political organization, the Convention People's Party, and coined the motto "Self-Government Now." To those who warned at home or abroad that Africans were not ready to face the perils of independent existence Nkrumah

replied: "We prefer self-government with danger to servitude in tranquillity."

The British stepped up the pace of change, but it was not fast enough. They introduced administrative reforms, allowing nationalist leaders to serve on legislative councils and encouraging the appointment of Africans to the civil service. But like the Indians, Nkrumah and his followers would accept nothing short of independence. For his obstructionist tactics, Nkrumah went to prison, but repression only made him a hero and intensified the demands for independence.

In 1957 the British yielded and granted the country its freedom. Nkrumah became prime minister, later president, of an independent state. To banish the memory of Western imperialism he renamed the Gold Coast "Ghana," recalling the splendid empire that had once existed in West Africa from the Eighth Century until the 13th, when it fell to invasion.

After that the British rapidly took steps to prepare the way for independence elsewhere. In the next few years Nigeria and Sierra Leone, Uganda, Kenya and Tanganyika (now Tanzania) all achieved independence and membership in the United Nations. Jomo Kenyatta of Kenya, Julius Nyerere in Tanzania, Nnamdi Azikiwe of Nigeria, all of them revolutionaries who had spent considerable time in British prisons, became heads of sovereign states. Once the move toward independence began, the roster of states in Africa grew fast. In 1945 there was hardly a state ruled by black Africans; by the middle of the 1960s there were more than 30.

The Africans who have at long last won independence are determined to use their hard-won freedom to build new societies, to absorb the best of Western technology—but not to be swallowed up by it. They proudly reassert the traditional principles of African civilization even as they modernize and improve the lot of their poor and hungry populations. "We do not seek freedom so that our people may remain in poverty and ignorance," declared Julius Nyerere, the Socialist-oriented, Edinburgh-educated president of Tanzania. They look not only to their own past, nor to a merely Western future, but to a fusion of the best of the old and the new. They adopt five-year plans or capitalist industrial organization, build cities, provide education and housing, create new industry. At the same time they would preserve their traditional culture, with its deep roots in the villages and tribes.

The new Africa has faced formidable problems. The infant states, often organized along the boundaries fixed by the European powers in the Age of Imperialism, have been plagued from the outset by tribal and ethnic rivalries. In Nigeria and the Congo disputes have led to civil war. A major obstacle to unity within the new states is the diversity of languages in each one. Official pronouncements over the radio and television commonly have to be made in five or six languages. Ironically, the only languages that can be understood throughout the continent are English and French, the tongues of the hated imperialists. Swahili has increasingly been used in the countries of East Africa, but it runs into opposition elsewhere because of local jealousies.

In each country democratic government has been more pretense than reality. The kind of leadership needed for heading an independence movement easily turns into dictatorship and autocracy after independence has been achieved. Nkrumah is the outstanding example. Insisting on complete obedience, exacting personal homage to his image on coins and in statues, he pushed the patience of his followers too far. In 1966 a military clique took advantage of his absence from Ghana to overthrow him. In many places—even in Nigeria, which

for a while seemed to be the most stable of the African states—military dictatorships moved into the political vacuums created by internal dissension.

Yet despite all the obstacles a new Africa is emerging. Trucks and bulldozers, pumps and generators, dams and hydroelectric plants have made their way into the countryside as the African bush is being pulled into a 20th Century economy. But the old and the new still exist side by side. Cars stand in front of mud huts. Villagers use hoes to widen dirt lanes to make their villages accessible from the outside. Women from the countryside, balancing bundles on their heads, walk past steel and plate-glass office buildings in the towns. Automobiles slow down to allow farmers to shepherd cattle across the highways.

Facing the overwhelming tasks of industrializing and of raising living standards, all the states have needed outside capital, management and technical knowledge. But they will not accept political control by the West.

International tensions heighten Africa's problems. At almost any time the new states might be drawn into the orbit of one of three groupings—the Communist world, Russian or Chinese; the non-Communist world, of which the United States has been the recognized leader; or the Islamic world, which entreats Black Africa to make common cause with Muslim nationalism.

The integration of modern technology and tribal cultures would have been difficult under the most propitious of circumstances. Faced now with untried political institutions and with international rivalries that threaten to engulf them, the new African states confront almost insuperable obstacles. Nevertheless, their decision has been made and they are resolved to face the future. They, like the newly created nations elsewhere in the world, have chosen "self-government with danger" over "servitude in tranquillity."

GRAFTING THE NEW ON THE OLD, *a woman uses the ancient art of embroidery to depict a hydroelectric plant, instead of traditional birds and flowers.*

破坏旧世界建设新世界

"DESTROYING THE OLD WORLD, BUILDING THE NEW."

In 1940, nine years before he gained control over the most populous nation in the world, Mao Tse-tung stated the aim of his Communist revolutionaries: "We wish to eradicate the old Chinese culture." Mao's specific goals—quoted in Chinese script above and on the following pages—may yet be fulfilled, although many aspects of the past life live on in new guises. Old China, a weak and complacent giant for two thousand years, is making a clamorous bid for modernity. Gone is the Confucian code of ethics that controlled society with inflexible laws. Gone is the godlike emperor, the prestigious class of scholars that staffed a labyrinthine bureaucracy, the landlords who kept millions of peasants working at subsistence levels. Unceasing trumpet-blares of propaganda now reverberate in the lowliest villages and the highest centers of learning as the Communist government takes the nation on a forced march toward industrialization. Although its future still hangs in the balance, China's quest for cultural change is clearly one of history's great experiments.

FARM MACHINERY TO SPUR EFFICIENCY *includes tractors of an old Soviet type as well as ingenious semiautomatic devices (right) that are used to transplant rice seedlings.*

发展农业的生产

"EXPANSION OF AGRICULTURAL PRODUCTION."

From time out of mind, China's millions have been enslaved to their land. Tilling patchwork fields in the flood-prone north or tiny rice paddies in the hills of the south, the peasants of old China had to feed at least 1,000 mouths from each square mile of cultivated land—after paying up to three quarters of their crops to landlords as rent.

Under Communism, the landlords are gone (farmers now work on communes) and machinery has boosted agricultural yield—although food production has barely kept pace with population. Because the specters of famine and peasant unrest are ever present, the government is giving priority to agriculture.

IN A PEKING NURSERY children learn from the mural above them that there are many different races in the world. Old China considered itself the geographical

THE NEW BREED OF SCHOLAR *studies science and technology in schools that graduated 230,000 engineers between 1949 and 1960.*

使儿童得到学习

GIVE CHILDREN A USEFUL EDUCATION

Education in old China was reserved for less than one per cent of the population—those few who had the time and intelligence to master the intricate, narrowly focused Confucian classics. A student spent years memorizing the thousands of symbols of the written language, then immersed himself in ancient texts so that he could pass an examination for government service.

Today, perhaps 100 million Chinese are in school, studying science, technology and foreign cultures—subjects never before considered worthwhile. Yet freedom of thought is still lacking. The Communists have replaced the Confucian orthodoxy with an equally rigid ideology: guidelines for Chinese schools come not from the Ministry of Education but from the Department of Propaganda.

ritual center of the world, and regarded all foreigners as backward and inferior.

要人家服只能
说服不能压服

"PERSUASION, NOT COMPULSION, IS THE ONLY WAY
TO CONVINCE THE PEOPLE"

Propaganda on a staggering scale, rather than force, provides the motive power for the Chinese Revolution. It is an ancient Chinese belief that the use of force is an admission of failure. Communism has therefore developed an enormous apparatus to instill political doctrine and fan enthusiasm at all levels of society. Just as old China was regulated by the words of Confucius, the 750 million people of modern China quote Mao on every occasion. Slogans for all manner of campaigns ("Onward to the Higher Stage of Co-operative Farming," "Kill Rats, Flies and Sparrows") are pronounced across the country in universal chorus. Children sing such songs as "The People's Communes Are Good" and "We Will Not Allow U.S. Imperialists to Ride Roughshod over the People."

Political meetings are part of the fabric of life. Policies are disseminated through mass organizations like the All-China Federation of Democratic Women and the Young Pioneer Corps. Factory laborers discuss politics during work breaks. Millions march through the streets of Peking to greet a foreign leader or celebrate a State occasion.

This high-pitched indoctrination, beginning in kindergarten and never letting up, has made possible sweeping changes in China's style of life. But the Chinese are accustomed to obeying civil authority—until a more promising authority offers itself. Whether or not Communism has a truly deep hold on the people remains to be seen.

A BARRAGE OF PROPAGANDA *extolling Mao Tse-tung and berating his enemies greets passers-by at a gate in Peking (top). Below, wildly enthusiastic Chinese patriots—a million in all—parade through Peking on the October 1st anniversary of the Revolution.*

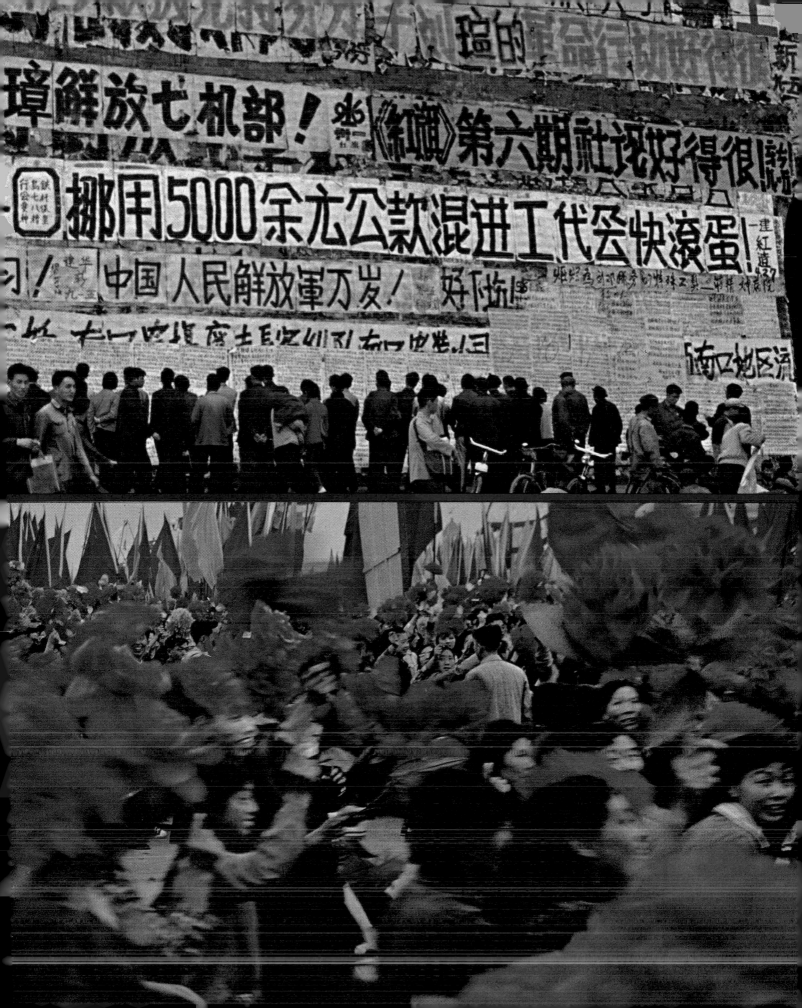

THE ALIEN SKILLS OF INDUSTRY *are practiced by two women laborers at a meter factory (above) and workers at a Russian-built trac- tor plant in northern China (left). The tractor workers were all once local farmers.*

我们现在正在进行技术方面的革命

"WE ARE NOW CARRYING OUT A REVOLUTION IN TECHNOLOGY."

Industrialization is a fledgling passion in China. Traditionally, manufacturers and merchants were regarded as parasites, at the bottom of the social scale. The ideal gentleman was one who devoted himself to leisurely scholarship, and the moneyed classes invested primarily in land. As a result, when Mao took control, China had less manufacturing capability than tiny Belgium.

The revolutionaries at first made factories rather than farms their paramount concern. In 1958 the government embarked on a crash program, "The Great Leap Forward," to accelerate economic growth. Workers put in 14-hour days, farmers tried to smelt steel in backyard furnaces, labor armies built railroads— but the lack of industrial skills turned the program into a fiasco. Recently, the government has had to pay more heed to agrarian problems, and the coveted goal of full-scale industrialization may take decades or even generations.

总路线万岁
大跃进万岁
人民公

FORWARD-LOOKING MASSES *in a huge Shanghai street poster praise the party's precepts, the commune and the economic revolution. Although such*

...ropaganda presents a naïve picture, most Chinese proudly regard their nation as setting an example for cultural change in all underdeveloped countries.

6

A NEW BALANCE OF POWER

As the second half of the 20th Century began, the world outlook was a mixture of optimism and mounting alarm. The great colonial empires were dissolving; new nations were being born. For many millions of people, dreams of independence and a less arduous life had become firm realities. But ominous clouds lurked on the horizon. International tensions, unless relieved, promised to destroy not only the nascent states but the old ones as well. The global population was mushrooming at an explosive rate, creating enormous social and economic dilemmas upon whose solution hinged the very existence of humanity itself. Augmenting these troublesome uncertainties was another significant cause for worldwide alarm—the rebirth of the Chinese nation under aggressive Communist rulers.

In 1900, China, once the leader of all East Asia, had been impotent—an enfeebled colossus, shrunken in territory, torn by civil violence, occupied and exploited by European and Japanese imperialists. Yet half a century later China was experiencing a political, economic and social miracle. Under its dynamic Communist regime, it was being transformed into a new and belligerent nation powerful enough to upset the entire international scene.

The sad fate that had overtaken Imperial China during the second half of the 19th Century had been avoided by neighboring Japan. The Japanese, quick to recognize the advantages of modernization, had adopted the technology, military methods and political machinery of the West. But 19th Century China, under the weak, tradition-bound Manchu Dynasty, resisted modernization. On into the present century it retained a feudal, hierarchical class structure thousands of years old, in which everyone had his proper place under Confucian prescriptions.

At the very bottom of this structure were the peasant masses—illiterate, tax-ridden, poor and badly exploited, but resigned to their lot. Far above them, power rested with the "scholar-officials," administrators chosen from the landlord class by an archaic system of civil service examinations that tested knowledge of Confucius' writings and other Chinese classics rather than practical ability. Although this ruling group refused by and large to admit new knowledge, a few high-ranking Chinese understood the lesson taught by Japan's adoption of modern ways and saw the possibility of learning from the West.

Some ministers had visions of reform within the existing Manchu framework. While their efforts met with only limited success, by 1905 they had managed to abolish the old examination system, thereby ending the power monopoly of the scholar-officials. At the same time they promoted a modern system of education. Steps were taken to write books in the language of everyday speech instead of in the erudite literary language understood only by the elite. The University of Peking and a few other Western-style universities were founded. From these new Western-inspired schools, and from Chinese educated in Japan, Europe and the United States, a truly revolutionary leadership emerged.

The most forceful of the new Chinese leaders was Dr. Sun Yat-sen, who headed a movement to overthrow the antiquated Manchu monarchy and establish a modern government capable of restoring China to a great and stable nation. Educated in an Anglican missionary college in Hawaii, Sun received medical training in British-ruled Hong Kong. He was at home in both Chinese and Western literature, and he read with special interest writers like Karl Marx and Henry George.

Sun's political creed, which he called the "Three Principles of the People," epitomized the needs of China in the contemporary age—Democracy, Nationhood and Livelihood. Although he called for eventual democracy, or sovereignty of the people, he stressed the necessity for a long period of government by political experts, with gradual steps toward popular government. In his appeal for nationhood he called on the Chinese to loosen their traditional ties to family and clan and to work

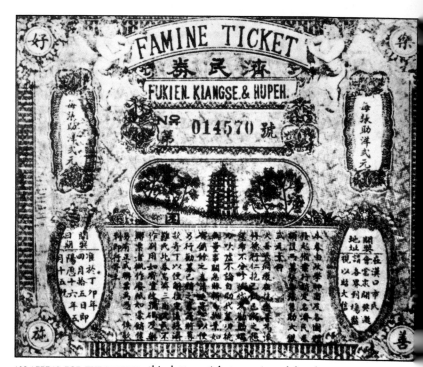

AN APPEAL FOR THE MASSES, *this lottery ticket was issued by the Communists in 1927 to obtain funds for famine victims in the Chinese provinces of Fukien, Kiangse and Hupeh. The Communists tried to attribute the famine to British economic imperialism.*

for the national solidarity essential for throwing off Western control. The Chinese, he said, never a strongly cohesive people, would have to make "cement" out of "sand."

By the third principle, "livelihood," Sun meant a fair distribution of land, the end of peasant poverty and a reformed society concerned with the welfare of all. Not a full-fledged Marxist, Sun nonetheless identified capitalism with imperialist exploitation. He was able, however, to win support for his nationalist cause among wealthy Chinese financiers and industrialists, and he married a daughter of C. J. Soong, a prominent Shanghai merchant.

For a time Sun toured the world, lecturing to sympathetic audiences in Europe and the United States, explaining his political program and raising money for his cause. In 1911 he hastened home to take part in a successful revolution against the Manchu Dynasty, and early the following year he became the first president of the Chinese Republic.

The new republic, however, did not live up to its promise of sweeping reforms and national solidarity. President Sun soon retired in favor of Yuan Shih-k'ai, a leader who he believed would carry on his democratic principles, but who instead established a military dictatorship headquartered at Peking. Sun then reorganized his revolutionary supporters into the Kuomintang, or National People's Party, and in 1917 established a rival and nationalist government in southern China.

Lacking a strong central authority, China fell into near-total anarchy. Bands of brigands terrorized the countryside almost at will and provincial warlords ruled their domains like feudal chieftains, fighting savagely with one another. More often than not, the armies they commanded were little better than rabble, and their appearance epitomized the confusion of the times. From Jean Bouchot, a Frenchman living in Peking, comes an eyewitness description of a typical body of troops in the service of a local warlord:

"The commander looked as tattered as his men, and you could not distinguish him except for the fact that every now and then he tripped over his exceedingly long sword. . . . The soldiers' rifles swayed back and forth with each step, and sometimes nearly hit their neighbor in the eye. . . ."

Despite their raggle-taggle appearance, however, such troops were ferocious, barbaric warriors. Reporting the assault of a provincial army on soldiers defending the city of Chengtu in western China, Sir Meyrick Hewlett, the British Consul, wrote: "There was a hideous massacre at the city gate which was closed against the retreating troops, who had been sent out of the city on the night of 3rd September. Among these unfortunates was a body of seventy mounted women; only seven escaped and the bodies of the slain were subjected to nameless indignities."

Adding to the chaos caused by civil warfare and the widespread depredations of bandits was the fact that China's long-standing humiliation at the hands of Western or Westernized nations was aggravated at the peace conference at the close of World War I. The victorious powers granted the Japanese territory and concessions in China which had formerly belonged to Germany: this triggered off a powerful protest in China. Organized and led by university students, the protest movement began in Peking, where some ten thousand youthful demonstrators openly voiced their anger and indignation, and it quickly spread among the Chinese masses. Known as the Fourth of May movement, it proved the depth of anti-Western feeling, and soon thereafter the Chinese delegates left the peace conference, refusing to sign the treaty.

Disillusioned with the West, and stimulated by the example of Lenin and the successful Bolshevik Revolution, Sun became more radical. He turned for help to the Soviet Union, which sent military and political advisers. He opened the ranks of the Kuomintang to the Chinese Communist party, which had been founded in 1921 by Leftist intellectuals and worker-peasant representatives. He set up a military college whose staff included Russian instructors, and placed at its head his lieutenant Chiang Kai-shek, an army officer who was also to marry into the wealthy Soong family.

Now that he had allied Nationalist China with the Soviet Union and the Chinese Communists, Sun sought to use the Kuomintang and its army to overcome the war lords. He also planned to introduce land reforms to win peasant support. But before he could accomplish these tasks he died in 1925, and Chiang Kai-shek succeeded him as head of the Kuomintang.

Chiang, a more dynamic and pragmatic leader than his predecessor, altered Sun's policies. Realizing that broad social reform could not come without national solidarity, he concentrated first on the military unification of China. His troops swept northward to defeat many of the independent war lords and the militarist regime in Peking, and by the end of 1928 he was on his way to unifying most of the country. Out of his new strength he negotiated with Britain and France to end the old imperialist treaty system, which gave Westerners special trade and legal privileges.

Meanwhile, Chiang had broken with the Communists. Sympathetic to the right wing of the Kuomintang—the conservative businessmen, financiers, landlords and army leaders who never had liked the Communist alliance—he purged the Kuomintang, the army and his government of Communists and Russian advisers, and ruthlessly suppressed a Communist workers' rising in Canton. The Communists then withdrew into remote parts of south-central China and formed a guerrilla army. They lived off the countryside, organized the peasants into local "soviets," and saw to it that they received arable land expropriated from recalcitrant landowners.

The Communists' leader was Mao Tse-tung, a former librarian, teacher and newspaper editor with both a classical Chinese and a Western-style education, who had been among the founders of the Chinese Communist party. In 1931 Mao felt strong enough to proclaim a Chinese Soviet Republic. Chiang's forces tried desperately to overcome the Chinese Red Army, and in 1935 they succeeded in forcing the Communists into a mass retreat—the celebrated "Long March"—in which they suffered incredible hardships as they made their way northward by a circuitous 10,000-mile route.

Some 300,000 Communist soldiers began this epic retreat, which lasted a year; decimated by disease, starvation and almost constant enemy assaults, less than 30,000 completed the journey. Edgar Snow, an American journalist who knew the Chinese Communists well, vividly records some of the horrors of the march:

"Passing into the Mantzu and Tibetan territories, the Reds for the first time faced a populace united in its hostility to them, and their sufferings on this part of the trek exceeded anything in the past. They had money, but could buy no food. They had guns, but their enemies were invisible. As they marched into the thick forests and jungles and across the headwaters of a dozen great rivers, the tribesmen withdrew from the vicinity of the march. . . .

"A few hundred yards on either side of the road, however, it was quite unsafe. Many a Red who ventured to forage for a sheep never returned. The mountaineers hid in the thick bush and sniped at the marching 'invaders.' They climbed the mountains, and when the Reds filed through the deep, narrow, rock passes. . . the Mantzu rolled huge boulders down to crush them and their animals."

The crossing of the vast grasslands north of the Tibetan mountains was equally terrible: "Almost perpetual rain fell over this swampland, and it is possible to cross its center only by a maze of narrow footholds known to the native mountaineers who led the Reds. More animals were lost, and more men. Many foundered in the weird sea of wet grass, and dropped from sight into the depth of the swamp. . . . But from this trial, too, they emerged triumphant. . . ."

Finally the exhausted Communists reached a previously established base in north central China, from which eventually they were to take over the entire country. There they managed to reinforce and reorganize their army and carry forward an agrarian revolution. A nation within a nation, the self-styled republic continued to repulse all of Chiang's efforts to destroy it. Only in 1937, after the Japanese had launched an invasion of northern China by way of Manchuria, did Chiang and the Communists suspend their civil war to create a "united front" against the common enemy.

This alliance lasted through World War II. At the War's end, partly on the basis of their fighting record against the Japanese, the Communists demanded a share in the Nationalist government. Chiang, who had meanwhile become more and more authoritarian, was unwilling to concede this. The Communists, for their part, refused to give up the northern Chinese provinces they had defended against the Japanese, or to accept control by Chiang. Moreover, they had been considerably strengthened by large supplies of captured Japanese arms.

So from 1946 to 1949 civil war raged again. This time the Kuomintang—rife with corruption, increasingly authoritarian, with few ties to the common people and suffering from enormous post-war economic problems—was no match for the Communists. The United States provided some $2 billion to aid Chiang, but to no avail. In 1949 the victorious Communists proclaimed the Chinese People's Republic. Chiang withdrew his badly mauled troops to the island of Taiwan, 100 miles from the Chinese mainland, where he established the seat of Nationalist China and awaited his chance to retaliate.

The gigantic task of modernizing China, which neither Sun or Chiang had been able to do, was now taken up vigorously by the Communist regime. To transform a nation of more than 3.5 million square miles and containing upwards of 500 million inhabitants—a fourth of the world's population—was probably the most ambitious enterprise in social engineering ever undertaken. Yet almost at once China, at long last under a strong central government, showed signs of becoming a power to be reckoned with. Late in 1950, when hundreds of thousands of Chinese Communist "volunteers" intervened in the Korean War to help the North Korean Communist regime, they amazed the world with their might and determination by halting the United Nations forces at the Yalu River and hurling them back down the Korean peninsula.

To industrialize agrarian China, the new regime, with Soviet aid, launched in 1953 the first of several Soviet-type Five-Year Plans. Some of the industrial accomplishments were impressive. Steel production rose from less than one million tons per year to more than 18 million tons by the mid-1960s. There were similar achievements in the production of coal, electric power and iron. In 1964 the Chinese further astonished the world with their technological and scientific skill by successfully making and exploding an atom bomb. In total production China now ranked among the top 10 industrial powers, although it would take decades, by Mao's own admission, before China would rival the principal ones, the United States, the Soviet Union, West Germany and Japan.

In agriculture, the Chinese record was less impressive. The Communists undertook an overly ambitious program in 1958—called the "Great Leap Forward." This program would have transformed the countryside into mechanized agricultural communes, but much of it had to be abandoned, largely because of peasant resistance and crop failures caused by floods or droughts. Thus China still faced the enormous problem of developing its economy and increasing food production rapidly enough to match the burgeoning population. With more than 700 million people in the mid-1960s, and growing at an annual rate of two to three per cent, China had at least 15 million new mouths to feed each year.

Yet despite its reverses—and the clouds of propaganda that obscured the true picture—the new regime seemed to be transforming the life of China. The Communists achieved significant advances in sanitation and public health, and reduced illiteracy by reforming and simplifying the Chinese written language. Reversing the practice of centuries, the regime gave women equality with men, outlawing child marriages and concubinage. Less admirably in non-Communist eyes, China's new leaders used "thought control" and modern propaganda techniques to indoctrinate an entire generation. Youth was encouraged to play an important part in defending the new government, even if that meant reporting disloyal neighbors and parents to the authorities.

The greatest success of the Communist regime was psychological: it restored the country's self-respect, reviving pride in its historic past and hope in its future destiny. The thoughts and sayings of Chairman Mao, put into the hands of millions, preached that through austerity and self-discipline the human spirit could triumph over all material obstacles, and that each individual must struggle against his own selfish instincts for the greater good of the community. At the same time there were signs of intra-party struggle and there ensued the "great proletarian cultural revolution," in which youthful "Red Guards" were mobilized to destroy any element that might interfere with supreme power for Mao and his ideas.

Communist China made it known that it did not intend to restrict its radical dogma to the homeland, but aspired to worldwide revolutionary leadership. Mao denounced Stalin's successors in Russia, not only because the Russians were revising orthodox Marxism, but also because their leaders resembled Western-style managerial types and preached the possibility of coexistence with the capitalist world. After 1960, Mao quarreled with Moscow, and China asserted itself as a dynamic new center of world Communism, with a special appeal to the nonwhite peoples of Asia and Africa and to all former colonial peoples struggling for equality, including those of Latin America. There were setbacks to the spread of the Chinese Communist influence: one occurred when the Communist regime, after taking over Tibet, came into open conflict with hitherto friendly India; another came when China broke with Castro in Cuba. But Mao's followers remained active in many parts of the world, ready to fish in troubled waters. Western Marxism was now mounted on a Chinese dragon.

Although the Communist regime had been clearly in control of the Chinese mainland since 1949, the United States refused to recognize the Chinese People's Republic and actively campaigned against giving it a seat in the United Nations. For their part, the Chinese Communists had denounced the American role in the Korean War and backed this denunciation with their "volunteer" troops.

More recently, they viewed American involvement in the Vietnam conflict as another Western intrusion in East Asia and responded by sending military advisers to aid the North Vietnamese government and by providing arms for the Viet Cong. Ironically, the United States—which had played the smallest part in 19th Century imperialism in Asia and had defended China against territorial partition—had become the chief target of the Communists, who accused it of reviving imperialism and attempting to suppress popular revolutions. The United States, on the other hand, believed that it was acting to contain Communism in Asia when other Western nations were not strong enough to do so.

Many observers of the international scene, however, maintained that it would be the better part of wisdom to open the United Nations to the Chinese Communists in view of China's long role and historic interest in East Asia. They felt that over the centuries many East Asian nations had learned to protect themselves from actual political domination—that in Vietnam and elsewhere it was not China that the West was confronting but a revolutionary movement that could not be put down by force of arms. It did not help matters when Mao proclaimed: "The east wind prevails over the west wind," nor when the American administration maintained that military solutions alone were possible in Asia. Still, some experts in foreign affairs proposed that the Chinese People's Republic be encouraged to "join the international world" and accept the responsibilities that all nations shared in avoiding new catastrophes that could, in this atomic age, mean the destruction of the entire planet.

If ever evidence were needed that an international world had come into being by the mid-20th Century, it was provided by the United Nations headquarters building towering above New York's East River. Here men and women of all nationalities, representing the newest states as well as the oldest and most powerful, mingled freely to work toward a common end—to preserve not only global peace but humanity as well.

Even before the close of World War II, the Allied powers had met at San Francisco to establish an international body that, like the earlier League of Nations, would dedicate its efforts "to save succeeding generations from the scourge of war." The United Nations as it emerged from that 1945 conference consisted of several organs, including the General Assembly, in which all of the 51 member nations had an equal voice, and the Security Council. The Council's permanent membership was made up of the five great powers—the United States, the Soviet Union, Great Britain, France and the Republic of China (Nationalist China)— and six lesser powers elected by the Assembly for two-year terms. Each permanent power enjoyed a veto, and action on any important matter therefore required unanimity among the great powers. But the two superpowers, the United States and the Soviet Union, overshadowed all others in the Security Council, and after 1949, when Chiang Kai-shek withdrew his nationalist government to the island of Taiwan, Nationalist China did not represent the hundreds of millions of Chinese on the Communist-ruled mainland.

It had been expected that wartime cooperation among the great powers would lead to their working together to preserve the peace. This idealistic hope quickly dimmed. The United Nations had hardly been founded when the United States and the Soviet Union had begun to confront each other in the bitter diplomatic and ideological struggle known as the Cold War. Among the early issues in that conflict were the post-war division of occupied Germany, the manner in which the

Russians consolidated their war gains in Eastern Europe and their blockade of the Western zone of Berlin. Each of the superpowers sought allies outside the framework of the United Nations. The Soviet Union, moreover, used its veto power so frequently in the Security Council that the Council could scarcely function.

In 1950 the Cold War turned hot when the action shifted from the diplomatic front to the battlefields of Korea. After World War II and the withdrawal of Russian and American occupation forces, Korea found itself divided at the 38th Parallel into a northern zone under a Russian-sponsored government and a southern republic headed by an American-appointed leader. Determined to extend Communist domination throughout the peninsula and fortified by Russian-supplied equipment that made an easy victory seem certain, the North Koreans struck the south in June 1950. It was widely believed at the time that the attack was instigated by Moscow to test the Americans' avowal to contain Communism. If so, the test produced quick—and for the Russians, unexpected—results.

Russia, in protest against the Western powers' refusal to admit Communist China to the United Nations, was at this time boycotting the Security Council. Russia's absence, and therefore the absence of the crippling Russian veto, enabled the United States to persuade the Council to sanction prompt military action against the aggressors. United Nations combat troops, consisting mainly of American soldiers with smaller contingents from 15 other nations, poured into Korea. In a dramatic three-year conflict that surged up and down the peninsula, they finally drove the North Koreans beyond the 38th Parallel and restored that line as the divider between the Communist and non-Communist governments. Confronted by such speedy and concerted action from the United Nations, the Russians and their allies would hence-

forth tend to be more cautious in their adventures.

The United Nations also acted as mediator in other trouble spots. In the Middle East, it arranged the armistices that ended the Israeli-Arab conflicts of 1948 and 1956, and after Egypt blockaded the Suez Canal a 10-nation United Nations Emergency Force cleared the vital waterway and patrolled the area to prevent further trouble. In Kashmir, fought over by India and Pakistan, a United Nations cease-fire checked hostilities in 1949. In Cyprus, when civil war seemed on the verge of erupting between the Greek and Turkish communities in the mid-1960s, United Nations personnel were instrumental in maintaining the peace.

From the Korean War onward, however, the United States and the Soviet Union no longer completely dominated the international scene. A new international order seemed to be taking shape in the world and with it new possibilities of influencing the course of international affairs. A clear reflection of this emerging order could be seen in the United Nations General Assembly. By the mid-1960s the Assembly had grown dramatically from its original 51 members to over 120. More than a third of its membership now represented the newly independent states of Asia and Africa, some of them no more populous than a medium-sized American city. Kuwait, for example, a small kingdom admitted in 1963, had a population of only 350,000. But it, as much as any of the others, had the right to an equal voice and full dignity as a sovereign state.

The new nations, many of them struggling to throw off vestiges of colonialism and racial discrimination, and nearly all of them economically underdeveloped, refused to make common cause with either the United States or the Soviet Union. Instead they allied themselves loosely in an important "neutralist" bloc. The Latin American member nations, long independent but suffering

PAKISTAN

SOUTH KOREA

MALAYSIA

SYMBOLS OF FAMILY PLANNING, *these circular designs, which depict parents with one or two children, are the official emblems of national groups contending with the touchy problem of overpopulation in various Asian lands.*

from the same social and economic problems as the former colonial countries, often shared the views of the Asian-African bloc. In addition, the United States lost some support among its allies in Western Europe. These nations, recovering from the War, cooperated among themselves in the Common Market and became increasingly independent of American influence. In the Russian camp, the East European satellites were also asserting themselves, and, despite the Russians' brutal crushing of the Hungarian revolt in 1956, were gaining an independent role in world affairs. The older Arab states looked to their own interests and were wooed by both the United States and the Soviet Union. Mighty as the superpowers were, they could not ignore the influence of these new power blocs.

As the world's political structure became more and more complex, so did the United Nations' task of preserving the peace. Evidence of this was seen in the Congo crisis of the early 1960s, when tensions between the superpowers promised not only to threaten this new state but to spread to others in Africa and Asia. Whereas in Korea the United Nations had intervened to curb military aggression from the outside, in the Congo it acted in the hope of holding together an inexperienced state beset by political and social chaos and therefore vulnerable to foreign political ambitions.

In 1960 the Congo had suddenly won independence from Belgium, and almost at once its richest province seceded and civil war threatened to tear the new country apart. The Soviet Union, hoping to seat a Congolese regime favorable to the Communists, was poised to intervene. So was the United States, which was intent on frustrating any Communist attempt to establish a foothold in Central Africa that might infect neighboring emergent nations. But the Congo was prevented from becoming a battleground of the great powers when 20,000 soldiers, drawn from 29 countries and wearing the blue berets of the United Nations, moved in. This international police force restored order and a degree of unity as well, and permitted the new Congo Republic to shape its own destiny.

Without United Nations efforts to confine or liquidate it, such a crisis—or any of those that preceded it—might easily have exploded into global war, since each directly or indirectly involved the interests of the major powers. And after 1949, when the Soviet Union as well as the United States had the atomic bomb, there was always the grave threat that some local crisis might lead to a confrontation that could escalate into nuclear holocaust. The danger of such a confrontation, in which even the peacekeeping capabilities of the United Nations might prove ineffective, was compounded in the 1950s when both the United States and the Soviet Union successfully developed the far more destructive hydrogen bomb.

By the mid-1960s Britain, France and Communist China also possessed nuclear arms. Many nations urged the banning of nuclear tests for they feared that radiation might endanger not only the health of the present population but that of future generations as well. Science, which had made possible man's conquest of nature, now threatened to destroy man himself.

As the United Nations has worked to ease political frictions that might otherwise flare into global conflict, humanity has been struggling with the no less alarming problem of the population explosion. In 1900 the world's population was one and a half billion. By 1960 it had doubled, and by the year 2000 it is expected to soar to six and a half billion—over four times as great as it was at the start of the century. Unless ways are found to feed this burgeoning population—or to control its growth—starvation looms as an ever-increasing specter for the majority of mankind.

The population explosion is especially spectacular in underdeveloped countries, where inroads against diseases, decimating plagues and famine are extending the life span and where birth rates continue to be much higher than in the industrial nations. The population of Brazil, for example, rose from 33 million in 1930 to 70 million in 1960. Mexico expects its population to double in 20 years' time. India's teeming masses are increased by more than 10 million new babies each year, and the rate of increase is steadily going up. Every three years China adds to its huge population some 45 million people, or the equivalent of the total population of France.

Only a rational attitude toward family planning and the introduction of simplified birth control techniques can check such soaring birth rates. Although there is religious and cultural resistance to birth control—not only in the Catholic nations of Latin America but in Hindu and Muslim countries, too—there are hopeful signs that this attitude is gradually being overcome. India, despite orthodox Hindu resistance, made the dissemination of birth control information official policy in 1961.

Meanwhile, the underdeveloped parts of the world have had to live with the frightening possibility that population growth would outrace efforts to build up their economies. In much of Asia, Africa and Latin America, where the population has expanded two or three per cent annually, a corresponding rate of economic growth is needed merely to keep up. To help these areas achieve adequate agricultural and industrial production and better standards of living, the more advanced nations, particularly the United States, have made economic and technical assistance available under a variety of auspices, among them the World Bank, the American Peace Corps and the Point Four Program (named after the fourth point of a foreign policy proclaimed in 1949 by President

AN INTERNATIONALISM OF STYLE *is offered by the proprietors of the Classical Barber Shop in Akure, Western Nigeria. Reflecting the converging influences in that new nation, the advertisement promotes nationalism in the "Sahara New Boy" and the "Bulewa Style" (named for the former Prime Minister); it also suggests such foreign possibilities as "Kennedy Style" and "English Ladies Boy."*

Harry S. Truman). In addition, economic planners sponsored by the United Nations have dedicated themselves to making the 1960s the "Development Decade," in the hope that by 1970 the underdeveloped nations may achieve an annual economic growth rate of five per cent.

But the prospects of attaining this goal seem bleak. With more people inhabiting the earth than ever before, more of them live in dire straits than at any time in history. At the start of the Development Decade, the economies of the less-developed countries were showing the slowest growth rate, while those of the wealthier nations were moving ahead faster than ever. The economic gap between the industrial nations and the less-developed countries was broadening, not narrowing. In 1945 the income of the average American was 20 times that of his counterpart in India; by 1960 it was some 40 times greater. United Nations sources estimated that half the world's population subsisted on a diet below minimum nutritional requirements, and that 10 to 15 per cent

143

was close to starvation. For three fifths of the human race the per capita annual output of goods and services in 1961 was below $300; for the peoples of the United States and Canada it was some $2,700. Technical aid, financial loans and widespread birth control may perhaps slow the race between developing economies and the spiraling global population, but there are few grounds for easy optimism.

Nevertheless, there is reason for hope in one respect. Mass education and literacy have aroused a hunger for cultural satisfaction, and this quest may eventually bring about a greater world unity. Music, art and literature, no longer the monopoly of the leisure class, have reached out to vast numbers of people. And, as culture has spread, it has brought about a mingling of the formerly heterogeneous and isolated.

As the far-flung parts of the world are brought closer together by jet planes and electronic communications, men everywhere are drawn to search out one another's traditions and ideas.

Stimulated by a younger generation, disillusioned with the shortcomings of the West, Westerners are turning to the traditional music of India and playing the *sitar*; others sit at the feet of *gurus* to learn of Hindu mysticism. Americans study African ivory carvings and listen to African chants and rhythms played on the *ngonga*; Europeans turn to the American Indian art of Mexico.

Clearly the next step is the intermingling and fusion of non-Western and Western cultural elements, regardless of language, people, nations and politics—a movement toward the creation of a common world culture, drawn from every continent and embracing all humanity.

Meanwhile, Western science and technology, and Western ideas of social justice and equality, have reached out to villages and hamlets from Bo-

livia to Borneo. Old religions are being revitalized, throwing off the outmoded; they are facing up to the world of the present, adding to their traditional values the new ones of racial and social equality and of individual freedom. Today the human goal is indeed the "Four Freedoms"—freedom of speech, freedom of religion, freedom from fear and freedom from want. For the first time in history it is possible to utilize the technology of the West to alleviate want, hunger and famine, to end pestilence and disease, to curb illiteracy and ignorance. To this end the new nations of Asia, the Middle East and Africa seek hydroelectric plants, steel mills, highways, airports, hospitals, schools.

Certainly the impact of Western technology has been disruptive as well as creative. It has undermined old and stable societies in Asia, Africa, the Middle East and Latin America—societies that had gone untouched for centuries. Life will never be the same for villagers, peasants and tribesmen who move into the city and the factory. As formidable obstacles emerge to thwart the promise of social and economic advance, frustrations and discontent will mount. But at no time do men grow more dissatisfied than at the dawn of a new era, when conditions show sufficient signs of improvement to cause aspirations to rise. It is then that ferment and impatience set in; in the 20th Century, this mood has been called "the revolution of rising expectations."

All over the world men and women are abandoning the old resignation to fate and destiny, the idea of submission to a wretched lot. The Western message that man must be master of his fate has fallen on receptive ears. The West no longer rules the world as it did at the opening of the 20th Century, but it has triumphed in another way. It has made possible the emergence of an interconnected world, and it has aroused new aspirations in the vast masses of mankind.

A 1914 work by Kasimir Malevich juxtaposes unrelated objects in an early break with realism

THE
ONE WORLD
OF MODERN ART

The rootless, searching nature of the 20th Century in its movement toward a common culture is nowhere so sharply revealed as in the kaleidoscope of modern art. "Painting is a thundering collision of different worlds destined to create a new world," wrote Wassily Kandinsky, one of the pioneers of nonrepresentational art. In the century's early decades, the collisions that produced the new painting exploded established traditions and produced canvases, like the one above, that defied easy interpretation. The new art also brought together such disparate influences as African tribal symbols, American pre-Columbian statuary, Oriental calligraphy and new scientific principles of color and space. Out of these encounters emerged works that have become increasingly international in feeling—so much so it is often difficult to determine their place of origin. Indeed, in its quest to express new values, art may be coming as close as any medium to creating a worldwide language of man.

THE IMPACT OF THE PRIMITIVE

In their dissatisfaction with tradition, painters and sculptors in the early 1900s began to ask what was basic and universal in art. This concern, in turn, led them to experiment with fundamental, often abstract forms instead of literal, photographic realism.

Modern art got a great forward push beginning about 1907, when artists like Pablo Picasso, Georges Braque and Jacques Lipchitz, exploring the geometry of forms, began to collect and study African tribal sculpture—not as interesting evidence of another civilization, but as an artistic inspiration. What most fascinated these Europeans was the way that African sculptors, in rendering a human figure, reduced the body to its simplest planes and portrayed the face as an expressionless, impersonal mask. Soon the African influence was making itself felt in powerful, even frightening, modern works.

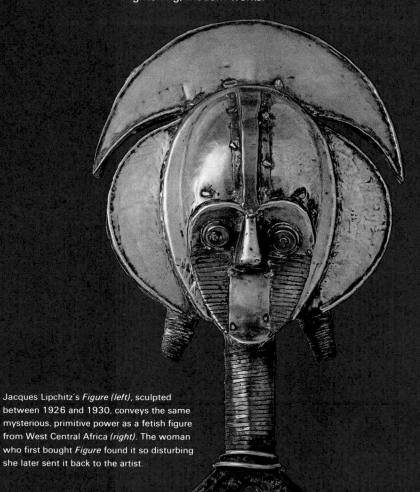

Jacques Lipchitz's *Figure (left)*, sculpted between 1926 and 1930, conveys the same mysterious, primitive power as a fetish figure from West Central Africa *(right)*. The woman who first bought *Figure* found it so disturbing she later sent it back to the artist.

Pablo Picasso's 1907 *Dancer*, with its oval mask and bowed legs, was probably inspired by burial figures made in the French Congo.

A REVOLUTION IN DESIGNS FOR EVERYDAY LIFE

The 20th Century artist's preoccupation with basic forms revolutionized not only painting and sculpture, but architecture and industrial design as well. In the vanguard of the revolution were the teachers and students of Germany's celebrated Bauhaus (literally "house for building"). This art school, probably the most influential in modern times, opened in 1919 in Weimar and immediately set about bringing a clean,

A coffee pot, designed by Christian Dell in 1925, and a silk wall-hanging woven by Anni Albers a year later, continue to look surprisingly "modern" after more than four decades.

Exquisitely crafted, Marcel Breuer's steel and canvas chair was designed for mass production.

Through-Going Line was painted by Wassily Kandinsky i

streamlined look to the artifacts of everyday life—coffee cups, furniture, even city plans. When Hitler, in his purge of "decadent" modern culture, forced the Bauhaus to close in 1933, the school's staff and students emigrated to other countries, spreading their ideas of good design.

During the 14 years of its formal existence, however, the Bauhaus achieved with striking success its goal of "form follows function." Its interest in pure form, which had been pioneered by Bauhaus painters like Wassily Kandinsky and Paul Klee, was extended to such crafts as weaving and furniture design. The school's founder and leading architect, Walter Gropius, was among the first to create buildings constructed with frameworks sheathed in walls of glass—prototypes of structures now common all over the world.

1920 when he was an instructor at the Bauhaus; the school's emphasis on pure design led Kandinsky to create free and colorful geometric abstractions like this.

Piet Mondrian's *Composition with Red, Yellow and Blue,* which the artist completed in 1942, is typical of the severe, abstract style he pursued from 1916 until his death in 1944. The emphasis on stark black lines, primary colors and a balanced but asymmetrical composition was an attempt to reduce painting to its basic elements.

Le Corbusier gave eloquent form to modern design principles in his buildings in India. He used asymmetrical rhythms in his Secretariat Building *(above, left)*, primary colors in the windows of a villa *(above, right)* and grid patterns in the Assembly Palace *(below)*.

THE SEARCH FOR A BASIC STYLE

At about the same time the Bauhaus was being formed in Germany, a group of Dutch artists, led by Piet Mondrian and Theo van Doesburg, were developing an art movement known as *de Stijl* ("The Style"). Like the Bauhaus artists, whom they influenced in many ways, *de Stijl* painters, sculptors and architects were interested in creating simple forms free of ornamentation. Unlike the Bauhaus group, however, *de Stijl* artists worked out a rigidly defined doctrine of art. They preferred working with only the painter's three primary colors— red, blue and yellow—and they produced nothing but abstract works. These abstractions, moreover, were dominated by vertical and horizontal lines and avoided symmetry.

De Stijl's principles were so confining that the movement lost vitality after little more than a decade, but the effect of its theories can still be felt. For instance, in the 1950s the famous Swiss architect Charles Édouard Jeanneret—better known as Le Corbusier— reflected *de Stijl's* patterns in the public buildings he designed for Chandigarh, the new capital of the Punjab in India, and for a private villa in Ahmedabad, north of Bombay *(right)*.

STRUCTURES FROM THE INNER SOUL

Before World War II, American artists had stirred little attention abroad. After the War, however, a group in New York City developed an explosive new style that was soon emulated throughout the world. The style was called, alternately, "Abstract Expressionism" (because it portrayed no objects in the real world) and "Action Painting" (because the method stressed the creative acts that the artist went through in painting a canvas more than it did the finished composition). Harold Rosenberg, the critic who invented the "Action" label, characterized the approach: "At a certain moment the canvas began to appear to one American painter after another as an arena in which to act—rather than as a space in which to reproduce, redesign, analyze or express an object, actual or imagined. What was to go on the canvas was not a picture but an event."

Although this movement was extraordinarily innovative, it owed much to early modernists, and to the bold structural shapes of modern architecture and engineering *(below)*. No less important an influence was Oriental calligraphy, particularly on such leading Action painters as Franz Kline and Jackson Pollock; centuries before, the Zen priests of China and Japan had also conceived of their picture-writing as spontaneous expressions of the human soul.

Swift, bold brush strokes render the word "self-discipline" in a Japanese Zen painting; such calligraphy was much admired by "Action" painters.

Stark patterns of technology, like the trussed girders of bridges, are echoed in the structured lines of much contemporary abstract art.

Painting with Stars, an early collage done by Kurt Schwitters in 1920, juxtaposes newsprint, string, wire mesh.

Negro faces peer out of a city scene in *Summertime*

ART
FROM THE DEBRIS
OF TODAY

The history of art in the 20th Century is a record of continuous assaults on the very definitions of art. The old notion that a canvas should show a "lofty" subject rendered in the "noble" medium of oil was demolished by artists who invented the new technique of *collage* (French for "gluing"). As early as World War I, artists like the German painter Kurt Schwitters began to incorporate into their works newspaper clippings, ticket stubs, torn bits of screen and other debris of the modern world. By placing these elements into arresting and sometimes elegant

by Romare Bearden, a leading U.S. artist of the 1960s.   In *Tracer*, Robert Rauschenberg silk-screened modern photographs onto a canvas with a Rubens nude

compositions, these artists attempted to show that any material could be "noble," or at least valid, if handled correctly. As for subject matter, the collage artists were as resolutely abstract as their contemporaries, but they went a step beyond. Kandinsky and others had believed that abstractions were expressions of inner feelings; Schwitters denounced even this "meaning" in art. "It now seems to me," Schwitters wrote in 1921, "that even striving for expression in a work of art is harmful to art. Art is as inexplicable as life, indefinable and without purpose."

Despite such formal disavowals, collage strikingly reflected the world in which it was created—if for no other reason than that it included the everyday products of that world. In a recent collage by the American Romare Bearden *(above, center,* fragments of photographs recreate the slum world of the city; similarly, another American, Robert Rauschenberg, selected a street scene and Army helicopters—then juxtaposed against them an American bald eagle and Peter Rubens' 17th Century painting of Venus, goddess of love *(above, right)*.

"OP": MARRIAGE OF ART AND TECHNOLOGY

Perhaps more than any other modern movement, "Op" art brings together many of the dominant esthetic trends of the 20th Century. As can be seen in the work at right— *Transparent Rhythms II*, by the Israeli painter Yaacov Agam—Op artists share with earlier *de Stijl* painters an interest in primary colors and geometric forms. Yet this large mural—painted on a corrugated surface so that its patterns change with the observer's position—reflects much of the new 20th Century landscape in its rhythms, which suggest everything from city skyscrapers to electronic circuits to IBM punchcards.

Like the members of the earlier Bauhaus, Op artists have tried to break down the barriers between art and technology. Some use luminous or quick-drying acrylic paints, first developed for industrial use; many create visual patterns based on optical principles; still others make their creations twitch, light up or even produce musical sounds by employing computers and electrical devices.

In another important way Op art is a product of its age—it is a truly global movement. Founded by the German Josef Albers and the Hungarian Victor Vasarely, Op is now practiced by leading painters from Israel to Iceland, and has influenced other art forms from fashions to interior design.

EPILOGUE:
THE DREAM OF WORLD CULTURE

by
WILLIAM H. McNEILL

BUILDING A WORLD OF STEEL, *workers wrestle with girders and scaffolds in this painting by Fernand Léger. By means of bright colors and a harmonious relationship between the men and their mechanical surroundings, Léger expressed his "optimistic acceptance" of a technological universe.*

The human adventure on the face of this planet has been an almost uninterrupted series of crises and disruptions of society's established order. Since the days of Plato and Confucius some 2,500 years ago, if not before, sensitive and learned men, with a truly remarkable unanimity, have viewed cultural changes with alarm. Therefore, those who survey the political, military and racial turbulence of the 20th Century with similar misgivings find themselves in excellent company—but that does not necessarily prove the accuracy of their estimate of the world situation.

It is, of course, undeniable that social change is accelerating all around the globe at a very rapid rate. Everywhere—in remote villages as well as in cosmopolitan centers—older patterns of conduct and traditional values are undergoing alteration, and some are being discarded entirely. Largely responsible is modern technology. A network of communications now links together into a single whole all the disparate peoples of Africa, Asia and the Western world. Day after day and year after year innumerable messages crisscross the earth to create a stream of stimuli and counterstimuli the like of which never existed before. Swift modern transportation is an equally important factor in spurring interactions among men on a scale unimaginable in earlier ages.

But worldwide interactions among men are not entirely new. Even when walking was the only mode of travel and face-to-face speech the principal means of communication, useful new tools and techniques spread relatively quickly and very widely. The uniformity of Stone Age hunters' tools around the globe can only reflect a process of interaction and borrowing from one hunting band to another that ran across very long distances.

Stone Age hunting bands left few clues to tell how much or how little they may have differed from one another in local rituals, family customs and the like. Possibly the principal differentiation among human societies evolved only after men could spare an appreciable part of their energies from the simple compulsions of seeking food. With the rise of a few unusually successful societies—the earliest civilizations—in the Middle East and elsewhere in Asia and in Europe, written

If mankind shares an essential unity, as philosophers have maintained, why and how were the earth's peoples split into racial divisions? And how, despite man's tendency to think in ethnocentric terms, can these obvious separations be overcome?

According to the Bible, all the races of man must have begun with the children of Noah, because everyone else on earth was destroyed in the Flood: Shem was the father of the Semitic people; Ham, the father of the Egyptians; Japheth, the father of the people of Asia Minor. This interpretation, which dates from about 1000 B.C., has endured longer than many others—such as the ancient Greek myth which held that black people are descendants of the driver of the dawn chariot, who passed too close to the sun. But the Bible still leaves a number of vexing questions unanswered.

The map, taken from a French geography book, is an early 19th Century attempt to meld Biblical teachings with objective observations and scientific explanations. It pictures the three racial sources (colored circles) as centers from which various subgroups branched out. The legend at lower right also claims that the map allows us to observe an anthropological principle: "the double and powerful influence of the times and climates on peoples." But, catholic as it may be, the map still leaves questions hanging: why are the Slavs (the purple band in Eastern Europe) unrelated to anyone around them? And what about the "unknown people of southern Africa"?

More recently, scientists have gone further in presenting a rational view of race by explaining physical differences as a dynamic factor in the complex processes of adaptation to new environments. One interesting theory, for example, holds that men are colored differently because of their need for vitamin D, the "sunshine vitamin," which is manufactured in the human body under the stimulus of ultraviolet rays. According to this theory, man first evolved in tropical Africa with a black skin to shield him from an excess of ultraviolet rays, which can be harmful; lighter-skinned people gradually evolved in more northerly and southerly latitudes because their bodies needed to absorb more of the scarcer sunshine in those regions to produce the requisite amount of vitamin D.

Perhaps as such theories are developed into a body of scientific agreement, man will begin to see physical differentiation and race itself as evolutionary accidents rather than as preordained barriers.

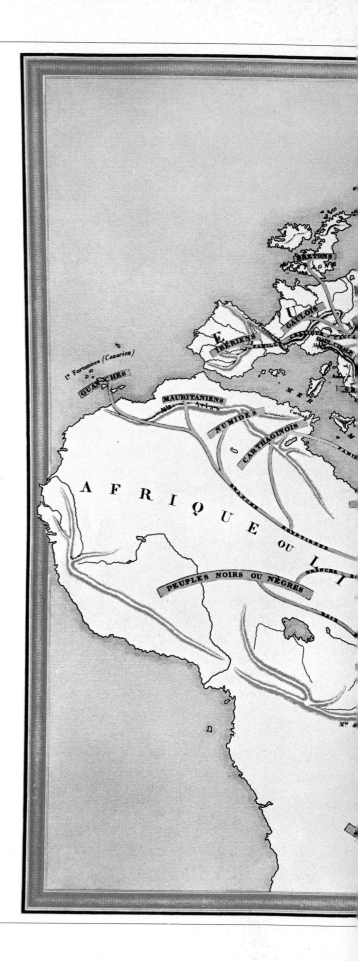

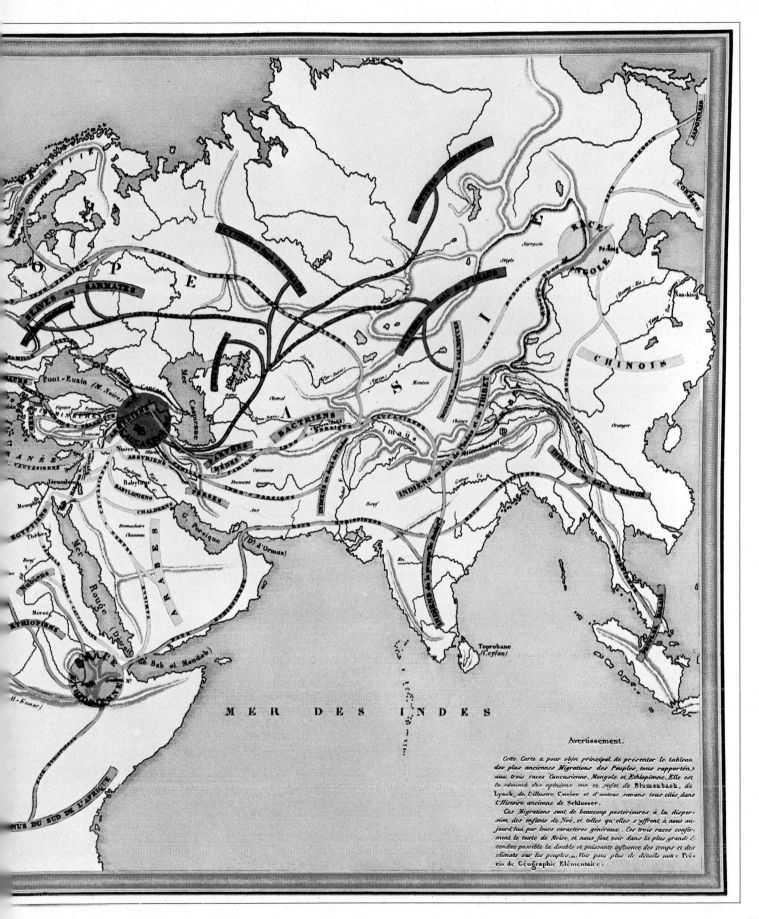

MER DES INDES

Avertissement.

Cette Carte a pour objet principal de présenter le tableau des plus anciennes Migrations des Peuples, tous rapportés aux trois races Caucasienne, Mongole et Éthiopienne. Elle est le résumé des opinions sur ce sujet de Blumenbach, de Lynck, de l'illustre Cuvier et d'autres savans tous cités dans l'Histoire ancienne de Schlosser.

Ces Migrations sont de beaucoup postérieures à la dispersion des enfants de Noé, et telles qu'elles s'offrent à nous aujourd'hui par leurs caractères généraux. Ces trois races confirment le texte de Moïse, et nous font voir dans le plus grande étendue possible la double et puissante influence des temps et des climats sur les peuples... Voir pour plus de détails notre Précis de Géographie Élémentaire.

records allow us to understand better how different men in different parts of the world organized their lives. Because these civilizations developed in circumscribed areas and contact among them was limited by geography, each was able to develop its own characteristics. Middle Eastern monotheism and bureaucratic empire, Greek ideas of natural law and the primacy of the territorial state, India's transcendentalism and caste, the decorum and dynastic empire of ancient China—each was fundamentally different from the others.

Each of those four main centers of high culture came in time to be flanked by offshoots and variants as bits and pieces of the civilized achievement mingled with local traditions of barbarian peoples. Largely responsible for this mixing of cultures were the civilized traders and soldiers who intruded into neighboring barbarian lands in search of goods or services they lacked at home. Presumably the complex interactions that took place among peoples in ancient Europe, Asia and Africa were duplicated in the New World. There, however, the absence of decipherable records, other than a few calendrical inscriptions, makes it harder to measure the impact of the high pre-Columbian cultures—those of the Aztecs, the Maya and the Inca—on neighboring peoples.

The spread of civilized influences in the Old World was encouraged by a series of major technological and geographical breakthroughs. In fact, civilization itself owes its beginning to one of them—the development of irrigated farms in desert river valleys of the Middle East some 5,000 years ago. This made settled towns possible. Another significant innovation came around 2000 B.C. By then men had learned how to raise sufficient crops, on ordinary rain-watered land away from the rivers, to allow them to maintain civilized societies beyond the valley confines.

In Europe, the invention of an improved plow played a key role in the spread of advanced culture. For a long time easily farmed lands bordering the Mediterranean were the sole seat of civilization on that continent. But between 500 and 1000 A.D. men using the new plow learned to cultivate the more fertile, water-soaked plains that drained into northern seas, and following the collapse of Rome as the prime focus of European civilization, the more active centers of civilized life tended to shift northward. In Asia, similar technological and geographical breakthroughs took place as civilization expanded from the Indus to the Ganges valleys and as the Chinese style of life moved southward from the Yellow River valley.

Each of these pulses of world history in ancient times affected only a single theater of civilization. But two more recent breakthroughs had worldwide significance, because they eliminated barriers that had previously separated major Old World cultures from one another. One occurred on land: the conquest of the Eurasian steppe by agricultural peoples. This great, open zone sparsely inhabited by pastoral nomads had always before separated Chinese, Middle Eastern and European civilizations. But beginning around 1500 A.D., civilized armies of Russian, Chinese and Turkish foot soldiers equipped with firearms gradually asserted their superiority over steppe-nomad cavalry. As a result, the grasslands of Eurasia opened for agricultural settlement as never before. By 1750 the vast open space that had once limited contact among the great cultures of the Old World ceased to play its accustomed role as insulator, filter and mediator.

At almost the same time that the steppe barrier was being breached, a second geographical breakthrough that revolutionized traditional relationships between civilizations was taking place: the opening of the oceans by European (and for a while also by Chinese) explorers. But the cultural confrontations and interactions that it produced were generally more drastic and abrupt than those accompanying the settlement of the steppe. The great discoveries not only brought European soldiers, missionaries, merchants and settlers to the New World, Africa and the East: they also inaugurated a worldwide colonial expansion by European peoples that was to last until the 20th Century.

Inevitably, however, as new peoples and regions brought new strands and attitudes into the enlarged circle of civilization, all the Old World societies began to feel serious strains upon their long-established ways. Among the earliest disruptive forces to have far-reaching impact were the silver and foods sent from the Americas. The influx of silver upset price systems the world around by making the precious metal so much commoner than before. Some economies profited, some suffered; and everywhere rapid shifts in prices compelled governments to overhaul tax systems and interfere with traditional economic activity in new ways.

An equally important transformation in traditional human life was wrought by the introduction of sweet potatoes in China, "Irish" potatoes in northern Europe and corn into almost all of Africa, southern Europe and parts of Asia. The global diffusion of these American crops affected the millions of peasants and farmers who raised them. In many regions the new crops produced more food per acre than had previously been possible, allowing populations to multiply.

In some areas, most notably in Western Europe, there was also a marked increase in agricultural efficiency—in the amount of food produced per farmer. Europe was therefore able to feed not only a peasant population but also the inhabitants of rapidly growing towns and cities where, by the middle of the 18th Century, the Industrial Revolution and new democratic ideas were beginning

to transform still other aspects of human life.

All these factors—geographical, economic, ideological and technological—that tended to unsettle traditional social structures came to a sort of crisis point between 1850 and 1865. During that era Western civilization further demonstrated the dynamic qualities that had characterized its stormy history since 1500. No part of the earth remained entirely exempt from the impact of the technology, military might and democratic concepts that now emanated from the West.

The political and psychological consequences of the new conditions showed themselves almost at once. Confronted by the sudden and dramatic spread of Western power and influence, one after another of the great civilizations of Asia suffered profound and unsettling shock to their traditional hopes, values, habits and beliefs. The Chinese empire experienced the Taiping Rebellion against its weak and corrupt Manchu rulers, and found its time-honored imperial institutions useless against the increasing scale of European intervention. Feudal Japan opened itself up to the Western world and undertook radical and rapid self-transformation in the hope of acquiring the military strength and economic power needed to maintain effective independence. India saw the waning of its old order with the failure of the Sepoy Mutiny, a revolt of native soldiers in the army of the British East India Company, the mercantile-military enterprise that then ruled most of the country. Thereafter a modernizing administration under the British Crown and a modernizing movement among small but influential circles of Hindus together repudiated important parts of India's past.

The realm of Islam, too, had to come to terms with the growing military and technological supremacy of Western nations. But Muslims, whose faith was consciously in opposition to Christianity, found it harder than other civilized peoples to go to school in the West. Such an act amounted to a confession that in some important respects the ways of the contemporary Christian world were superior to those of Islam.

As for the West, it is a disputed matter whether what has happened since 1865 is best described as a fundamental breakdown of traditional structures or as a transformation of institutions and patterns of conduct comparable to those wrought by the Renaissance and Reformation or by the industrial and democratic revolutions that erupted in Europe between 1750 and 1850.

Amid such uncertainties, what lies ahead for mankind as a whole? Continuing and endless social chaos? A return to barbarism brought about by dependence on technological advances that might suddenly collapse in the event of international, scientific war? Or are we living through a period whose effervescence and accelerating change will in the long run prove basically creative—an era that future generations will rank among history's Golden Ages?

Perhaps society in the 20th Century is on the verge of a general mutation as revolutionary as the one that came when men shifted from hunting to farming as the ordinary basis of their daily lives. Certainly if the possibilities of raising food by machines (a technique already highly developed in the United States and certain other countries) eventually spread all around the earth, the basis of human societies will have changed in the most fundamental sense.

Ever since neolithic times, when men first discovered how to cultivate the soil, the overwhelming majority of the world's population have been farmers. But in a society where machines operated by a few specialists could raise the food farmers now produce—at less cost and probably in greater abundance per acre—for most men there would no longer be any need to raise their own food.

As we in the United States know, men can live in cities hundreds or thousands of miles from the place where their daily diet has been coaxed out of the earth—and never miss a meal or go hungry for lack of anything but money. Thus rural life, the mainstay of mankind down through the ages, may be headed for eclipse, to be supplanted by an almost totally urbanized society.

Traditional civilizations were all built around the radical difference between town and country. Towns sustained themselves by the produce of the countryside, part of which they exacted as rents and taxes. In return they offered a fragile public peace and sometimes a few artisan goods of use to the peasants. From the peasants' point of view, this relationship was always fundamentally unjust; some men ate what they did not raise by taking food from those who earned an honest living by laboring in the fields.

This ancient relationship between town and country, already breaking down in some of the more technologically advanced areas of the globe, seems likely to break down still further. Modern communications are reaching into all the world's villages to stir the peasants' discontent. Even in the most remote hamlets, radios bring to their attention the advantages of urban living as well as new ideas of political and personal rights. Coinciding with increased dissatisfaction among the peasants is the fact that machines could take over their work in the fields and do it even more efficiently. The result of these combined factors may be a peasant movement toward cities more massive than any that the world has seen before. It staggers the imagination to consider the disorganization of traditional societies that would ensue if the teeming peasant millions of Asia, Africa and South America were to follow the North American subsistence farmer into the cities, there to seek a new way of life. In the United States

THE MIGRATION FROM COUNTRYSIDE TO CITY

As ever-increasing numbers of farmers and laborers have deserted their fields and flooded the cities of the world, they have been forced to take up new, and sometimes exotic, ways of earning a living. The young West African shown above, for instance, has left his native village to set himself up as a photographer in Niamey, capital of the Republic of Niger. In the mural behind him, which advertises his services, both the photographer and his subject combine aspects of their tribal identity—long robes and the ritual scars on his cheeks—with symbols of their new status as city dwellers: a wrist watch, high-heeled shoes, a purse and eyeglasses.

Wherever it has occurred, the migration from the country to the city has disrupted old patterns of existence and has frequently created grave problems. Although the industrial centers of the Western world have usually, in time, provided jobs for migrants, the less-developed cities of Asia, Africa and Latin America have had much less success in absorbing the influx. Nevertheless, the drift toward the city continues at an increasing rate. In 1900 only 5 per cent of the world's population lived in large cities, but by 1960 the proportion had leaped to 20 per cent as more and more families came to town seeking wealth, freedom from physical toil or just excitement.

we had difficulty in fitting poor white farmers into the megalopolitan structure of the nation during the depression years of the 1920s and 1930s, when hundreds of thousands of family farms were abandoned. We are facing even greater problems in accommodating the millions of Negroes who in the 1940s and 1950s drifted from the cotton fields of the South toward our big cities. But the problems posed by these shifts are comparatively trifling when compared to those that would arise were a similar abandonment of rural life to take place in any of the heavily populated countrysides of the earth.

Technologically, it seems possible that a small percentage of the working force of the world could supply food for all the rest. Perhaps in time the possibility will become fact, and mankind will in its majority leave the fields and plunge into a new kind of life centered on cities, emancipated at long last from the curse of Adam: "In the sweat of thy face shalt thou eat bread."

On the other hand, the fundamental hypothesis may be wrong. Abandonment of the fields may not lie ahead for most men; the future may hold instead a drastic collapse of cities and of the extraordinary network of communication and transport that sustains modern high technology. What, for example, would happen to the United States if organized, armed and persistent civil conflict or nuclear war were to interrupt the flow of gasoline for as little as six or eight months? Tractors would cease to operate; fields would not be sown; crops would disappear; famine would quickly cease from being a forgotten myth and become the liveliest sort of reality. Distribution of all other commodities would be so disrupted as to make nearly all manufacturing processes impossible. Our society would, in short, face disaster of enormous magnitude. Such vulnerability may mean that urbanized, technologically sophisticated,

post-peasant society of the kind that the United States has experimented with in recent decades will not spread very widely. It may even founder where it now exists, to be supplanted by more "barbarian" patterns of social organization.

But the overall record of the human past supports a more optimistic judgment. Most men, most of the time, have wanted and liked the wealth and power that technological skills impart. Peasants prefer to be free from the pains of cultivation. Artisans prefer to be spared the muscular exertion required in handicraft production. Consumers prefer cheap and abundant goods, and managers and entrepreneurs prefer more efficient ways of production. Hence, history seems to show that more elaborate forms of social integration do prosper because they combine larger numbers of men in more multifarious ways, allowing fuller scope for special skills and for all the gains that flow from specialization.

In the perspective of history, then, there appears no intrinsic reason why a shift away from the age-old structure of civilized society—the division of mankind between a peasant majority and a privileged minority of specialists—will not come to pass. Certainly every part of the world is today straining toward such a result, seeking technical modernization—airports, factories and scientifically equipped armies—with the same energy that other ages put into building cathedrals or palaces.

Let us therefore assume that transition to a world based on machine technology and attuned to urban life is indeed the vision of the future. But so vast a changeover will not be sudden. The archeological record suggests that it took men in the Middle East several centuries to develop a more or less stable set of tools for the tasks of agriculture. Presumably other kinds of invention went along with this period of radical change. New patterns of work, new religious ideas, new family structures—these and other innovations must have caused much anguish, disruption of deeply rooted habits and frustration of deeply felt values. A shift away from the fields by mankind's majority in the years ahead will no doubt require comparably painful and wide-ranging changes in nearly every aspect of life before workable readjustments to the lineaments of a new society begin to emerge.

How such reorganization of the human scene might proceed is far from clear, however. Obscuring its course are a multitude of dilemmas and ambiguities. Some of them are physiological and psychological, others political. Still others concern the struggle for survival of existing cultural or national identities in an age already tending toward worldwide uniformity.

In fact, our vision of a machine-powered world emerging two or three centuries hence holds scarcely any certainties, unless a diminution of expenditure of muscular energy in work is counted so. But this certainty is itself troubling. What will men find to do with their muscles? And with the psychological drives their muscles once expressed? When it no longer means using human strength, what will work become? How will men spend their time to avoid boredom?

The question can be put another way. How adaptable is man? If our inherited physiological arrangements are attuned fundamentally to hunters' requirements, as seems likely, clearly great changes were made—and successfully—when men started to farm. Can similar adjustments be expected when men cease to make a living by using their heavy muscles in farming or other occupations?

And assuming that men succeed in adapting physically to their new experience, there still remains the problem of their psychological reconditioning. What new kinds of expression will be found for ancient aggressive instincts and kinesthetic itchiness? Can making marks on paper,

talking on telephones or intercoms and lounging in front of a TV satisfy us all? Sex and sport are obvious outlets that are already elaborately developed supplements to white-collar routines. Yet one must wonder if sex and sport can supply the moral equivalent for such aggressive impulses as now find outlet in war and crime.

Political ambiguities that lie ahead are just as troublesome. The breakneck social and economic change that is going on in most of the world today is scarcely compatible with democratic government, and is likely to become less so if its pace continues to accelerate. A drift from government by consent toward some form of authoritarian rule is apparent now in countries of Africa and Asia where older styles of life are in full retreat and new ones are full of uncertainties.

The reason for this drift from democracy is clear. In a democratic society public debate can focus on only a few, and comparatively very simple, issues at any one time; when too many things are up for decision, confusion sets in. The best that can then result from democratic methods of government is a plebiscite on personalities. But this will work only as long as the defeated personality and his adherents agree to abide by the upshot. Casual inspection of the world's new governments is sufficient proof of how seldom this agreement actually exists. Consequently, military dictatorships of one sort or another already rule almost all the new nations of Africa and much of Asia. Where acknowledged military rule is absent, as in Communist countries, party rule prevails; and most of the ruling parties are themselves modeled on military lines so that their members act more or less like soldiers in mufti.

Internationally, the political scene is no less full of contradictory portents. In countries only recently freed from colonial chains fierce local nationalisms clash with the economic realities that make such states less and less capable of effective independence. Yet the truly great powers in recent years have shown themselves afraid to use their full military potential lest atomic warfare ricochet and endanger those who started it. This tends to equalize great powers and small, particularly when a small power such as North Vietnam can depend on weapons and supplies from abroad.

These political circumstances are likely to be comparatively transitory, however. International alliances and enmities alter repeatedly even within a single lifetime. The fervent nationalism that has recently characterized most new nations will likely prove to be a passing stage also, as men find other loyalties to which to devote themselves.

Probably far more significant for the long-range future of mankind than its political relations and national allegiances are loyalties based on the cultural differences that have given structure and form to civilizations in the past. Will these age-old distinctions fade and disappear as modern communications make the world increasingly one? Or will they reassert themselves in some fashion and maintain a degree of cultural diversity among men into the indefinite future?

Here again the auguries seem contradictory. On the one hand, universal technological uniformity on a Western pattern appears certain. Where technical considerations dictate form and details of design, there is never likely to be much local variety in style; airports are remarkably similar in all lands, so are radio towers, machine tools and automobiles. Any useful and valuable changes in design will probably continue to spread very widely around the globe to maintain a general sameness comparable to that exhibited by the tools of Stone Age hunters.

On the other hand, long-standing distinctions between cultures and the local loyalties they foster show a tenacity that is not apt to be easily overwhelmed by the advance of Western-style modernization. All of the world's nations are today busily exhuming or creating a past that they can call their own. The impulse is as old as nationality itself: the self-consciousness of Italians, French, English and Germans in late medieval and early modern times was supported by learned explorations into their respective pasts. In the 19th Century, the study of history and language was the device by which such submerged peoples of Europe as the Czechs, Slovaks, Croats and Bulgars reasserted their respective cultural difference and peculiar identity.

During the early decades of the 20th Century this impulse spread beyond European boundaries. For example, after World War I, when the polylingual Ottoman Empire shrank to Turkey itself, the followers of Kemal Ataturk, leader of the new Turkey, set out to rediscover an ancient and purely Turkish past. Since the loss of a great empire was psychologically difficult for the Turks to accept, their historians and philologists were tempted to exaggerate the glories of the Turkish heritage. They even claimed credit for the origin of civilization by counting the Sumerians, the earliest civilized people, among their ancestors.

More recently, since World War II, the urge to prove a venerable and distinctive ancestry has touched all the new nations of Africa and Asia. One instance of this was seen when the first independent government of what the British had called the Gold Coast chose the name Ghana because that had been the name of the oldest known West African state. The fact that the territory controlled by the ancient rulers of Ghana lay almost entirely outside that of the new Ghana was not important. What was important was the name itself, which not only implied a decent antiquity but also claimed for the newborn republic an independent cultural tradition.

A MERGING OF CULTURES IN A CHANGING WORLD

In developing lands around the globe, the intermingling of ancient ways and 20th Century technology often produces incongruous scenes. Here, in the courtyard of a Buddhist temple not far from Bangkok, Thailand, a Volkswagen belonging to the temple's abbot stands in contrast to the serene, gilded figure of the Buddha and the saffron-colored robes of the monks. But despite such modern inroads, deep-rooted local customs and beliefs show a remarkable capacity to endure—as the Thai inscription on the car attests. It announces that "women are not allowed to sit or drive," thus affirming the age-old Buddhist conviction that an object used by the priestly class suffers contamination if touched by a woman.

Similar mélanges occur in other areas of the world where the trusted ways of the past refuse to be wholly eclipsed by Western techniques and innovations. Young university graduates in the Ivory Coast use tape recorders to preserve African tribal tales for posterity; a new airport at Kandahar in Afghanistan perpetuates the shape of mud huts in outlying villages; and highland Indians of Peru travel by plane to markets largely unchanged since the day of the Inca. Such mixings of modernity with the traditional past ultimately provide new scope and vitality to local cultures.

Efforts to discover a unique national past—actual or fictitious—is one aspect of each nation's desire for cultural autonomy at home and abroad. One reflection of this drive is the emphasis most countries place on their traditional style of art or literature. Where a truly creative and distinctly national artistic or literary legacy was lacking or had been eclipsed by modern influences from the West, public officials have tried to summon one into existence. Only in a few instances, however, have they achieved any notable success. The outburst of artistic creativity in revolutionary Mexico during the 1920s and 1930s, for example, effectively combined ancient Aztec motifs with machine-inspired modernity to evolve a local and distinctive style. More recently, African authors writing in French have created a body of poetry celebrating *négritude* that has commanded considerable admiration outside as well as within French-speaking Africa.

Much more often official patronage of cultural creativity has produced abortive, strained results. This appears to be the case in all Communist countries, although it may be premature to pass judgment on some of the newer regimes. The effort of Irish nationalists to revive the ancient Gaelic tongue and literary tradition lies closer home to English-speaking lands. This movement, begun in the late 19th Century and officially supported since the 1920s, has had to live with the ironic fact that all the principal Irish writers of the 20th Century have written their important works in English.

During the past century or so, the major Asian civilizations—Muslim, Indian, Chinese and Japanese—have seen experiments in combining Western-inspired art and literary forms with traditional ones as a means of stimulating cultural creativity.

In China and Japan and among the Muslim peoples, however, creative cultural innovation has been in short supply. Men of sensitivity and learning have instead gravitated to either of two poles: a rigid adherence to old beliefs and styles that conflicted sharply with those of the West, or a ravenous and uncritical effort to appropriate Western ideas and skills as fast as possible and without much regard for the quality or finer nuances of what they were trying to make their own.

Somewhat more successful attempts at blending Eastern and Western cultural elements appear to have been made in India, where the traditions of Hindu mysticism and Western practicality could recognize each other as superior in its chosen field, and each could claim to supplement the deficiencies of the other. Yet hardly anything that the rest of the world easily recognizes as freshly creative has come out of modern India.

Perhaps there has simply not been enough time for cultural leaders of the great non-Western civilizations to get over the initial shock they felt when, scarcely a hundred years ago, they recognized that the West had outstripped them in essential and important ways. Eventually there is almost bound to be some relaxing of the tension between a naïve whoring after Western ways and the impulse to maintain, reassert or create local cultural uniqueness. Thus it may be the great work of the 21st Century to see a more complex and fruitful interaction between the major cultural traditions of mankind than has yet been manifest.

But whether any viable cultural pluralism will develop from such interaction remains to be seen. So much that is rooted in the past is already being swept away that a revival of any distinctive culture may have a fragile and artificial character.

Moreover, there is the possibility that the years ahead may bring a radical alteration of a fundamental bond that has been even stronger than nationality or artistic and historical traditions in unifying cultural groupings. All such groupings in the past depended largely upon locality as the basis of association. In ages when easy and rapid movement and communication were impossible, this bond to geographical propinquity was hard to escape. But in the modern world, locality has become much less confining. Some groupings have already been widely diffused geographically, yet each is still bound by a common tie. For example, scientists and scholars of many lands who work on the same or closely related problems keep in touch with one another and easily surmount barriers of language, cultural differences and often even antagonistic political allegiances. A variety of technical specialists until now nearly all of them trained in the West—also move to and fro in the world, erecting or servicing specialized equipment of many kinds. What holds members of that community together is the uniformity of the machines and installations they create or maintain and by which they are spreading Western-style modernization throughout the globe.

Armies are another kind of world-girdling community that may turn out to be far more important than others as a basis of association. They already embrace larger numbers of men and in principle can easily expand their ranks to include men of diverse racial and cultural origins. To be sure, modern armies tend to be national and prefer to recruit manpower from a single people. The Russians, however, draw upon all the different nationalities of the Soviet Union, and nothing intrinsically prevents a Western power from raising an Asian or African army, as the French and British proved as recently as World War II.

Like a monastic order or an international corporation, such an army—polyglot and culturally diverse though it may be—creates and carries with it a moral and technical society that is unified by army regulations and is a sort of halfway house between the elements that constitute its ranks. In accordance with the fundamental military principle of "replaceable parts," the elements of that society, men as well as equipment, can be shifted here and there across the face of the earth quickly while retaining a corporate identity and power of coordinated action.

It is easy to imagine other possible bases of association that might eventually transcend the old-fashioned bond of locality and nationality based on locality. Religious sects or other ideological parties have a long history as rivals to territorial solidarity. In the Western world, loyalty to a religious doctrine has clashed with political allegiance ever since pre Christian days. A similar conflict between the pursuit of holiness and obedience to political authority arose repeatedly in all Muslim lands. In more recent times, Communist and other revolutionary parties in the West and in the East have tried to create a class unity that would transcend national and state boundaries. They succeeded, however, only insofar as they put doctrinal purity above the exercise of power.

Still another potentially important framework for human organization may result from an already noticeable tendency to break down barriers that formerly separated mankind into more or less distinct racial blocs. To be sure, newly emancipated peoples often use their political power to exclude racially different minorities, particularly those that formerly held privileged social positions · among them. But it is an open question whether such impulses toward local segregation will be able to resist the pressures created by the ease with which people move around the world today. Political barriers to human migration are no stronger than the organized force that supports them. New and backward nations regularly find that their best hope of increasing wealth and power at home is to invite foreigners, regardless of race, to practice and impart special skills not yet mastered by their own peoples. Increased technical and commercial involvement in the great world is not likely to reduce this influx of foreigners, and societies that refuse to tolerate outsiders are almost certain to fall behind those that open themselves to foreign stimulus and immigration.

Thus racial segregation by and within political boundaries could conceivably become obsolete in the future. And in racially plural societies loyalty to nationality may find a potent competitor in allegiances based on race. This has already been suggested by such movements as the American Negro's recent stress on Black Power.

With so many ambiguous portents beclouding the future of mankind, it is foolish to predict what may lie ahead. Yet there are some obvious limits that mankind cannot exceed. Human numbers is one of these. Experts have long been forecasting a check to spiraling population growth as the earth runs out of room to support humanity. Another limit is man's capacity to communicate. Messages can never be sent more rapidly than those that already travel with the speed of light from any part of the globe to any other. Nor is the mind's ability to react to messages unrestricted. Even today the enormous inflow of information necessary to the conduct of human affairs makes it difficult for world leaders to filter out the unessential in order to concentrate on matters of prime importance. As the human community continues to grow larger and more complex, the greater the likelihood becomes that the system of message filtering will work to retard change. It may select information to be passed upward in the ladder of bureaucratic hierarchy in a way that protects and justifies what is already being done and makes sudden important change improbable.

These examples—a curtailing of the population boom and the control of information—are only two of a multitude of ways in which men set out, half unconsciously, to protect themselves from too much uncertainty and too rapid change. Yet it seems inconceivable that the present pace of social change can accelerate indefinitely into the future. If the possibility of a machine-powered world of urban-dwellers does indeed become reality, a general slackening of the pace seems sure to set in once the initial shock of transition from traditional peasant-based social structures begins to fade. Bureaucracy is a great and ready instrument for routinizing action of every kind. By refusing licenses to innovators and by policing the world against rebels and criminals with computer-like precision, interlocking bureaucracies—even if they are professedly antagonistic to one another—might bring the gallop of today's technical and social change under control rather quickly.

In that event, men a century or more from now will look back upon the 20th Century as a truly extraordinary Golden Age, when everything was open, everything up for grabs, and the guidelines of the future were laid down by us poor fools, little witting for the most part what we were doing. Like ours, Golden Ages of the past have always been times of vast and fundamental confusion. They were times when old truths foundered and ancient guidelines disappeared. And they were ages when men faced the tragic nakedness of their condition with panic but also with wide-eyed energy, seeking new certainties for old, and when that proved impossible, learning to live with mere probabilities or agreed conventions.

Our age belongs in the high company of those times when men found themselves forced, willynilly, into far-ranging, fundamental creativity. It is naïve and short-sighted not to recognize our age for what it is. Only the weak and timorous can regret being alive in a time when so many avenues lie open and so much remains to be done.

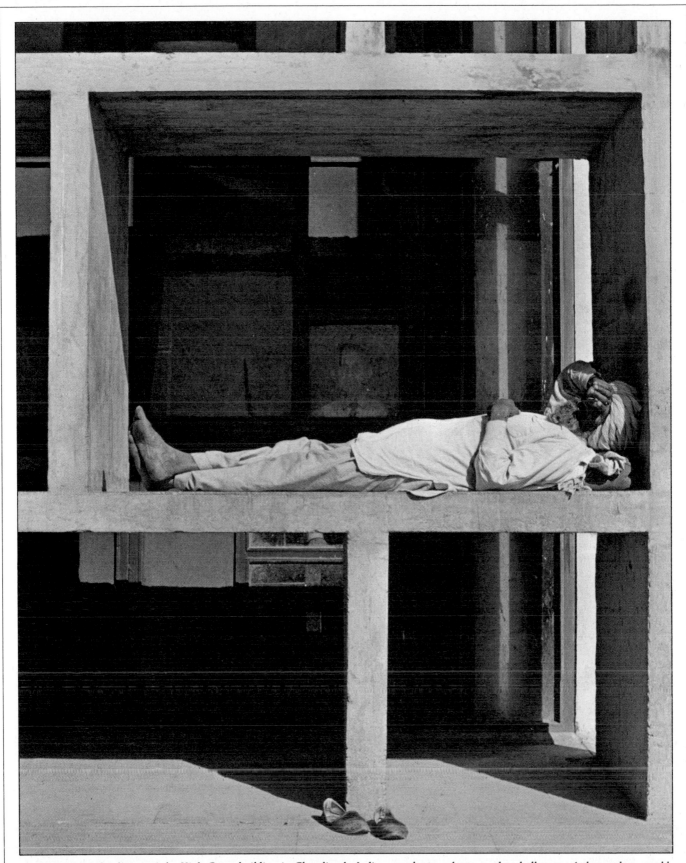

Making use of the design of the High Court building in Chandigarh, India, a workman adapts to the challenges of the modern world.

BIBLIOGRAPHY

The following volumes were selected during the preparation of this book for their interest and authority, and for their usefulness to readers seeking additional information on specific points. An asterisk (*) marks works available in both hard cover and paperback editions; a dagger (†) indicates availability only in paperback.

GENERAL READING

Aron, Raymond, *The Century of Total War*.† Beacon Press, 1955.
Barraclough, Geoffrey, *An Introduction to Contemporary History*.* Penguin Books, 1967.
Brinton, Crane, John B. Christopher and Robert Lee Wolff, *A History of Civilization*, Vol. II, *1715 to the Present*. 3rd ed. Prentice-Hall, 1967.
Chambers, Frank P., *This Age of Conflict*. 3rd ed. Harcourt, Brace and World, 1962.
Commager, Henry S., ed., *Contemporary Civilization*.† Issue Three. Scott, Foresman, 1963.
Crouzet, Maurice, *Histoire Générale des Civilisations*, Vol. VII, *L'Époque Contemporaine*. Paris, 1959.
Findlay, James F., ed., *Contemporary Civilization*.† Issue Four. Scott, Foresman, 1967.
Halle, Louis J. *The Cold War as History*. Harper & Row, 1967.
Hauser, Philip M., *The Population Dilemma*.† Prentice-Hall, 1963.
Holborn, Hajo, *The Political Collapse of Europe*. Alfred A. Knopf, 1963.
Hughes, H. Stuart, *Contemporary Europe: A History*. Prentice-Hall, 1966.
Kohn, Hans, *Political Ideologies of the Twentieth Century*.* 3rd ed. rev. Harper & Row, 1966.
Lafore, Laurence. *The Long Fuse*.* Lippincott, 1965.
McNeill, William H.:
 The Rise of the West.* University of Chicago Press, 1963.
 The Contemporary World: 1914/Present.* Scott, Foresman, 1967.
New Cambridge Modern History, Vol. XII, *The Era of Violence, 1898-1945*. Cambridge University Press, 1959.
Palmer, R. R., and Joel Colton, *A History of the Modern World*. 3rd ed. Alfred A. Knopf, 1965.
Robertson, Charles L., *International Politics Since World War II: A Short History*.* John Wiley and Sons, 1966.
Ropp, Theodore, *War in the Modern World*.* Duke University Press, 1959.
Roth, Jack J., ed., *The First World War: A Turning Point in Modern History*.† Alfred A. Knopf, 1967.
Ware, Caroline F., K. M. Panikkar and J. M. Romein, *History of Mankind: Cultural and Scientific Development*, Vol. VI, *The Twentieth Century*. Harper & Row, 1966.

AFRICA AND THE MIDDLE EAST

Antonius, George, *The Arab Awakening*.* G. P. Putnam's Sons, 1965.
Balfour, Patrick (Lord Kinross), *Ataturk*. William Morrow and Co., 1965.
Carter, Gwendolen, *Politics in Africa*.† Harcourt, Brace and World, 1966.
Easton, Stewart C., *The Twilight of European Colonialism: A Political Analysis*. Holt, Rinehart and Winston, 1960.
Emerson, Rupert, *From Empire to Nation: The Rise to Self-Assertion of Asian and African Peoples*.* Harvard University Press, 1960.
Fisher, Sydney Nettleton, *The Middle East: A History*. Alfred A. Knopf, 1966.
Kenworthy, Leonard, and Erma Ferrari, *Leaders of New Nations*. Rev. ed. Doubleday, 1968.
Kenyatta, Jomo, *Facing Mount Kenya*.† Vintage Books, 1962.
Lewis, Bernard, *The Emergence of Modern Turkey*. Oxford University Press, 1961.
Nkrumah, Kwame, *Ghana*. Thomas Nelson and Sons, 1957.

EUROPE AND AMERICA

Bauer, Raymond A., Alex Inkeles and Clyde Kluckhohn, *How the Soviet System Works*.* Harvard University Press, 1956.
Bird, Caroline, *The Invisible Scar*.* David M. McKay, 1965.
Fairbank, John K., *The United States and China*.* Rev. ed. Harvard University Press, 1962.
Galbraith, J. K., *The Great Crash*.* Houghton Mifflin, 1955.
Herring, Hubert, *A History of Latin America*. Alfred A. Knopf, 1962.
Kennan, George F., *American Diplomacy, 1900-1950*.* University of Chicago Press, 1951.
Levin, Nora, *The Holocaust*. Thomas Y. Crowell, 1968.

ASIA

Azad, Maulana Abul Kalam, *India Wins Freedom*. Longmans, Green, 1960.
Beasley, W. G., *The Modern History of Japan*.* Frederick A. Praeger, 1963.
Brown, W. Norman. *The United States and India and Pakistan*. Rev. ed. Harvard University Press, 1963.
Cady, John F., *Southeast Asia: Its Historical Development*. McGraw-Hill, 1964.
Clyde, Paul H., and B. F. Beers. *The Far East*. 4th ed. Prentice-Hall, 1966.
Fairbank, John K., Edwin O. Reischauer and Albert M. Craig, *East Asia: The Modern Transformation*. Houghton Mifflin, 1965.
Fitzgerald, Charles P.:
 Flood Tide in China. Dufour Editions, 1958.
 Revolution in China. Frederick A. Praeger, 1951.
Furnivall, J. S.:
 Colonial Policy and Practice. New York University Press, 1956.
 Netherlands India. Cambridge University Press, 1944.
Gandhi, M. K., *The Gandhi Reader*. Ed. by H. A. Jack. University of Indiana Press, 1956.
Hall, D.G.E., *A History of South-East Asia*. 2nd ed. St. Martins Press, 1961.
Hu Chang-Tu, ed., *Chinese Education under Communism*.† Teachers College, Columbia University, 1962.
Latourette, Kenneth Scott, *A Short History of the Far East*. 4th ed. Macmillan, 1964.
McAleavy, Henry, *The Modern History of China*.* Frederick A. Praeger, 1967.
Mao Tse-tung, *Quotations from Chairman Mao Tse-tung*.† China Books and Periodicals, 1966.
Myrdal, Gunnar, *Asian Drama*.* 3 vols. Pantheon Books, 1968.
Nehru, J., *Toward Freedom: The Autobiography of Jawaharlal Nehru*.† Beacon Press, 1958.
Pelissier, Roger, *The Awakening of China*. G. P. Putnam's Sons, 1967.
Snow, Edgar, *The Other Side of the River: Red China Today*. Random House, 1962.
Spate, O.H.K., and A.T.T. Learmonth, *India and Pakistan*. 4th ed. Barnes and Noble, 1967.

ART

Geldzahler, Henry, *American Painting in the Twentieth Century*. Metropolitan Museum, New York Graphic Society, 1965.
Neumeyer, Alfred, *The Search for Meaning in Modern Art*.* Transl. by R. Angress. Prentice-Hall, 1964.
Rosenberg, Harold:
 The Anxious Object: Art Today and Its Audience. Horizon Press, 1964.
 The Tradition of the New.† McGraw-Hill, 1965.
Seitz, William C., *The Art of Assemblage*. Museum of Modern Art, Doubleday, 1961.

ACKNOWLEDGMENT OF QUOTATIONS

Page 22: Letter of Sir Thomas Raffles to the Duchess of Somerset, 1820, from *Raffles of Singapore* by Emily Hahn, Doubleday, 1948, p. 410. Pages 24-25: from *Life in Java* by William Barrington d'Almeida, Hurst and Blackett, 1864, pp. 260, 261, 298. Page 26: from *Travels in the Central Parts of Indo-China (Siam), Cambodia, and Laos* by Henri Mouhot, John Murray, 1864, I, pp. 279, 282. Page 28: from *Java, Sumatra and the Other Islands of the Dutch East Indies* by Antoine Cabaton, transl. by Bernard Miall, Charles Scribner's Sons, 1911, pp. 304-306. Page 30: Extract of letters of Francis Garnier from *Tonkin or France in the Far East* by C. B. Norman, Chapman and Hall, 1884, pp. 111, 130, 131. Page 32: from *Java, Sumatra and the Other Islands of the Dutch East Indies* by Antoine Cabaton, transl. by Bernard Miall, Charles Scribner's Sons, 1911, p. 179. Page 96 (in the order in which the quotations appear): Dr. Jindřich Flusser from *Terezín*, ed. by František Ehrmann, Otta Heitlinger and Rudolf Iltis, Council of Jewish Communities in the Czech Lands, 1965, p. 277. From *Jewish Survivors Report #3: THERESIENSTADT and From Theresienstadt to Auschwitz* by Max E. Mannheimer, Jewish Central Information Office, 1945, p. 1. From *Jewish Survivors Report #6: TEREZÍN: The Daily Life, 1943-1945* by Dr. Jacob Jacobson, Jewish Central Information Office, 1946, p. 7. F.R. Kraus from *Terezín*, ed. by František Ehrmann, Otta Heitlinger and Rudolf Iltis, Council of Jewish Communities in the Czech Lands, 1965, p. 147. Page 100 (in the order in which the quotations appear): Dr. Norbert Frýd from *Terezín*, ed. by František Ehrmann, Otta Heitlinger and Rudolf Iltis, Council of Jewish Communities in the Czech Lands, 1965, p. 207. From *Jewish Survivors Report #3: THERESIENSTADT and From Theresienstadt to Auschwitz* by Max E. Mannheimer, Jewish Central Information Office, 1945, p. 2. Mordechai Ansbacher from *Justice in Jerusalem* by Gideon Hausner, Harper & Row, 1966, pp. 158-159. Page 104: Josef Polák from *Terezín*, ed. by František Ehrmann, Otta Heitlinger and Rudolf Iltis, Council of Jewish Communities in the Czech Lands, 1965, pp. 25, 38, 44. Pages 121-129: Adapted from *Quotations from Chairman Mao Tse-tung*, China Books and Periodicals, 1966.

ART INFORMATION AND PICTURE CREDITS

The sources for the illustrations in this book are set forth below. Descriptive notes on the works of art are included. Credits for pictures positioned from left to right are separated by semicolons, from top to bottom by dashes. Photographers' names which follow a descriptive note appear in parentheses.

Circa is abbreviated "ca." The works on pages 52, 53, 54-55, 60-61, 147, 158, are published by arrangement with SPADEM, by French Reproduction Rights, Inc. The work by Wassily Kandinsky on pages 148-149 appears by arrangement with ADAGP, by French Reproduction Rights, Inc.

COVER—Detail from Sky Cathedral III by Louise Nevelson, painted wood, 1960, courtesy Kroller Muller Museum, Otterlo (Eddy Van Der Veen). 8-9—Map by Milton Glazer, Push Pin Studios.

CHAPTER 1: 10—Poster-covered wall in Hong Kong (Harry Redl from Black Star). 14-15—Map by Rafael D. Palacios. 18—Japanese woodcut depicting Commodore Matthew Perry, 1854, The Granger Collection, New York. 22-23—Photograph from album *Sumatra's O.K.*, courtesy Cornell University. 24-25—Library of Congress. 26-27—Courtesy Gernsheim Collection, University of Texas. 28-29—J. Lynn Ball. 30-31—Roger Viollet, Paris. 32-33—Courtesy E. Breton de Nijs.

CHAPTER 2: 34—Detail from *Gassed* (Scene at Dressing Station on the Doullens-Arras Road, August 1918) by John Singer Sargent, oil on canvas, 1918, courtesy of the Trustees of the Imperial War Museum, London (Derek Bayes). 37—Map by Rafael D. Palacios. 40—The Bettmann Archive; Culver Pictures. 41—Keystone View; Culver Pictures. 46—Map by Rafael D. Palacios. 49—Courtesy Mr. and Mrs. Elihu Rose, New York (Walter Daran). 50, 51—Courtesy Mr. and Mrs. Elihu Rose (Walter Daran). 52—Poster by Abel Faivre, courtesy Metropolitan Museum of Art, New York (Robert S. Crandall). 53—Poster by Abel Faivre, courtesy Mr. and Mrs. Elihu Rose (Paulus Leeser). 54-55—Poster by Georges Sem, courtesy the Victoria and Albert Museum, London (Derek Bayes). 56, 57—Courtesy the Gallery of Modern Art including the Huntington Hartford Collection, New York. 58—Courtesy Metropolitan Museum of Art, New York (Robert S. Crandall). 59—By James Montgomery Flagg, courtesy Mr. and Mrs. Elihu Rose (Paulus Leeser). 60-61—Poster by Abel Faivre, courtesy Gallery of Modern Art including the Huntington Hartford Collection, New York.

CHAPTER 3: 62—Untitled work by George Grosz, ca. 1923, courtesy the Estate of George Grosz, Princeton, New Jersey. 65—Ink drawing of flapper girl by John Held Jr. from *Held's Angels*, published by Thomas Y. Crowell, New York, 1952, courtesy Mrs. John Held Jr. 68—Cartoon from *Punch*, April 6, 1932, courtesy *Punch*. 73—Margaret Bourke-White. 75—Underwood and Underwood—United Press Associates—United Press International. 76—Underwood and Underwood—Black Star—Missouri Historical Society. 77—United Press International—Underwood and Underwood—Underwood and Underwood. 78-79—The Press Association Limited, London—National Air and Space Museum, Smithsonian Institution; Underwood and Underwood; Ralph Crane—Culver Pictures. 80—The Press Association Limited, London—Bettmann Archive; United Press International—United Press International. 81—Ullstein Bilderdienst, Berlin; United Press International. 82—Brown Brothers—Wide World Photos—Culver Pictures. 83—Underwood and Underwood.

CHAPTER 4: 84—Detail from *The Last Moments of Admiral Yamaguchi at Midway* by Renzo Kita, oil on canvas, ca. 1943-1945, courtesy Department of the Army, Washington, D.C. (Ichiro Nakagawa). 89—Russian poster by "Kukriniksy," 1942, (Novosti Press Agency, Moscow). 92-93—Map by Rafael D. Palacios. 95-107—Details from drawings of Terezin, charcoal and India ink, all courtesy State Jewish Museum in Prague and Hawthorn Books, New York (Frank Lerner). 95—*Incoming Transport* by Bedrich Fritta, 1943. 96-97—*Registration* by Karel Fleischmann, 1943. 98-99—*Going to Work* by Bedrich Fritta, 1943. 100-101—*Entertainment* by Bedrich Fritta, 1942. 102-103—*In Terezin*

by Bedrich Fritta, 1943. 104-105—*Awaiting Transport to Auschwitz* by Bedrich Fritta, 1942. 106-107—*Transport Leaving* by Bedrich Fritta, 1943.

CHAPTER 5: 108—Alfred Eisenstaedt. 112—Statue of Gandhi enshrined among Hindu goddesses, Durga Temple at Pariyur, Coimbatore District, Madras, India, 1948 (G. Nanja Nath from Black Star). 116-117—Map by Rafael D. Palacios. 121—Paolo Koch from Black Star. 122-125—Marc Riboud from Magnum. 126-127—Gerda Endler—Emil Schulthess from Black Star. 128-129—Emil Schulthess from Black Star. 130-131—Marc Riboud from Magnum.

CHAPTER 6: 132—Fluidic computation circuit photographed at Corning Glassworks, Corning, New York (Henry Groskinsky). 134—Famine ticket distributed in Shanghai in 1927 by Communists (Keystone). 139—Planned parenthood symbols for Pakistan, Korea and Malaysia (courtesy Planned Parenthood-World Population). 143—Barber shop sign in Akure, Western Nigeria (Marc and Evelyne Bernheim from Rapho Guillumette). 145—*An Englishman in Moscow* by Kasimir Malevich, oil on canvas, 1914, Stedelijk Museum, Amsterdam (Robert S. Crandall). 146—*Figure* by Jacques Lipchitz, bronze, 1926-1930, courtesy Joseph H. Hirshhorn Collection, New York (Eric Schaal); African (Bakota) fetish figure, courtesy Gaston T. de Havenon, New York (Eliot Elisofon). 147—*Dancer* by Pablo Picasso, oil on canvas, 1907, courtesy Walter P. Chrysler, Jr. Collection, New York (Robert S. Crandall). 148-149—Coffee pot designed by Christian Dell, silver and grained wood, 1925, courtesy Busch-Reisinger Museum, Harvard University (Lee Boltin); Silk wall hanging designed by Anni Albers, 1926, courtesy Busch-Reisinger Museum, Harvard University (Lee Boltin)—Armchair designed for mass production by Marcel Breuer, chromed tubular steel and canvas, 1925, courtesy Busch-Reisinger Museum, Harvard University (Lee Boltin); *Through going Line* by Wassily Kandinsky, oil on canvas, 1923, Musée du Vingtième Siècle, Dusseldorf, courtesy Nina Kandinsky, Paris (Eric Schaal). 150—*Composition with Red, Yellow and Blue* by Piet Mondrian, oil on canvas, 1935-1942, courtesy Mr. and Mrs. James H. Clark, Dallas (Frank Lerner). 151—Façade of the Secretariat Building in Chandigarh, India, designed by Le Corbusier (Brian Brake from Rapho Guillumette); Interior of the Villa Shodham in Ahmedabad, India designed by Le Corbusier (Lucien Hervé)—Façade of Assembly Palace in Chandigarh, India designed by Le Corbusier (Tapio Wirkkala, courtesy *Domus* Magazine). 152—Two large characters by the Priest Unchū of the Zen Buddhist Daitokuji Temple, Japan, calligraphic scroll, Edo Period, Private Collection (Herb Orth); Cornell Capa. 153—*Slate Cross* by Franz Kline, oil on canvas, 1961, the Estate of Franz Kline, (photograph courtesy Marlborough-Gerson Gallery, New York). 154-155—*Merz 25: A Painting with Stars* by Kurt Schwitters, montage, collage and assemblage with cardboard, 1920, Kunstsammlung Nordrhein-Westfalen, Düsseldorf, courtesy the Estate of Kurt Schwitters (Pierre Boulat); *Summertime* by Romare Bearden, collage, 1967, Mr. Jesse Shanok, courtesy Cordier and Ekstrom Gallery, New York (Robert S. Crandall); *Tracer* by Robert Rauschenberg, collage and silk-screen, 1964, courtesy Mr. and Mrs. F. Titelman (Sabine Weiss). 156-157—*Transparent Rhythms II* by Yaacov Agam, oil-painted on aluminum relief, 1967, courtesy Joseph H. Hirshhorn Collection, New York (Frank Lerner).

EPILOGUE. 158—*The Builders* by Fernand Léger, oil on canvas, 1950, Musée Fernand Léger, Biot, France (Jacques Mer from Rapho Guillumette, Paris). 160-161—Map done in 1838 purporting to show migration routes of three major races, from Tome II, Fascicule IV of *Atlas Antiquus et Index*, published in 1933, New York Public Library (Lee Boltin). 165—Marc Riboud from Magnum. 169—John Launois from Black Star. 173—Paolo Koch from Black Star.

ACKNOWLEDGMENTS

For help given in the preparation of this book, the editors are particularly indebted to Leonard Krieger, Professor, Department of History, University of Chicago, who has also been Series Consultant for *Great Ages of Man*. The editors are grateful as well to James T. Siegel, Assistant Professor, Department of Anthropology and Asian Studies, Cornell University, Ithaca, New York; Theodor Reff, Professor, Department of Art History and Archeology and Donald W. Klwin, Research Associate, East Asian Institute, Columbia University, New York City; Paul Mocsanyi, Director, New School Art Center, New School for Social Research, New York City; Harry J. Alderman, Library Director, Blaustein Library, American Jewish Committee, New York City; Dina Abramowicz, Head Librarian, Yivo Institute for Jewish Research, New York City; Robert Wood, Chief, Information and Research Divisions, National Air and Space Museum, Smithsonian Institution, Washington, D. C.; Ruth Field, Curator, Picture Department, Missouri Historical Society, St. Louis; Gerard Alexander, Chief, Map Division, New York Public Library, New York City; Roland Jones, Engineering Manager, Industrial Applications, Bowles Engineering Corporation, Silver Spring, Maryland; Lucie Prinz, Assistant Director, Department of Information and Education, Planned Parenthood-World Population, New York City; New York Society Library, New York City; Cynthia W. Nachmani, New York City; Lucien Hervé, Paris; Laurent Laporte, Service Culturel de la Mairie, Levallois-Perret, France, Marie-Antoinette Menier, Conservateur des Archives Nationales, Section Outre-Mer, Paris; Ando Gilardi, Fototeca Storica Nazionale, Milan; Carlo Fabi, Museo Numismatico della Zecca, Rome; Marianne Lorenz, Domus Magazine, Milan; Ufficio Stampa (Press Office), Olivetti S.P.A., Ivrea; Ufficio Stampa, IBM Italia, Milan; Museo del Risorgimento, Milan; Raccolta Civica Bertarelli, Milan; Otto Steinert, Professor, Volkwangschule, Essen, Germany; Deutsche Akademie der Kuenste zu Berlin, East Berlin, Roland Klemig, Staatsbibliothek, Berlin; Friedrich Rauch, Munich; Rob Nieuwenhuys, Koninklijk Institut voor Taal-Land en Volkenkunde, Leiden, Netherlands; Yukio Kobayashi, Director, National Museum of Modern Art, Tokyo; Kanae Tanaka, Chairman, Mainichi Shimbun, Tokyo; Seiichi Iwao, Professor of History, Hosei University, Tokyo; Mrs. H. de Vries, Netherlands Embassy, Tokyo and Yukio Yashiro, Director, Yamato Bunkaken Museum, Nara, Japan.

INDEX

* This symbol in front of a page number indicates an illustration of the subject mentioned.

INDEX TO THE SERIES

The following 31 pages comprise a comprehensive index of the 20 volumes of the Great Ages of Man Series. Page numbers in Roman type indicate text references; numbers accompanied by an asterisk indicate architectural illustrations. Abbreviations in capital letters specify the volumes to which each reference is made (a full list of these abbreviatiions appears at the foot of every page of the index). Thus, the index entry Amenhotep III, King of Egypt, AE *55, 58 directs the reader to the *Ancient Egypt* volume, where he will find an illustration of Amenhotep on page 55 and a text reference on page 58.

But this index is more than an A-to-Z compendium of names and subjects. Incorporated in it are a number of master entries—each a major area of study—that facilitates finding information about broad subjects. Under Architecture, for example, are listed a number of paragraphs that break down the subject of architecture into categories identified by subheadings: architectural elements, Byzantine, Chinese, Gothic and Greek. By looking first for a master entry, checking its subheadings, and then glancing over the list of references under each of the subheadings, the reader will very quickly be led to special information in any book in the Great Ages of Man Series.

Ayllu (Inca social unit), AA 106, 170
Aymara Indians, AA 85, 87
Ayodhya, HI *map* 93; kingdom, HI 116
Aztecs, AA 62-68, 101-104, EX 11, REN 105; Spanish conquest of, AA 60, 68, *map* 140, 141-146, 163, 164, EX 19-20, 60, 100, *176-177. For details see index of Vol. AA

B

Ba (vitality), AE 81, 88, *89
Babur, Mughal Emperor, HI *158, 159-161; empire of, HI *map* 160
Baby-faces, Olmec, AA *19, 31, *32, 33, 82
Babylon, CC *map* 9, CG *map* 162; Alexander in, CG 160, 162. For details see index of Vol. CC
Babylonia, AE 15, CC 31, 51, 52-56, maps 58-59, 61, 147, CG 13, 69; astronomy, AE 147, CC 125, 159, CG 15; calendar, AE 146, CC 125; cuneiform, AE 58, 141, CC 122, 132, *133; gods and goddesses, CC 32, 53, 56, 62, 88, 107-108, 151, 154; history of, see index of Vol. CC; houses, CC 152, *153; irrigation, CC 53, 61; law, CC 52, 53, 82, 160, *170, CG 13; mathematics, AE 147, CC 124-125, 159; sculpture, CC 143, *147
Babylonian Captivity, at Avignon, AF 161, 164, 165-166, REN 14
Babylonian Captivity of the Church, The, Luther, REF 41
Babylonian Captivity of Hebrews, CC 62, 158-159, 160
Bacchus, IR *138
Bach, Johann Sebastian, AE 126, EN 122, 124
Bacon, Francis, EN 16-17, 18, 20, KIN 11, 59, 105
Bacon, Roger, AF 149-150, AK 105, EN 14-15
Bactrian Greeks, invasion of India by, HI 91, 92, 155
Baffin, William, EX 126
Baga people, snake worship, AK *122
Baghdad, AE 164, CC *map* 9, EI *map* 164; ancient sites near, CC 12, 16, 35, 52, 55, 140, 147; capital of Islam, BYZ 163, EI 83, 64, 79-80, 88, 101, HI 156; Mongol destruction of, EI 11, 163-164, 166, HI 158; trade center, AF *map* 72, BE *map* 127, CC 88, EI 83, 97, RR 14, *map* 19. For details see index of Vol. EI
Bailey, P. J., PRO 24
Bairam Khan, HI 161, *168
Baker, Sir Samuel, AK 62
Bakufu, EJ 60, 61, 62, 64
Bakunin, Mikhail, PRO 121-122
Balboa, Vasco Núñez de, AA 146, EX 96-97, 100
Baldwin of Boulogne, King of Jerusalem, AF 56, EI 146
Baldwin of Flanders, Latin Emperor of Constantinople, BYZ 166
Balkans, BE 167, 172, BYZ 55, 60, 61, 62, *map* 164, 166, PRO 81, RR 20; Bulgars in, BYZ 60, 61, 62; Byzantine cultural heritage, BYZ 12, 22, 145, *156-157, 170; Europe's trouble spot, PRO 168, 170-172; historical source on, BYZ 137; Islam in, EI 141, *map* 164, 166, KIN 166; Visigoths in, BE *map* 12, 17, 19, 36; Wars (1912, 1913), PRO 170-171
Ballad of Reading Gaol, Wilde, PRO 175
Ballet, EJ 84, KIN *71, 84, *127-137
Ballista, IR *94-95
Balloon flight, Blanchard, EN *chart* 17
Baltic Sea, RR 40, 81; Swedish-German power struggle, KIN *map* 32, 40; Swedish-Russian power struggle, KIN 169, RR 158, 159; trade, AF 78, BE *map* 127, 134, RR *map* 19
Baluba people, fetish, AK *120
Bambara people, sculpture of, AK 148
Bandello, Matteo, REN 166, 170
Bank of England, KIN 167, PRO 13
Banking, REF 167, REN 36, 38, 80-81, PRO 13, 53, 54-56; big families, AF 78, PRO 54-56, REF *72-73, REN 75, 80, *89; crises, PRO 58; development of, AF 74, 78, 79, *83, EI 84; a medieval legacy, AF 11
Bantu languages, AK 21
Baptism, AF 36, 106, CC 161, REF 41, 59,

180. *See also* Christianity, conversions to
Baptism of the King, The, Carpaccio, REN *149
Baptista, Pedro João, AK 170-171
Barbarians, *entire vol.* BE, IR *30; contributions to art and culture, AF 119, BE 13; in Roman army, BE 18, *22-23, *28, IR 30, 142; invasions of Byzantine Empire by, BE *map* 12, BYZ 56, *map* 59; See also Germanic tribes; *and individual tribes*
Barbarossa. *See* Frederick Barbarossa
Barbarus, BE 18
Barberini ivory plaque, BYZ 142, *152
Barcelona, AF 71, *map* 72, BE 102, *map* 106-107; Cathedral, AF *map* 8
Bardas, Caesar, BYZ *67, *68
Bardi family, AF 78, REN 75, 80
Barents, Willem, expedition of, EX 16, *116, 117, *map* 121, *125, 126
Barley, AC 12, *map* 36, 37, AE *map* 30, CC 13, 42, 83-84, 145, HI 32
Barmakids, rule of, EI 82-83
Baroque art, KIN 13, 77-84, 121, REF *100, 148-149; architecture, EN *30, KIN 79-81, 121, 147, REF *100; development of, KIN 79; origin of term, KIN 78; painting, KIN *80, 81, 83; sculpture, KIN *30, *76, 77-78, *79, 81, 83, *85-95, REN *30; techniques of, KIN 81
Baroque music, EN 121-128, *129-139, KIN 81, 84
Barrel vault, AF 122, CC 141, BYZ 139, IR 162
Barrisons, The Five, PRO *180
Barter economy, AA 102, 107, AF 17; demise, AF 60, BE 97, 166, EJ 167, REF 14, 65
Bartholomew, Dom, EJ 120
Bartolommeo, Fra, REN 122, 126
Bas-relief. *See* Relief sculpture
Basham, A. L., HI 77, 78, 95
Bashkirs, RR 122, *132, *map* 162
Basil I, Byzantine Emperor, BYZ 61, *63-73
Basil II Bulgaroctonus, Byzantine Emperor, BYZ 61-62
Basilicas, AF 32, 118, BE 111, BYZ 138, 139-140, IR *18-19, 175, REF 18, REN *72-73
Basiliskianos, BYZ *69
Basonge mask, AK *160-161
Basques, BE *map* 34, 102, 113
Bass, EN *135
Bastet (goddess), AE 73
Bastille, storm on, EN 168
Baths, public, BYZ 35, 114, HI 32, *34-35, IR 86, *87, 88, 135
Battering rams, BYZ 86, *87, CG *70
Battle of the Books, The, Swift, EN 80
Battle of the Camel, EI 60
Battle of Nude Men, Pollaiuolo, REN 99
Battle of the Sea Gods, Dürer, REF *48-49
Battleships, KIN *181, PRO 169
Batu Khan, RR 11, 38, 39, 40, 55, 56, 59, *126, 127
Baudelaire, Pierre Charles, PRO 142
Baule people: masks, AK 144, *160-161; mouse oracle, AK *124
Bavaria, BE 103, *map* 106-107, KIN *map* 32, 42, 171, PRO 102, *map* 103
Bavarians (tribe), BE *map* 34, 64
Bayaka initiation masks, AK *127
Bayeux Tapestry, AF *152-153, BE *146, 156
Beardsley, Aubrey, PRO 145, 157
Beasts of burden, AA 28, 87, *120, AC 14, 33, *178-179, AE *37, *47, *109, AK 46, *78, 81, 89, *map* 90-91, *92-93, *97, CC *42-43; absence in Middle America, AA 10, 64; harnessing, invention of, AC 132, BE 94, 166
Beau Dieu (sculpture, Amiens), AF 126
Beauvais Cathedral, AF 124
Beaux-Arts, Salon des, PRO 140, 141-142
Beccafumi, Domenico, REN 128
Beccaria, Cesare, EN 20, 55, 56
Becket, Thomas à, AF *57, 144
Bécquerel, Antoine Henri, PRO 166
Bede, the Venerable (historian), AF 94, BE 177, BYZ 118
Bedouins. *See index of Vol.* EI
Beese, Melli, PRO *177
Beethoven, Ludwig van, AF 126
Beggar's Opera, Gay and Pepusch, EN 125
Behistun, Rock of, CC 119, 120-121, *136-137
Belalcázar, Sebastián de, EX 99

Belgian Congo, PRO 56, *map* 104
Belgium, AF 11, 88, PRO *map* 102-103; Franks settled in, BE 19, 34; independence, PRO 98, REF 86; *See also index of Vol.* PRO
Belisarius (general), BE 42, BYZ 38, 58
Bell, Alexander Graham, PRO 39
Bellarmine, Robert Cardinal, KIN 103
Bellerophon, CG 36, 104, 183
Belloc, Hilaire, AK 173
Bellini, Gentile, painting by, REN *46-47
Bellini, Giovanni, REN 113, 126; painting by, REN *113: Jacopo, REN 126
Benedict of Nursia. *See* St. Benedict
Benedict XIII, Pope, AF 165-166
Benedictines, AF 34-35, 43, 93, BE 61-64
Benevento, Duchy of, BE *map* 106-107, PRO *map* 100
Benin. *See index of Vol.* AK
Benin sculpture, AK *16, 22, 103, *109-119, 144-145, *147, EX *174
Benjamin of Tudela (writer), BYZ 47
Bentham, Jeremy, EN 109-110, 121; Panopticon, EN *108, 109
Benz, Karl, PRO 46, 47
Beowulf, BE 126, 134
Berbers, AK 20, BE 14, BYZ *map* 57, EI 75, 77, 125, 142, 148, IR 143
Berchtold, Count Leopold von, PRO 172
Berlin-Baghdad railway, PRO 166
Berlin: in 16th Century, EX 100; in 18th Century, EN *9, 11, 141, 142; in 19th to 20th Century, PRO 10, 15, 36, 74, 102, *map* 103, 128, *182
Bernard of Clairvaux, AF 59, 95, 122
Bernhardt, Sarah, PRO 154, *158, *180
Bernini, Gianlorenzo, KIN 77-79, 81, 98; design for Louvre, KIN 77, *120, 121; sculptures by, KIN *76, *79, *80, *85-95, REN *72-73
Bes (god), AE *75, *126
Bessarion, Cardinal, REN *24-25
Bessemer, Henry, PRO 39, 41
Bessemer process, PRO *40, 41
Bestiaries, EI 107, 131; Persian, AE *97, EI *131-139
Bethlen Gabor, Prince, KIN 34, 36
Beust, Count Friedrich Ferdinand von, PRO 167
Bevis of Hamton, Sir, AF 103
Beyeren, Abraham van, painting by, EX *42
Bhagavad Gita, HI 119-121, 136
Bhakti (Hindu worship), HI 121, 122, 165
Bharata (writer), HI 96
Bhuvaneshvar, HI 93, *102-105, 106
Biruni (scientist and traveler), EI 130
Bijapur, HI *map* 160; Kingdom of, HI 163
Bilal (first muezzin), EI 18
Bildungsroman, EN 118
Bimbisara, Magadhan King, HI 74
Bindusara, Mauryan Emperor, HI 75
Bingham, Hiram, AA 137
Biology, CG 142, EN 21, *22-23, *158-159, PRO 30
Biondo, Flavio, REN 22
Birds, The, Aristophanes, CG 123
Bishops: as administrators, BE 58, *chart* 64, 104; in Church organization, AF 31, BE *chart* 64, BYZ 95-96, 100, IR 159; in feudal

system, AF 37-38, BE 149, 150; relations with Frankish kings, BE 58-60; selection of, AF 38, BE 60; simony, AF 38
Bismarck, Prince Otto von. *See index of Vol.* PRO
Bisticci, Vespasiano da, REN 56, 82
Black Death, AF *88-89, 162-163, BYZ 166, EX 17, 32, REF 11, 113, REN 14, 36, 77, 99
Black Noba, AK 38, 41
Black Sea, CG 66, 71, *map* 72, BYZ *map* 164, RR 159; Greek colonization and trade, CG 52, *map* 53, 64, 89, 98, 122, 124; "private lake" of Ottoman Turks, EI *map* 164, RR 157; trade, BE *map* 127, BYZ 31, *map* 32, RR 14, *map* 19
Blaeu, Willem, map by, EX *70-71
Blake, William, sketch by, EN *19
Blanchard, Jean-Pierre, EN 17
Blenheim, Battle of, KIN 171
Blériot, Louis, PRO *176
Block printing. *See* Woodblock printing
Blois (château), REF 149, *151
Blomert, Samuel, AK 104
Blood feuds, BE 83, 154, EI 12
Blum, Léon, PRO 126
Boats: for coastal exploration, EX 75; ironclad, early, EJ 141; iron hulls, introduction of, PRO 13; Marsh Arabs, CC *87, 92, *93-97; river, AE *28, 32-33, *42, 43, AF *83, *84, IR *70-71, RR 48; steam, PRO 13, 30, 38, 52; of Wako pirates, EJ 105;
SAILING: AC *160-161, AE 32, *42, 43, *66-67, AK 42, CC *84, CC *88-89, *122-123, EX 14, *41-42, *48-49, *85-93, IR *154-155; caravel, AK *28, 29, *90, 91, EX 36, 53, carrack, EJ 106, *118, EX *87-89; Chinese junk, EX 14; clipper, PRO 13; curragh, EX 51; dhow, AK *28-29, *91, *94-95, EX 14; merchantmen, 16th to 17th Century, EX 74, *92-93; northern (Clinker-built) vs. southern (carvel built), EX 14, *86-87; Viking knorr, EX *86-87; Viking longship, BE 126, *128-129, 135, *138, *144. *See also index of Vol.* EX, Sailing vessels. *See also* Shipping; Warships
Boccaccio, Giovanni, AF 102, HI 95, IR 164, REN 18, 75, 166
Boccioni, Umberto, PRO 145
Bodhi tree, HI *62, *63, 64
Bodhidharma (Buddhist monk), EJ 83, 101
Bodhisattvas, in sculpture, AC *72-73, *76-77, 172
Bodiam Castle, AF *169
Boeotia. *See index of Vol.* CG
Boer War, PRO 106
Boerhaave, Hermann, EN 55
Boethius (writer), AF 94
Bogolyubsky, Andrei, Grand Prince of Vladimir-Suzdal, RR 28, 37
Bohemia, AF *map* 142, 165, KIN 31, *map* 32, 35; elects Protestant king, KIN 18, 34, REF 168; part of Habsburg Empire, EN 13, KIN 42, 166, REF 168, 170; rebellion in (1618), KIN 32-33, 36, 37; religious strife, KIN 31-32, 37, REF 109, 168
Bohemond, Norman prince, AF 56, BYZ 165
Boileau, Nicolas, KIN 122, 123
Boleyn, Anne, REF 80, 81, 82, 93
Bolivia. *See index of Vol.* AA
Bologna, IR *map* 66, PRO 127, REN *map* 12, 13; Concordat of, REF 86-87; trade center, AF *map* 72; University of, AF 96, 175
Bolotnikov, Ivan, RR 117, 122
Bolsheviks, PRO 125
Bonampak, AA *map* 35; murals, AA *109-117
Bonaventura, AF 99
Boniface VIII, Pope, AF 159-161, REN 14
Bonnard, Pierre, painting by, PRO *65
"Book of Changes" (*I Ching*), AC 103, *table* 149
Book of Common Prayer, KIN 143, REF 82, 83
Book of Ecclesiastes, EN 37
Book of Genesis, CC 103, 154, 160, 161
Book of Good Examples and Good Manners, Certaldo, REN 58
Book of Gospels, BE *56, RR *90
"Book of History" (*Shu Ching*), AC 144-145, *table* 149
Book of Kells, AF 119, BE *108
Book of Kings (Old Testament), CC 61
Book of Kings (Persia), AF 97

H

Habsburg Dynasty, EN 13-14, 165, 166, KIN 16, 20, *24-25, IR 160, REF 13; Austrian, KIN 16, *map* 32, 41; challenged in Bohemia, KIN 31, 32, 33; demise of, PRO 171-172; French relations with, KIN 33, 36, 39-40, 41, 42, 68, 165, 166, 168-172, PRO 99, REF 78; hereditary owners of crown of Holy Roman Empire, KIN 16-17; and Hungary, EN 13, PRO 167, REF 88; intermarriage, KIN 11, 168; lands of, EN 13, KIN *map* 32, 42, 166, PRO 99, 167, REF 14, *map* 17, 170; power of, KIN 16, 20, 38, 39; power checked, KIN 40, 42, REF 170; Spanish, KIN 16, *25, *map* 32, 36, 37, 38, 39, 41, 168, PRO 102, REF 168, 169; in Thirty Years' War, KIN 24, 33-42, REF 120, 168, 169; and War of Spanish Succession, KIN 168-172
Hachiman (war-god), EJ 20, 60, 77
Hadi, Caliph, EI 82
Hadith (Traditions), EI 38-39
Hadrian, Patriarch, RR 161
Hadrian, Roman Emperor, IR *64, 65, 67-68, 110, 166, 182; villas of, IR *24-25, *116
Hadrian's Wall, BE 14, IR *32-33, 64
Hagia Sophia, AF 119; effect on Russians, RR 32, 95; Muslim takeover, EI 147. *For details see index of Vol.* BYZ
Haile Selassie, Emperor of Ethiopia, AK 41, 168
Hakim, Caliph, EI 145
Hakluyt, Richard, EX 13, 79, 124
Halaf culture, CC 16
Hall, Christopher, EX 123
Hallaj (mystic), EI 87
Halley, Edmund, EN 18, KIN 107, *115
Halley's Comet, AC 126, KIN 115
Hallucinogenic potions, AA 76, HI 36
Hals, Frans, EX 46, KIN 83; painting, KIN *80
Hamburg, AF 75, BE *map* 127, PRO *88-89, *map* 103; trade, AF *map* 72, BE 168
Hamburg Dramaturgy, Lessing, EN 144
Hamilton, Alexander, PRO 57
Hamlet, Shakespeare, REF 131, 132
Hammurabi, King of Babylonia. *See index of Vol.* CC
Han Dynasty, BYZ 95. *See also index of Vol.* AC
Han-Shan (poet), AC 155
Han Yü (writer), AC 146, *table* 149
Handbook of Sacred and Secular Learning, The, Cassiodorus, AF 94
Handel, George Frederick, EN 122, 124, 125
Handwriting: Art of, EN *85; overhaul of styles, BE *108, 110
Hanging Gardens of Babylon, CC 62
Hangö, Battle of, RR 160
Hanifs (ascetics), EI 14
Hannibal, IR 38, 107, 127
Hanover, House of, in Britain, EN 32
Hanover, Kingdom of, PRO *map* 103
Hanseatic League, AF *map* 72, 78, RR 60
Harappan (Indus Valley) civilization, CC 158, HI 31, *map* 32, 33-35. *For details see index of Vol.* HI
Haremhab, tomb of, AE 127
Hargreaves, James, EN 103, PRO 14
Hariot, Thomas, EX 120
Harness, invention of, AC 132. *See also* Horsecollar
Harold, King of Saxons, AF 13, 152-153
Harp. *See* Musical instruments
Harsha, Emperor of India, HI 98
Hartley, David, EN 101-102
Harvey, William, EN 15, 104, KIN 105-106, 113
Hasan, Caliph, EI 61
Hasse, Ernst, PRO 106
Hassuna culture, CC 16
Hastings, BE *map* 155; Battle of, AF *152-153
Hathor (goddess), AE 72, 175, *185; temple of, AE *map* 9
Hatshepsut, Queen. *See index of Vol.* AE
Hawkins, John, AK 102-103
Haxthausen, Baron von, RR 138
Haydn, Franz Joseph, AF 126, EN 122, 127, 128, 129, 131, 133, 134
Head deformation, Maya practice, AA 25
Head markings, Indian, HI *59, *120
Headhunting, AC 15
Headless people, myth of, AK 18, EX *map* 9, 163
Hebrews, AE 36, 80, CC *chart* 54; Babylonian captivity, CC 62, 158-159, 160; calendar, CC 35; conquest of Canaan (Palestine), AE 95, CC 158; Kingdom of Israel, CC 59, 61, CG 33; literary influence on Egypt, AE 144; Mesopotamian influence on, CC 126, 159, 160-161; settlement in Egypt, AE 160, 161. *See also* Israel; Jews; Judaism
Hector, CG 35, 41, 43, 183
Hecuba, CG 120
Heian Age. *See index of Vol.* EJ
Heian-kyo. *See index of Vol.* EJ
Heidelberg Castle, REF *156-157
Heike, The Tales of the, EJ 76
Heinrichsbau, Otto, REF 156
Helen of Troy, CG 32, 44, 47, 183
Heliodorus (writer), AK 38
Hellenistic Age, AE 162, CG 160, 163-164, 165, *166-173; kingdoms, CG 163, IR 37
Helvétius, Claude Adrien, EN 109
Henriette, Princess of England, KIN *26
Henry I, King of England, AF 143
Henry II, King of England, AF 100, 143, REF 87, 150
Henry III, King of England, AF 146
Henry III, King of France, REF 128
Henry IV, Holy Roman Emperor, AF 40
Henry IV (of Navarre), King of France, KIN 13, 84, REF 62, 87-88, 128
Henry IV, Shakespeare, AF 53
Henry V, King of England, EX 86
Henry VI, King of England, AF 166
Henry VI, Shakespeare, REF 128
Henry VII, Holy Roman Emperor, REN 14
Henry VII, King of England, EX 99; tomb of, KIN *152-153
Henry VIII, King of England, KIN 141, REF 39, 80-81, *82, 83, 87; Holbein portraits of, REF 147, 148, REN 166
Henry, Joseph, PRO 33-34
Henry the Navigator, Prince, EX 32-33, 34
Hephaestus (god), CG *16-17, 181; temple at Athens, CG *106-107
Hera (goddess), CG *16-17, 44, 180, 181, 182, IR 124
Heraclea, IR *map* 8; battle of, IR 37
Heracles, CC 162, CG 36, *86, 181, 182, 183
Heracles, Euripides, CG 123
Heraclitus (philosopher), CG 59, 185, HI 51
Heraclius, Byzantine Emperor, BYZ 59-60, 80, 81, EI 54, 56, 57
Herberstein, Count Sigmund von, RR 62-63, 134, 138, 140
Herculaneum, EN 96, 97
Hercules and Anteus, Pollaiuolo, REN *110
Herder, Johann Gottfried, EN 141, 146, 147
Herder period, Saharan peoples, AK 19, 46, 48-55
Heresy, AF 32, AK 111, BE 57, BYZ 21, REF 12, 36, 58, 102, 107, 164; Albigensians, AF 95; Arianism, BE 38, 39, 57, 58, 59, BYZ 97; Hus, REF 41; iconoclasm, BYZ 97-98, 142-143; Joan of Arc, AF 166; Luther, REF 40, 41, 42; Monophysitism, BYZ 58; Savonarola, REN 62. *See also* Inquisition
Herjolfsson, Bjarni, EX 12
Hermes (god) CG *16-17, 181, IR 131, of Praxiteles, CG *13
Hermits, AF 33, BYZ 26-27, 98, *101, 174, 175, RR 98; Hindu stage of life, HI 137-138. *See also* Asceticism
Herodian, quoted, IR 142, 143
Herodotus, AE 32, 51, 52, 77, 82, 112, 134, 148, AK 36, 55, CC 141, CG 70, 72, 78, 103, 104, 184, HI 74, RR 16, 20; quoted, AE 11, 29, 31, AK 33, CC 149, CG 71, 73, 74, 75, 76, 77
Heroic tales, CC 114-115, 126, CG 31, 36-38, 182-183. *See also* Epics
Herschel, William, EN 24, 25
Hesiod (poet), BYZ 55, CC 162, CG 33, 180, 185
Hesse, Hans, painting by, REF *162
Hetman (cossack commander), RR 120, 121
Hevelius, Johannes, KIN 107, 114
Hidalgo, EI 143-144
Hidetada. *See index of Vol.* EJ, Tokugawa family
Hideyoshi. *See index of Vol.* EJ, Toyotomi family
Hierarchical order, in church decoration, BYZ 102, 143, 144
Hieratic script, AE 142, 151, 156
Hieratic style of art, BYZ 143, 144, *148-149, *152-153, *155, 156
Hieroglyphic staircase, Copán, AA *48, 49
Hieroglyphs: defined, AE 141; Egyptian, AE 16, 141-142, 148, *149-157, AK 37, CC 119, *165; Maya, AA 25, 40, *48, 49, *118, 126; Meroitic, AK 37; Olmec, AA 40, 126; phonographic (early phonetic), AE *152-155; pictographic, AE 141, *154-155; Zapotec, AA 35
Higashiyama pieces (art collection), EJ 102
High God, African, AK 123-124
Hildegard of Bingen, AF *61, 66, 68
Himalayas, EX 102, HI *map* 8-9, 14, 21; mountain passes, HI *map* 15
Himeji, EJ 148; White Heron castle at, EJ *147-159
Hindi (language), HI 39
Hindu algebra, EI 128, HI 97-98
Hindu art: eroticism in, HI *108, *132-133; motifs in Taj Mahal, HI 143, *146-147; painting, HI *123-133, 164; sculpture, HI *10, 18, *48, 92, 94, 95, *112, *118, *137; temple carvings, HI 102, *103-108, 110
Hindu Kush, CG 161, *map* 163, HI *map* 8-9, 14, 21, 74, 92; mountain passes, EI *76-77, HI *map* 15, *16-17
Hindu temples. *See index of Vol.* HI
Hinduism, EX 167, HI 113-122. *For details see index of Vol.* HI
Hindus, mistaken for Christians by Da Gama, EX 37, 38, 162
Hippocrates of Cos, AE 12, CG 16, 103-104, 185, EI 121, 125; oath of, CG 103
Hippodrome, BYZ 35, 37, 38, *map* 43, 45, *48-49, 79, 114-115, CG 126
Hippomenes (mythological hero), CG 183
"On the Historical Progress of the Human Mind," Turgot, EN 167
Histories, Tacitus, IR 109
Historiography, BYZ 137, EN 85-86, REN 75, 164; ancient, AE 12, 15, CC 36, 126, CG 16, 38, 103, 104, 117, IR 15, 103, 104, 106-107, 109-110; Chinese texts, AC 144-145, *table* 149; Indian lack of reporting, HI 36, 94; and legend, CG 16, 36, 37, IR 15-16, 35; Muslim, AK 79-80, 82-85, EI 110, 130; Russian texts, early, RR 18, 19-20, *21-29
History and Description of Africa, The, Leo Africanus, AK 85
History of Animals, Gesner, REF 165
Hittites, AE 15, 23, 58, 60, 95, CC *chart* 54, 123, 158, CG 33, 35; Empire, AE *map* 57, CC 55, *map* 58, CG 32; language, CC 36
Ho Chart, AC 103
Hobbes, Thomas, EN 38, 101, KIN 12, 55, 56, 106
Hofmann, August von, PRO 31
Hogarth, William. *See index of Vol.* EN
Hohenstaufen Dynasty, AF 12
Hohenzollern Dynasty, EN 13, 14, KIN *28, PRO 102-103, 172
Hohenzollern family, REF 39
Hojo family, EJ 60-61, 64, 75, 104, 146
Hokkaido. *See index of Vol.* EJ
Hokke sect, EJ 82
Holbach, Baron Paul d', EN 37, 53, 55-56, 125
Holbein, Hans, REF 147-148, 149, REN 166; chalk sketch by, REF *146
Holland. *See* Dutch; Netherlands
Hollerith, Herman, PRO 38
Holy Ghost, REF *111; dove symbol, AF 35, BYZ *106; *filioque* dispute, AF 36-37, BYZ 162
Holy Grail, AF 101, 114
Holy Land: Crusades, AF 53-54, 106, 107, EI 145, *map* 146; pilgrimages, AF 55, 59, REN 34
Holy League, KIN 166
Holy Roman Empire, AF *map* 142, BE 112, EN 141, IR 160, REF *map* 17, 55, RR 31; Catholic-Protestant struggle within, KIN 17, 18, *map* 32, 33 (*see also* Reformation, Thirty Years' War); character of, EN 13, 37, BE 104; church and state, AF 19, 37-40, REN 32, *33; Electors system, KIN 16, 18, 31, REF 14; Habsburg Dynasty, KIN 16-17, REF 13-14; Italian interests, AF 19, KIN 16, REN 13, 141; Ottonian revival, AF 19, BE 155, IR 160; paralyzed by Peace of Westphalia (1648), KIN 42, REF 170; Reichstag, KIN 17; termination, BE 112. *See also* Germany
Holy Trinity-St. Sergius Monastery, RR 61, 82, *85, 92, 117
Homage, feudalist ritual, AF *17, BE 151
Homer, BYZ 18, 19, 55, CG 35, 37-38, 103, 164, 185, EI 85, EN 82, IR 103; *Iliad*, BYZ 136, CG 37, 39, 41, 43, 60, 157; *Odyssey*, BYZ 136, CG 37, 39, 47, 60, IR 103; quoted, CG 39, 43, 111, 181
Honduras, Columbus in, AA 9, EX *map* 54, 59. *See also index of Vol.* AA
Honen (Buddhist monk), EJ 81-82
Honnecourt, Villard de, EN 15
Honorius, Western Roman Emperor, BE 15, 37-38, *145, IR 64
Honshu. *See index of Vol.* EJ
Hood, Thomas, PRO 83
Horace, EN 80, 126, IR 15, 16, 75, 84, 105, 106, 107, 111, 116, 164, 183, PRO 144; *Odes*, IR 107; quoted, IR 11, 52, 76, 107, 116
Horites. *See* Hurrians
Horse: domestication of, AK 46; fighting and jousting, AF *108-109, BE *133, BYZ *48-49; first acquaintance of American Indians with, AA 141-142, 148-149; in hunting, AF *111, BE *98, CC *63, *66-67, REN *158-159; introduction to Western Asia, CC 55; medieval knight and, AF *108-109, *151-153; racing, BYZ 114-115, CG 126, 131, PRO *66, REN 149, *154-155; sacrifice, Aryan, HI 39; sources, AC *map* 36, 49, *map* 168, in warfare, AC *48-49, CC 55, 57 (*see also* Cavalry)
Horse period, Saharan peoples, AK 46, 55
Horsecollar and horseshoe invented, BE 94, 166
Horsemanship manuals, EN *161, KIN *104
Horseshoe arch, EI *46; origin, BE 111
Horus (god), AE *70, 72, 73, 74, 163, *184, 185; temple of Edfu, AE *map* 9, 122, *158
Horyuji monastery, EJ 16, *17
Hosios Loukas, monastery church, BYZ 101, *102-103; mosaics, BYZ *101, 102, *104-109, 110, 143, *146-147
Hospitallers (religious order), AF 57
Hospitals, AF 12, 150, BE 88, 166, BYZ 37, 41, 57, 116, EI 124, 127, 147
Houdon, Jean-Antoine, sculpture by, EN *10
"House of Wisdom," EI 121, 122, 129
Housing: African huts, AA *175-177; medieval, AF *80-81, *88, BE *160-161; 19th Century model housing, PRO *76, 77-78, 82; plans of homes, AE *104-105, AK *64-65, CC *33, *81, CG 35, EJ *37, IR 84; reed huts of Marsh Arabs, CC *88-92; tenements, AF *88, BYZ 36, *46, IR 147, 154, PRO 75, 82;
EARLY: adobe, AA 66, 79, 80, CC 16; brick, AF 14, *44, *104-105, CC *33, 79, 85, HI 32; mud, AC 12, AK *65, *68-69, CC 13, 33; sanitary facilities, AC 40, AE 35, AK 107, CG 31, HI 32-33; stone, AA 66, AK 88, BYZ 36, CG 31; wattle-and-daub, AA 18, BE 16; wood, AC 12, 20, AF 89, BE 170, EJ 36. *See also indexes of Vols.* AA, AC, AE, AK, BE, BYZ, CC, EJ, IR, RR
Howells, William, AK 122
Hrabanus Maurus (scholar), BE 109
Hsia Dynasty, AC 79, 80, 102
Hsiao T'ung (poet), AC *table* 149
Hsieh Ho (painter), AC 111, 113, 115, 116, 119, 120, 122
Hsien, AC 63
Hsiung-nu (tribe), AC 49, 166
Hsüan-Tsang (pilgrim-explorer), AC 170
Hua people. *See index of Vol.* AC
Huari (ceremonial center), AA *map* 81, 85
Huascar, Inca Emperor, AA 90, 147, 151, 152
Huayna Capac, Inca Emperor, AA 90, 147
Hudson, Henry, EX 15; expeditions of, EX *map* 121, 124-125
Hugh, Abbot of Cluny, BYZ 164
Hugh Capet, King of France, BE 132
Hugo, Victor, PRO 16, 157, *175

EJ Early Japan; EN Age of Enlightenment; EX Age of Exploration; HI Historic India; IR Imperial Rome; KIN Age of Kings; PRO Age of Progress; REF The Reformation; REN Renaissance; RR Rise of Russia

191

141, EX 17; compared to Hinduism, HI 13, 155, 165-166; conversions to, EI 58, 76, 77, 142, 164, HI 156, 166, RR 17, 56, 57; persecutions of, EI 16-17, REF 85, RR 31; rejection of icons, BYZ 97; *for details see index of Vol.* EI, Religion;
TRADE: BE *map* 127, 128, EI 83-84, 97, 148, EX 18, 32, 35, 37-38; African, AK *78, 81, 84, 87, *89, 170, EI 83, 97, 141; with China, AC *map* 168, EI 83, 97. *See also* Arabs; Mosques; Saracens; Turks
Islamic art, EI 101-110, *111-119; arabesque, EI 12, *86, 105-106, 107, HI *146-147, 150, miniatures, AF *97, EI *21-29, 107-108, *140, *172, *174, *176, *178. *See also* Architecture, Islamic; Persian art; *and for details see index of Vol.* EI, Art; Decoration
Islamic literature, AK 84, EI 12, 85, 101, 108-110. *For details see index of Vol.* EI, Literature
Isma'il I, Khedive of Egypt, EI 169
Isocrates (orator), CG 143, 184
Israel, Kingdom of, CC 59, 61, CG 33, HI 51; Mosaic law, CG 13. *See also* Hebrews
Issus, battle of, CG 160, *map* 163
Isthmian Games, CG 125, 134
Italian language, REN 18, 32, 166, 167-168
Italian League, REN 12
Italian literature, AF 102, REN 18, 164, 166-168; behavior books, REN 56-57, 58, 59, 168
Italian music, REN 168-170; Baroque, EN 122; opera, EN 125, *136, KIN 84, PRO 146, REN 170
Italian painting, AF 126, REN 11-13. *See also* Painting, Renaissance
Italian Wars, REN 139-144
Italic tribes, IR 36, *map* 37, 122
Italy, Arabs in, AF 18; banking families, AF 78, REN 75, 80, *89; Byzantine possessions in, BE 42, BYZ 22, *map* 57, 58, *map* 61, 162, 163, *map* 164; Catholic Church in, AF 33-34, BE 61-64, KIN 12, REF 103, REN 60-62; Charlemagne's warfare in, BE 102; church architecture, AF *map* 9, BYZ *22-23, 40, 140 (*see also* Architecture, Renaissance); colonies of, PRO *map* 104-105, 106; contributions to exploration, EX 19; early history, IR 16, 35; education, BE 165, REN 15-17, 53-55, PRO 82; emergence of Rome, CG 141, IR 16, 35, 36-37; English tourists in, EN 87, *map* 88-89, *92-99; Etruscan domination, IR 35-36; flag, PRO *111; Greek colonization and trade, CG 52, *map* 53, 124, IR 35, *map* 37; Hannibal in, IR 38; Holy Roman Empire and, AF 19, KIN 16, REF *map* 17, REN 13, 141; humanism, REF 36-37, REN 13, 15-16, 18-19, 21, 22, 161-164, industrial *vs.* agrarian regions, PRO 50; Inquisition, REF 107, 164; law court, AF *90; nationalist movement, PRO 97, 98, 99-101, *107-115; Normans in, BE *map* 127, 172, BYZ 62, 162; political thought, EN 56, REN 147-148, 168; and pre-World War I politics, PRO 168, 170; railroads, PRO 51; Renaissance, BYZ 11 12, EN 16, EX 17 18, *entire Vol.* REN, REF 18, 151, *152-153; Roman roads, IR *map* 66; slavery and slave trade, EX 165-166; socialist movement, PRO 80; southern, empire of Dionysius, CG 143; Spanish holdings in, KIN *map* 32, 169, 170, REN 14, 140, 142, 143; strike of 1904, PRO 121; urban migration, PRO 74;
BARBARIANS IN: AF 14, BE *map* 12, 25, BYZ 11, IR 146, *map* 158; Huns, BE 40; Lombards, BE 42, 61, 62, 66, 102, *map* 106-107, BYZ *map* 59; Magyars, BE 133; Ostrogoths, BE *map* 34, 41-42, BYZ 56, *map* 57, 58, IR *map* 158; Vandals, BE 40, IR 146, *map* 158; Visigoths, BE *map* 12, 20, 36 37, IR 146, *map* 158;
CITIES OF: 11th Century, BE 168, 172, BYZ 162; Roman Empire, IR *map* 37, 40, 41, *map* 66; *see also* City-states, Italian;
POLITICAL DEVELOPMENT: communes, AF 75, REN 33, 38; feudalism lacking, BE 155; fragmentation, AF *map* 142, PRO 99, REN *map* 12, 33; kingdom of 888, BE *map* 107; republican government, REN 33, 35-36, 38, 77, 78; resistance to monarchy, AF 141, 147 148; revolution of 1848, PRO 99, 108; revolution of 1860, PRO 97, 100-101; suffrage, PRO 101; unification, PRO 98, 99, *map* 100, 101, *114-117;
TRADE: AF *map* 72, BE 167-168, EX 19, 38; fairs, AF 82; maritime republics and city-states, AK 84, 85, BE 168, 169, BYZ 62, 162, 166, EI 145, EX 35, 79, 170, REN 14, 34, 35, 36, 80-81; protectionism, PRO 57.
See also Papal States
Ivan (co-Czar of Peter), RR 131, 156
Ivan I, "Kalita," Grand Prince, RR 58, *127, 167
Ivan III (the Great), Czar, BYZ 170, RR 59-64, *128. *For details see index of Vol.* RR
Ivan IV (the Terrible), Czar, REN *167. *See also index of Vol.* RR
Ivory: artifacts, EI 107, *114; carvings, AF *35, *108-109, *113, 120, BE *164, BYZ *15, *35, *39, *129, 135, 141, *142, 144, 145, *150, *152-153, CG 99, 114, EI 12, *83, EX *175; trade, AF *map* 72, AK 29, 42, *86, 87, 88, 91, 94, 102, BYZ 31, *map* 32, CG 89, EI 84, EX 32, HI 28, 32, PRO 56
Iwan (architecture), EI 103-104

J

Jabir ibn Hayyan, EI 127-128
Jackman, Charles, EX 79, 124
Jade, AC 12; lapidary methods, AA 123-124; Olmec figurines, AA *19, 31, 123-124, ornaments, AA *8, 25, 61, 62, 67, 123-124, *177, AC *80; sources, AC 166, 167, *map* 168
Jaguar cult. *See index of Vol.* AA
Jahangir, Mughal Emperor, HI 43, *154, 162-163
Jainism. *See index of Vol.* HI
Jalal al Din Ruomi (Sufi poet), EI 110
Jamal al-Din al-Afghani, EI 169
James I, King of England, KIN 33, 34, 38, 139-142, REF 64, 167
James II, King of England, EN 13, 32 KIN 26, *27, 139, 148, 167
Janissaries, BYZ 167-168, 170, EI 166, 167; massacre of, EI 169
Jansenists, EN 35, 36
Japan, AF 97, *entire Vol.* EJ, EX 75; Chinese influences on, AC 150, 165, 170, EJ 11, 14-20, 33, 34, 103; Europeans in, EJ 106, 115-124, 139-140, *map* 142-143, *160, 162, 163, EN *145, EX 55, 56, 167-168, *172-173, REF *115; Europeans expelled, EJ 145-146, 162, 164; Portuguese exploration and mapping of, EX 104; 17th to 19th Centuries, EN 145; spread of Buddhism to, AC 170, EJ 15, HI 11, 61; at time of Renaissance, EX 11, 20, 100; war with Russia, PRO 123, 125
Japanese art. *See* Architecture, Japanese; Painting, Japanese; *and see index of Vol.* EJ, Arts
Japanese literature: drama, EJ 103, 168, *169-181; Kamakura war tales, EJ 76-77; novel, AF 97, EJ 34, 38-39, *43-53, 168; poetry, EJ 34-36, 84, 125-135
Jarmo, CC *map* 9, 13, 15, 16
Jason, CC 162, CG 183
Java, EI 148, EX *map* 138; Dutch in, EX *48-49, 141, PRO *map* 105; mapping of, EX 103; native dance, EX *169; slaves from, AC 179; trade, EI 141, 148, EJ 106
Jefferson, Thomas, EN 36, 38, 131, IR 161
Jenkinson, Anthony, EX 120-121
Jerusalem, BYZ 18, *map* 32, *map* 57, 59, CC 35; Assyrian conquest, CC 61; Babylonian conquest and destruction of (586 B.C.), CC *map* 59, 62, 159; believed center of world, EX 31, 60; Church of the Holy Sepulcher, EI 57, 145; Crusaders' Kingdom of, AF 57, BYZ 165, EI *map* 146; Crusaders in, AF 56, 107; dispersal of Jews from, IR 126, RR 31; Dome of the Rock, EI 102; Libyan plunder of Temple of Solomon (930 B.C.), AE 160; Muslims in, AF 53, 59, 60, BYZ *map* 59, 165, EI *map* 55, 57, *map* 164; Patriarch, RR 99; Persians in, BYZ *map* 59, EI 54; uprising of 66 A.D., IR 126
Jesuits, EN 36, 38, 166, REF *100, 104-106, 107, 112, *114, RR 116; in England, KIN 140; in France, EN 34, 35; in Japan, EJ 115, 116-124, 139-140, *map* 142-143, *160, 162, 163, EX 167, REF *115; Japanese expulsion decrees, EJ 145-146, 162, 164; landmarks in Rome, REF *106; role in education, REF 105-106, 109
Jesus Christ. communion, AF 164, REF 41, 57, RR 92; divine *vs.* human nature, BYZ 58, 97; expected Second Coming, BYZ 16; *filioque* dispute, AF 36-37, BYZ 162; honored in Islam, EI 25, 32; quotations, AF 31, BYZ 26, 94; regarded as incarnation of Vishnu, HI 115; rejection of secular authority by, BYZ 94; relics of, BYZ *24-25, 34; True Cross of, BYZ 17, 25, 59;
DEPICTIONS OF: AF *10, *64-65, *69, 119, *128-133, AK *41, *138, BE *108, BYZ 102, *104-111, *129, 141, 143, 144, *145, *148-149, 151, *153, *155-157, *159, IR *167-174, REF *50-51, *110-111, *135, REN *15, *52, *70, 94, 100, 104-105, *108-109, *111, *114-116; in catacomb art, BYZ 141, IR *167, *170; on coins, BYZ 24, 80; Germanic art, AF *13, BE *60, *72, 73, *78-79; in icons, BYZ 143, RR *108-109
Jews, BE 101, BYZ 16, CC 158, EI 167, EN 166, REN 34; dispersal of, IR 126, RR 31; Inquisition and, REF 85; massacred by Crusaders, AF 56, EI 146; merchants and moneylenders, AF 77, AK 85, BE 105; Muslim policies toward, AK 85, EI 19, 57, 58, 102; in Muslim Spain, EI 142; reject Muhammad, EI 17-18; Voltaire on, EN 39. *See also* Anti-Semitism; Hebrews; Israel; Judaism
Jiménez de Cisneros, Francisco, Archbishop of Toledo, REF 102-103
Jimmu Tenno (half-legendary Japanese emperor), EJ 14
Jina (*or* Mahavira, religious leader), HI 55, *56, 57
Jingoism, PRO 169
Ji-samurai, EJ 100, 104
Joan of Arc, AF 156, *165, 166
Job, Sumerian prototype of, CC 105, 109 *117
Jocasta (mother of Oedipus), CG 182
Jodo sect, EJ 81
John I, King of Portugal, EX 32
John II Comnenus, Byzantine Emperor, BYZ 80, 116, 162, 165
John II, King of Portugal, EX 34, 35, 36, 53, 79
John IV, Byzantine Emperor, BYZ 76
John V, Byzantine Emperor, BYZ 166, 167
John V, King of Portugal, EN 21
John VI Cantacuzene, Byzantine Emperor, BYZ *74, 137
John VII, Pope, AF 38
John Frederick the Magnanimous, Elector of Saxony, REF *54
John Lackland, King of England, AF 144-145, AK 60-61
John of Ephesus, AK 39-40
John Sobieski, King of Poland, KIN 166
Johnson, Samuel, EN 78, 79, 82, 95, 107
Jojuen garden, EJ *94-95
Jonson, Ben, REF 91, 131, 132
José, Amaro, AK 170, 171
Joseph, in Egypt, AE 31
Joseph II, Holy Roman Emperor, EN 166
Joseph of Arimathea, AF 114
Joseph of Volokolamsk, Abbot, RR 99, 100
Josephus (Jewish historian), IR 89
Journals, EN 56, 79-80
Journeymen, AF 77, 78
Joyce, James, PRO 148
Judaea, IR *map* 67; insurrection of 66-70 A.D., IR 62, 126
Judah (part of Israel), CC 61
Judaism, AC 101, CC 159, EI 14; comparisons with Indian thought, HI 13, 53; icons rejected, BYZ 97; influence of Mesopotamian religion on, CC 35, 159, 160-161; Khazars, BYZ 163, RR 16, 31-32; in Roman Empire, BYZ 16, IR *126. *See also* Hebrews; Jews
Judges, AA 102, BYZ 117, EI *93, IR 40, *161, 165; aristocracy as, AF 17, 144, BE 82, 86, IR 42, RR 139; England, AF 144, 146; France, AF 146
Judicial combat, AF 20, 75, BE 86-87
Jugurtha (African chieftain), IR 40, 41
Jujitsu, EJ 68
Julaha (Muslim "caste"), HI 166
Julia (daughter of Caesar), IR 42-43
Julian (missionary), AK 39-40, 42
Julian the Apostate, Roman Emperor, BYZ 55, IR *64, 128
Julian calendar, AE 146, 148, IR 44, REF 165
Julianus, Roman Emperor, BYZ 13-14
Julius II, Pope, REF 18, 19, 38, REN 18, 60, 73, 126, 143
Jundishapur, Persia, medical school, EI 122, 123, 124, 127
Jung, Hermann, PRO 81
Juno (goddess), IR 123, 124
Jupiter, BYZ 15, IR 11, *58, 122, 123, 124
Jupiter Amon (god), AE 185
Juries, CG *108, AF 17, 144, 146, EN 105, 109, IR 40; ballots, CG *99
Justin I, Eastern Roman Emperor, BYZ 56, IR 64
Justinian I, the Great, Byzantine Emperor, AF 119, AK 40, 42, BE 42, CG 173, EI 147, IR 64, 182. *For details see index of Vol.* BYZ
Justinian Code of Law, AF 147, 148, BYZ 20-21, 58, 117, CG 13, IR 146, 159, 166; frontispiece, BYZ *21
Jutes, AF 14, BE *map* 34; migration, BE *map* 12, 34; territory in England, BE 35 *map* 155
Juvenal (writer), BE 110, IR 14-15, 108-109; quoted, IR 25, 82, 85, 109, 154

K

Ka (spirit), AE *81
Kaaba. *See index of Vol.* EI
Kabuki, EJ 168, *169-181
Kali (Hindu goddess), HI 114, 116, 136
Kalidasa (poet and dramatist), HI 97
Kama (Hindu goal of life), HI 138
Kamakura and Kamakura Age, Japan. *See index of Vol.* EJ
Kamasutra (book), HI 139, 140
Kammu, Japanese Emperor, EJ 20, 31
Kanem-Bornu, Kingdom of, AK *map* 81
Kanishka, King of the Kushans, HI 92
Kanissa'ai, King of Ghana, AK 80
Kansa (demon), HI 126, 130, *131
Kant, Immanuel. *See index of Vol.* EN
Kapital, Das, Marx, PRO 16, REN 168
Kara Mustafa, Grand Vizier, KIN 166
Karl August, Duke of Weimar, EN 141, 150
Karlowitz, Treaty of, EI 167, KIN 166
Karma, concept of, EJ 80, HI 13, 40, 54, 114, 122; Buddha and, HI 60; defined, HI 54; in Jainism, HI 55-56
Karnak. *See index of Vol.* AE
Kashan pottery, EI 116, *117, *119
Kassite Babylonia, CC 54-55, 56, *map* 58
Kautilya (Indian official), HI 76
Kazembe, Mwata, AK 171-172
Kazimov, principality of, RR 60
Keats, John, IR 164
Kells, High Cross of, BE *78-79
Kemal Ataturk, EI 170
Keng Shou ch'ang (astronomer), AC 127
Kenoticism, RR 96, 98, 102
Kent, Kingdom of, BE 35, 63, *map* 155
Kepler, Johannes, EN 15, KIN 37, 39, 98, 99-100, 101, 102, REF 166
Keyboard instruments. *See* Musical instruments
Khadija (first wife of Muhammad), EI 14, 15, 16, 17, 20, *23
Khafre (Chephren), King of Egypt, AE 18, 52; pyramid of, AE *map* 8, *20-21, 52, 118
Khajuraho, HI *map* 93; Hindu temples at, HI *108-109
Khalid ibn al-Walid, EI 56, 57
Khalid ibn Barmak, EI 82
Khanates, RR *map* 59, 60, 62, 80, 84
Kharijites (Seceders), EI 61, 63
Khazars, BYZ 163, RR *map* 12, 16-17, 31
Khmelnitsky, Bogdan, RR 121, *130
Khosrau I, King of Persia, EI 59
Khufu (Cheops), King of Egypt, AE 52, 129, 136, 138; pyramid of, AE *map* 8, *21, 52, 118, 129, 130, *132-139
Khwarizmi (mathematician), EI 129
Kiev. Byzantine influence on church architecture, BYZ 40; Christianization, BYZ 61, RR 20, 21, 37, 95, 97; Monastery of the

EJ *Early Japan;* EN *Age of Enlightenment;* EX *Age of Exploration;* HI *Historic India;* IR *Imperial Rome;* KIN *Age of Kings;* PRO *Age of Progress;* REF *The Reformation;* REN *Renaissance;* RR *Rise of Russia* 193

Caves, RR 34, 95; Viking trading port at, BE *map* 127, 128. *For details see index of Vol.* RR
Kievan Russia. *See index of Vol.* RR
Kilwa. *See index of Vol.* AK
King James Bible, REF *124, 125
King of Heaven (sculpture), AC *68-69
Kings and kingship, AC 79-88, AE 93-94, AF 12, AK 34, 111, CC *168-169, CG 49, KIN *20-21, IR 35-36, 121, 122; birth of institution of, AC 79-80, CC 35, 159, 168; decline, CC 168; divine sanction (and heredity), AC 79, 80, 84, 86, AE 94, CC 47, 80, 159-160, 168; dynastic changes under Mandate of Heaven, AC 79, 81, 83, 85, 88; Germanic, BE 16, 33-34, 66; elective, CC 47, 80; tribal *vs.* sanctified, BE 66. *See also* Monarchy; *and see indexes of Vols.* AC, Son of Heaven, *and* AE, Pharaoh
Kingsley, Charles, PRO 86
Kinship, AK 60, 63, 65, 66, 106, BE 81
Kircher, Athanasius, EX 166
Kirwan, Daniel, PRO 73, 75
Kish, CC 33, 35, 36, *map* 38; excavations, CC 12, 142, 144
Kiyomori. *See index of Vol.* EJ, Taira family
Klimt, Gustav, PRO 145, 161, *179; painting by, PRO *161
Klinger, Friedrich, EN 147
Kluchevsky, V. O., RR 37, 38, 119
Knapton, Ernest, PRO 104-105
Knights and knighthood, AF 17, 18, *103-115, BE 150, 152-153; armor, AF 56, *151-155, BE *149; chivalry, AF 103, 105, 114, BE 154, EI 144, 146; Crusaders, AF 56-57, *106-107; Rajputs compared to, HI 98; samurai compared to, EJ 57, 65, 68
Knights Hospitallers, AF 57
Knights of the Sword, RR 81
Knights Templars, AF 57, 107
Knives, ceremonial, AA 39, 61, 67, *95, AE *172-173
Knorr (ship), EX *86-87
Knox, John, REF 62-64
Knudstad, James E., CC *20-21
Ko Hung (alchemist), AC 129
Koken, Japanese Empress, EJ 20
Koldewey, Robert, CC 147, 148
Kollwitz, Käthe, drawings by, PRO *83-91
Königgrätz, battle of, PRO 102, *map* 103
Konarak, HI *map* 8-9; Temple of the Sun, HI *106-107
Kongo, Kingdom of, AK 101, 105, *171
Koran. *See index of Vol.* EI
Korea, EJ *map* 142; Buddhism, EJ 14-15, HI 61; Chinese influences on, AC 150, 165; Han colony, AC 17; Japanese invasions of (1592, 1597), EJ 161-162; kingdom of Paikche in, EJ 14-15; Mongol invasion of, EJ 61, RR 39; T'ang conquests of, AC 20, *map* 86; trade, AC *map* 169
Korongo (Nuba tribe), AK 67
Koryaks (tribe), RR *map* 162
Kossovo, battle of, BYZ *map* 164, 167
Kossuth, Louis, PRO 99
Kota people, AK 144, 145, 148
Kotoku, Japanese Emperor, EJ 15, 17, 41
Kotzebue, August von, EN *148
Krater, CG *56
Kremlin, EX *100. *For details see index of Vol.* RR
Krishna (Hindu god). *See index of Vol.* HI
Krivichians (tribe), RR *map* 12, 19
Krupp, Alfred, PRO 15
Krupp, Fritz, PRO 57
Krupp family, PRO 41
Kshatriya class, HI 119, 136, 137, 138, 139
Kuan-hsiu (painter and poet), AC 110
Kuan-yin (Buddhist deity), AC *116
Kublai Khan, AF 78, EI 148, EJ 61, 62, 64, EX 32, 100, *103, RR 39
Kucha and Kuchans, AC *map* 168, 172
Kufic script, EI *39, *109, *152-153
Kulikovo Pole (Snipes' Field), Battle of, RR 58, *map* 59, 61, 98
Kumaragupta, Gupta Emperor, HI 98
Kuo P'u (poet), AC 157
Kuru tribe, HI 118
Kush, Kingdom of. *See index of Vol.* AK
Kushans, HI 91; empire, HI 92, *map* 93
Kylix, CG *56
Kyoto. *See index of Vol.* EI
Kyushu. *See index of Vol.* EI

L

Labná, AA *map* 35, *50,51
Labor, EN *162-163, PRO 50, 56, 74, 76-77, 124; Adam Smith on, EN 105-106; child, EN 78-79, 107, PRO 74, 77, 78, 84, 86; combinations, EN 107-108; conscription, AA 34, 107, 134, AE 13, 34, 44, 51, 129, 134, EJ 17-18; construction, AA 34, 42, 107, 134, AE 13, 31, 34, 44, 52, 101, 129, 134, IR 162; demonstration, PRO *92-93; dislocation by mechanization, EN 108; division of, EN 101, *diagram* 105, 106; farm, AE 40, 44, 102, AF *21-29, CG 60, EN 107, 108, IR 86, 146, 149, PRO *84-85; legislation, PRO 77-79, 81, 93, 94, 167; mining, AA 164, 168, CG 94-95; planning, Inca Empire, AA 106-107; respectability of, attitudes, CG 87, IR 13; seasonal division, Egypt, AE 31; Statute of Laborers (England), AF 163; strikes, PRO 77, 78, 93, 121, 123, 124-125; unions, EN 107-108, PRO 77, 78, 81, 93, 94, 121; wages, EN 105-106, PRO 10, 74, 77, 79, 82, 84, 94; women, PRO 77; working conditions and hours, EN 78-79, 107, PRO 10, 76, 84, 94, 123. *See also* Serfdom; Slavery and slaves; *and see index of Vol.* PRO, Working class
Lacedaemonians, CG 76
Lactantius, quoted, IR 145
Lade, battle at, CG 70, *map* 72
La Fontaine, Jean de, EN 142, HI 95, KIN 122
Lagash. *See index of Vol.* CC
Laharpe, Jean-François de, EN *151
Laissez-faire, EN 104, 108, PRO 76, 80
Lakshmi (Hindu goddess), HI 116, 117
Lalibela (king *and* town). *See index of Vol.* AK
Lalique, René, PRO 154, 155
La Mettrie, Julian Offroy de, EN 55
Land: as base of wealth, replaced by money, AF 159-160, REF 65, REN 38; reclamation, BE 166, 167, EJ 60; use, Inca planning, AA 106, 121;
REFORMS: Akbar, HI 162; Peisistratus, CG 60; proposals of Gracchi, IR 40; Taika, EJ 17, 18, 41;
TENURE AND RIGHTS: Byzantine aristocracy, BYZ 62, 162; colonial, papal arbitration, EX 34, 56, *map* 57; colonial, taking possession, EX 34, 84; feudal grants (fiefs), AF 16, 103, BE 148, 149-150, 151, 152, EJ 60, 61, 64; Kievan Russia, RR 35; Mesopotamia, CC 82; peasants and, AE 102, AF 21, BE 152, 153, 160, BYZ 62, 162, IR 146, 149, RR 79, 119; Roman *coloni*, IR 146; Roman "thirds" system, BE 38
Landseer, Sir Edwin, PRO 139-140
Landucci, Luca, REN 60
Langland, William, AF 101
Languages: African, AK 21, 29, 42, 138; Carolingian Empire, BE 106; Indian, HI 34, 39, 58, 92, 95, 96, 165; Mesopotamian, CC 32-33, 36, 52, 120-125; monosyllabic *vs.* polysyllabic, AC 142, 150, EJ 34; Semitic, CC 52, 121, 122; vernacular, use of, BE 165, HI 60, 165, REF 44, 123, 125, 132, REN 18, 166, 167-168;
COMPARISONS: Chinese and Japanese, EJ 34; Chinese and Western, AC 142-143; Sanskrit and Indo-European, HI *table* 39. *See also* Writing systems; *and individual languages*
Lao Tsu (Taoist book), AC 62, 64, 65
Lao Tzu (Chinese philosopher), CG 77
Lares (deities), IR 121, *122
Larsa, CC *map* 38, 52, 53, *map* 58
Las Casas, Bartolomé de, EX 28
Lasso, Orlando di, REN 169
Lateen-rigger, EX 14, 36, *74, *86-87
Lateran Council, Fifth, REN 62
Latin alphabet, AE 148, CG 36, 38
Latin Empire of Constantinople, BYZ 166
Latin Kingdom of Jerusalem, AF 57, 59, EI *map* 146
Latin language, BE 106, 109, IR 103, 104, REN 167; Bible translations, IR 110, REF 124; in Byzantium, BYZ 80, 135, IR 159; comparisons with Sanskrit, HI *table* 39; Greek works translated, IR 103; heritage of, IR 110, 157, 164; humanists' use of, REN 21; in Roman Catholic Church, AF 13, *124, IR 159; *vs.* vernacular, REF 44, 123, 125, 132, REN 18, 166, 167-168
Latin League, CG 141
Latin literature. *See* Roman literature
Latin right, IR 61, 63, 68
Latins (tribe), IR 16, *map* 37
Latitudinarians, EN 32, 33, 34, 36
Launcelot, Sir, AF 101, 114
La Vallière, Mlle. de, KIN *23
Lavater, Johann, EN *68, 69
La Venta, AA *map* 16, 32-34
Lavoisier, Antoine, EN 26, *27, PRO 37
Law, John, EN *74
Law: African, AK 82-83, 104, 171, 172; blood feuds, BE 83, 154; case-law, CC 82, IR 166; civil, AF 144, BYZ 21, CG 50, IR 165, 166; Code of Hammurabi, CC 40, 52, 53, 56, 82, 126, *170; Code of Ur-Nammu, CC 40, 82, 122; codifications, AF 148, BE 82-83, CC 40, 82, 163, CG 38, 50, IR 146, 166, RR 35, 119-120 (*see also* Justinian Code of Law); common, IR 166; concept of justice, AE 94-95, AK 82-83, CG 13, IR 165, 166; constitutional, AF 143-146 (*see also* Constitutions); criminal, AA *157, AF 75-76, 90, 144, 148, BE 84, 87, BYZ 21, 117, CC 82, CG 50, EN 56, 59, 60, 78, 109, 115, 165, 168, IR 165, REF 12, 35, RR 35 (*see also* Capital punishment; Debtors); custom and tradition in, AF 147, BE 81, 82, 83; Draconian Code, CG 50; due process, AF 146, CC 163; early medieval, AF 20, BE 82-88, 104, 171; family, AF 75, BYZ 21, 116, 117, IR 36, 73, 80-81, 165; feudal, AF 17, BE 84, 153; Greek, character and influence of, CG 13, 50, 168; humanitarian gains, EN 78, 109, 165, 168; inheritance, AF 75, 148, BYZ 21; Islamic, EI 170 (*see also index of Vol.* EI, Koran); labor, AF 163, PRO 77-79, 81, 93, 94, 167; Legalists of China, AC 83; medieval towns, AF 75-76, *90-91; mercantile, AF 82; Mesopotamian legacy, CC 160, *170-171; Mosaic Code, CC 163, CG 13; Napoleonic Code, CC 163, IR 166; reform, EN 55, 109, 166; reform demands, EN 11, 56, 59, 60, 143; role of Church in, BE *80, 87, 88; Roman, *see* Roman law; Salic, BE 84; Talmud, CC 160; tribal, AK 65-66, BE 82-83. *See also* Civil liberties; Courts of law; Judges; Juries; Trial
Law schools, AF 147, 175, REN 15
Laws, The Spirit of the, Montesquieu, EN 57-59, 102-103, 166
Laws of Manu, HI 136-137, 138
Lay investiture, AF 38, 39-40
League of Augsburg, EN 12, KIN 165
League of Corinth, CG 144, 157, 158, 163
League of the Greeks, CG *map* 72, 74, 78; disunity, CG 74, 76, 77, 78
Lebanon, CC 56, 62, EI *67; trade, AE 34, 128
Lecky, William, quoted, BYZ 13
Lecomte, Claude, PRO *133
Lefèvre d'Etaples, Jacques, REF 37, 44, REN 163
Legend, and history, CG 16, 36, 37, IR 15-16, 35. *See also indexes of Vols.* AA, CG, IR, Legends; *and indexes of Vols.* AC, AE, BE, CC, CG, EJ, EX, HI, Myths
Leibniz, Gottfried Wilhelm, EN 142, 143, KIN 172, RR 156, 161
Le Kain, Henri Louis, EN *46-47
Lely, Sir Peter, KIN 109
Lenaean festival, CG 101, 153
Lenclos, Ninon de, EN 37
Lenin, Vladimir Ilyich, PRO 120, 123, 125
Leo I, Eastern Roman Emperor, BYZ 34, IR 64
Leo I, the Great, Pope, AF 32, REN 127
Leo III, Byzantine Emperor, BYZ 60, 97
Leo III, Pope, AF 19, 37, BE 102, 103-104, BYZ 60
Leo V, Byzantine Emperor, BYZ 76, 97
Leo VI, the Wise, Byzantine Emperor, BYZ 61, *72-73, RR 20
Leo X, Pope, AK 17, 84, 86, REF 38-39, 40, 42, 56, 112, REN 22, 60
Leo XIII, Pope, PRO 80-81
Leo Africanus. *See index of Vol.* AK
Leonardo da Vinci, AF 166, REF 153, 154, REN 84, 97, 98, 99, 102-103, 122, 124, *129, 146, 169; anatomical studies, EN 15, REN *130-131, *133; drawings by, REN 104, *129-137; paintings by, REN 104-105, *115; scientific studies, PRO 39, REF 165, REN 20, 129, *132, *134-137. *For details see index of Vol.* REN
Leonidas, King of Sparta, CG 75-76, 184
Leopardi, Alessandro, sculpture by, REN *113
Leopold I, Holy Roman Emperor, EN 13, KIN *10, 20, *21, 165-166, 168-170
Leopold II, King of Belgium, PRO 56
Leopold, Grand Duke of Tuscany, PRO 114
Leroy-Beaulieu (historian), RR 135
Lesbos. *See index of Vol.* CG
Lesser Vehicle (Buddhist sect), HI 60
Lessing, Gotthold Ephraim, EN 57, 84, 121, 143-145, 150
Le Tellier, Michel, KIN 57-58
Le Vau, Louis, KIN 121
Leviathan, Hobbes, KIN 12, 55, 56, 106
Lexicography, AC 142
Lhote, Henri, AK 43, 44, 45, 49, 51, 56
Li Ho (poet), AC *table* 149
Li Lung-chi, T'ang Emperor, AC 65-66, 87, 88, 105, 107, 141, 165, 182
Li Po (poet), AC 38, *table* 149
Li Shang-yin (poet), AC *table* 149
Li Shao-chün (alchemist), AC 128-129
Li Te-yü (minister-gardener), AC 110, 141
Li Tsu, T'ang Emperor, AC 88
Liberal arts, AF 94, BE 109, REN 123
Liberalism, EN 56-64, 168, IR 39, PRO 77, 97-98, 102, 104; *laissez-faire*, PRO 76, 80
Libraries, AK 84, IR 83, REN 16, 24; monastic, AF 34, BE 110; public, EN 79, *82, IR 65, 83, *87, PRO 38, RR 163; university, AF *174, 175
Libyan Dynasty, AE 159-160
Libya and Libyans, AF 100, PRO *map* 104; nomads, AK 35; plunder of Temple of Solomon (930 B.C.), AE 160; settlement of, AK 35; wars with Egypt, AE *61, *68-69
Lichtenberg, Georg Christoph, EN 102
Licinius, Roman Co-Emperor, BYZ 18
Liebknecht, Wilhelm, PRO 79
Life expectancy, PRO 75, 90; explorers, EX 15; medieval peasants, AF 21
Life-Force, religious concept, AK 123, 145, 146, 151
Life forms, concept of interchangeability of, AC 62, 128
Lillo, George, EN 84
Lincoln, Abraham, PRO 144
Lindos, CG *map* 9; temple at, CG *21
Linear B script, CG 32
Linen, AE 34, 143, BE *97, 167, BYZ *map* 32, CC 145, EI 83, PRO 14
Linnaeus, Carl, EN 22
Lion of Judah. *See* Solomonid dynasty
Lippi, Filippino, REN 127; painting by, REN *118
Lippi, Fra Filippo, REN 75, 84, 122, 128
Lisbon, AF *map* 142; Moors ousted from, AF 59; role in exploration, EX 36, *map* 37, 38, 75, 103; trade, AF *map* 72, EX 118, 170, REF 166; Viking raids on, BE *map* 127
List, George Friedrich, PRO 51
Lister, Joseph, PRO 82
Liszt, Franz, PRO *145
Literacy, AK 82, 103, 107, 108, EJ 168, REF 84, RR 138; rise of, AF 19, EN 79, PRO 38, 50, 82, 169, 172, REF 13, 123, 132, 176
Literature, AF 99-102, EN 79-86, 141-150, KIN 122-125, PRO 139, 143-146, 148, REF 123-132, REN 163-168, 170; classical Greco-Roman, preservation of, AF 34, BE 110, BYZ 11-12, 135-136, IR 159-160, REN 16, 21, 54; essay, REF 126-127; history writing, *see* Historiography; monastic, BYZ 59; Naturalism, PRO 143-144, 145; oral memorized, AA 58, 125-126, AK 150, CG 38; of *philosophes*, EN 39-40, 53-54, 57-58, 62-64, 77, 78, 85-86; popularization of, EN 79-80, 81, *82, 84, REF 132; Realism, PRO 143, 145; rulers as patrons of, EN 12, 141, HI 162, KIN 73, 121-122, 123, 125, REN 163; short story, REN 166; Symbolism, PRO 145-146, 148; vernacular, BE 165, HI 165, REF 123, 125, 132, REN 18, 166, 167-168; "wisdom," AE 36, 86, 144, CC 128, 162. *See also* Drama; Epic; Novel; Poetry; Satire; *and see individual literatures, e.g.* Chinese literature; English literature; Islamic literature; Medieval literature; *etc.*
Lithuania and Lithuanians. *See index of Vol.* RR

194 AA *Ancient America;* AC *Ancient China;* AE *Ancient Egypt;* AF *Age of Faith;* AK *African Kingdoms;* BE *Barbarian Europe;* BYZ *Byzantium;* CC *Cradle of Civilization;* CG *Classical Greece;* EI *Early Islam;*

x

PRODUCTION STAFF FOR TIME INCORPORATED

John L. Hallenbeck (Vice President and Director of Production),
Robert E. Foy and Caroline Ferri
Text photocomposed under the direction of Albert J. Dunn and Arthur J. Dunn